releasing the creative spirit

Unleash the Creativity in Your Life

*To Joan
with best wishes
at Rancho La Puesta!
Dan Wakefield
5/27/03*

DAN WAKEFIELD

Walking Together, Finding the Way

SKYLIGHT PATHS PUBLISHING
WOODSTOCK, VERMONT

Releasing the Creative Spirit:
Unleash the Creativity in Your Life

Library of Congress Cataloging-in-Publication Data
Wakefield, Dan.
Releasing the creative spirit : unleash the creativity in your life / Dan Wakefield.
     p. cm.
Includes bibliographical references and index.
ISBN 1-893361-36-5 (pbk.)
1. Spiritual life. 2. Creative ability—Religious aspects. I. Title.

BL624.W32 2001
153.3'5—dc21   2001003724

10 9 8 7 6 5 4 3 2 1
Manufactured in the United States of America

SkyLight Paths, "Walking Together, Finding the Way" and colophon are trademarks of LongHill Partners, Inc., registered in the U.S. Patent and Trademark Office.

Walking Together, Finding the Way
Published by SkyLight Paths Publishing
A Division of LongHill Partners, Inc.
Sunset Farm Offices, Route 4, P.O. Box 237
Woodstock, VT 05091
Tel: (802) 457-4000   Fax: (802) 457-4004
www.skylightpaths.com

To the memory of my parents,
Brucie Ridge Wakefield and
Benjamin Harbison Wakefield,
who created me, and created a place for me to grow.

And to my wise, kind, and dedicated teachers at wondrous
Public School #80 in Indianapolis (like the era itself, the school
is no longer extant, the building now a condominium):
Roxie Lingle Day, Leta C. Shute, Jane Seal, Grace Grimes,
Louise McCarthy, Louise C. Wheeler, and principals Fern Hall
and Wallace Montague; and the librarians at the Broad Ripple
Branch Library, Miss Hodapp and Mrs. Logan.

With love to them all, and their counterparts today and
tomorrow—the parents, librarians, and public school teachers
who create the creators—this book is dedicated.

———————————

Contents

Acknowledgments

FIRST AND FOREMOST I THANK CHERYL WOODRUFF, THE EDITOR OF THIS BOOK, who pushed me far beyond its original conception; whose greater vision led me to many creative revisions and resulted in a far richer, more useful book than I had originally imagined, and which I am especially proud to send out into the world.

Thanks to Clare Ferraro, for important encouragement, communication, and moral support.

To Reverend Carl Scovel, of King's Chapel in Boston, who taught me how to teach, as well as how to keep the faith.

To the people who have enabled me to offer and develop the workshop on creativity in their own institutions: Reverend Florence Pert and Reverend Ann Benefield of Marble Collegiate Church in New York City; Reverend Roger Cowan of the First Unitarian Church of Palm Beach, Florida; Reverend William Tulley of St. Bartholomew's Church in New York City; Reverend Forrest Church of All Souls Unitarian Church in New York City; Paul Valenti of the Omega Institute; Nancy Lunney of the Esalen Institute; Roger Paine of Interface; Reverend John Buchanan of the Fourth Presbyterian Church in Chicago; Robert Reber, dean of Auburn Theological Seminary; Phyllis Pilgrim and Victoria Larrea of Rancho La Puerta, in Tecate, Mexico; as well as those others who have graciously hosted my workshops in Spiritual Autobiography and Expecting Miracles throughout the country, in Belfast, Northern Ireland, and at Sing Sing prison.

To Les Standiford, and my colleagues and students at Florida International University in Miami, for giving me a base and a home.

To Lynn Nesbit, most creative agent and friend, and Tina Bennett, whose creativity and spirit brought me into the "audio" world for the first time.

To my old and always growing circle of friends, who are family.

PART I

Creation—Works in Progress

I
_____

Creating Our Daily Lives

NOT ONLY ARE WE ALL CREATED, WE ALL CREATE. WE CREATE OUR LIVES, AND then create stories to explain them, and make art, music, and drama to make sense of our experience and our world. In our creating, we ask questions, pose answers, and celebrate our humanity. We often forget that every day is a creation—not only for us, but by us. We wake to it, step into it, and take our part in creating it by what we think and say and do. We don't regard our daily activities as "creation" or "being creative," it's just "what we do," it's just "life." We take our days for granted, as if they were not moment-by-moment miracles.

To enhance our lives, to give them meaning and color, rhythm and narrative, form and beauty, we engage in activities we call creative—writing, painting, singing, dancing, playing a musical instrument—and we seal them up in a special compartment and keep them isolated from the rest of our experience. We're not alone. Even though professional writers, artists, and musicians think of their work as creative, they usually view that work as a separate realm of doing and being apart from their daily, or "real" lives; so do many creative people in business, medicine, science, and technology.

Do you gulp down good food while you talk, read the paper, or watch television without even noticing the taste of what you're eating?

Do you "go on automatic," move in a kind of waking coma through the rituals of the day? I know how easy it is to fall into these routinized bad habits because I do it myself, unless I pay attention, bring myself back to wakefulness. Most of us dismiss as boring the nitty-gritty of waking, eating, washing the dishes, carrying on relationships with loved ones, paying the bills, answering the phone, solving problems, mowing the grass, tending the garden, feeding the cat, walking the dog, going to bed and to sleep again, waking anew each morning.

Seeing these ordinary activities as part of our creative lives, related to everything else we do, and seeing all we do as creation, infuses us with power. If we realize that we create our very reality, then we have a new relationship to it, and we can take more control of our lives. We can alter them and refine them as we would a work of art, like adding more color to a painting; or adding more characters to a story, or changing the end, or perhaps the setting; singing a song in a new key; doing a dance with a different rhythm.

Unlocking Creativity

Just as we sometimes feel blocked and shut off from the flow or animating principle in our "officially" creative activities, we also sometimes get "stuck" in our lives, our relationships. We seem stale, in a rut, burned out, locked up. When it comes to "artistic" creative activities, we know techniques to help us loosen up, refresh, and unblock, but we seldom think to apply those methods to other parts of our experience. Looking upon the whole of our experience as creative frees us from such restrictive, compartmentalized thinking. If we see our lives as art, as story, as dance, and as song, we can apply the techniques of the creative arts to make all our activities more creative, more enlivened by our own spirit—that force which animates each of us and makes us vital.

Just as we sometimes feel blocked and shut off from the flow or animating principle in our "officially" creative activities, we also sometimes get "stuck" in our lives, our relationships.

When we recognize that all aspects of our lives are open to creation, the creative spirit is no longer confined and is free to flow into new and unexpected areas, bringing change, making us aware, waking us from the numbing sleep of rote behavior, the mechanism of addiction.

"The whole secret of the spiritual life," wrote the English author Gerald Heard, in *The Human Venture,* "is just this painful struggle to come awake, to become really conscious. And, conversely, the whole process and technique of evil is to do just the reverse to us; to lull us to sleep, to distract us."

This book is based on that premise, that coming awake is a necessary and essential human struggle. Life is filled with spiritually sleep-inducing distractions and diversions. They account for our sometimes frustrating inattentiveness and impatience; they may lead some of us into a reliance on drugs and alcohol, sexual promiscuity, overeating, anorexia, bulimia, and other attitudes and behaviors that deaden our senses and stifle our spirit, the source of our creativity.

Making Creative Choices

Every act is a choice, and our choices determine the path we take. I used to scoff at the warning that "soft" drugs like marijuana lead to hard drugs like cocaine or heroin, laughing it off with my friends (we thought we were hip) as "square" propaganda put out by the Establishment. I'd forgotten that back in college I'd quickly progressed from beer to bourbon. It did not dawn on me for a long time that after a while one form of stimulation grew stale and I was ready for bigger, more dangerous nirvanas. One thing really does lead to another; none of our decisions is an isolated act, enclosed in some airtight chamber.

I'm a slow learner. Even after I finally recognized the truth of my experience with steps that led me progressively downward, I didn't see that the same principle operates in the other direction. Just as marijuana may lead to the search for a new high with cocaine or heroin, and beer may be the prelude to bourbon or vodka, so a little exercise leads to a desire for greater use of the body. Once I started using an Exercycle, I found myself getting interested in t'ai chi and yoga. After attending church for a while, I wanted to go on a retreat for prayer and meditation. A little exercise may lead to one of the martial arts, or running so many miles a day; a little prayer naturally leads to a thirst for deeper spiritual exploration, or involvement in a faith community. Once we get a taste of something powerful, we want more. Just as some paths lead to oblivion, other paths lead to an awakened spirit. That is the way of creativity.

All of us are endowed with spirit—which means that all of us are naturally creative. Yet you've heard people say, with frustration or despair, sometimes with perverse pride or in other cases false modesty, "Oh, I'm not creative." That's like proclaiming, "Oh, I'm really not human—I may look human, but it's just a costume."

A woman in one of my workshops in Spiritual Autobiography sat with her hands folded in her lap while everyone else was busy with crayons drawing a picture of a room from their childhood home. I went over to her and asked if there was some reason that she couldn't or didn't want to draw.

"Oh," she said, "I'm not visual."

At first I thought she meant something was wrong with her eyesight, but that was not the case. Her eyesight was fine, but her I-sight—the vision she had constructed of herself—needed refocusing. Maybe someone long ago had told her she was "not visual," or maybe someone had criticized a childhood drawing, so she had decided she couldn't—wouldn't—try to draw anything ever again. She decided she lacked "visualness."

What a waste to construct, or let others construct, blocks in our lives that really don't exist until we accept them and live by them. It's not uncommon. In one of my interviews with creators, singer Judy Collins recalls how a high school teacher's accusation of plagiarism froze her from writing her marvelous songs for many years. A priest I met at a workshop in Ireland told me how a grade school teacher advised him he wasn't "college material," and it put a damper on his academic work, delayed his education, and siphoned his creative energy off into anger.

Once we get a taste of something powerful, we want more. Just as some paths lead to oblivion, other paths lead to an awakened spirit.

CREATORS TALKING

"My access points are my dreams and my journal. Those are consistent threads. The most crucial point is consistent discipline—to write down my dreams, and to keep the journal on a regular basis. The opening line from a journal can be the beginning of a song."

—JUDY COLLINS, SINGER, SONGWRITER, NOVELIST

When I was starting out as a writer, the publisher who brought out my first book—a nonfiction work—read fifty pages of my first attempt at a novel and told me over a lavish lunch (designed to console me), "You're not a novelist." It was like a sentence from a literary court of law—a death sentence to a dream—and for a while I accepted it. But happily I began writing fiction again, finishing and publishing my first novel a decade later, followed by four others (with more to come).

When people say they are not creative, it may mean someone has branded them with that mistaken opinion. Or it may simply mean they don't know how to access their creativity.

Finding New Ways

To get hold of something that seems to be eluding us, we first need to know what it is. I like the definition in my new Random House Unabridged Dictionary: Creativity is "the ability to transcend traditional ideas, rules, patterns, relationships, or the like, and to create meaningful new ideas, forms, methods, interpretations, etc." Looking at how professional creators do this in their work gives us clues about viewing freshly our own issues, our own behavior. We often search for ways to change our circumstances, ways to jump from the worn grooves of life's daily record. Similarly, creative artists search for ways to break through "the way it's always been" in their own work, to shatter some of those "set in stone" rules.

Someone who transcended traditional rules in our recent cultural history is Tom Wolfe. He helped create the "new journalism."

Meeker souls might well have feared that styles and methods that broke the old rules would be rejected.

Wolfe said he was bored by writing what he called "totem journalism," which was standard procedure for daily newspapers, the plain, dry, "just the facts, ma'am" tradition of newsroom "objectivity," which purposely omitted irony, humor, and the personal vision and style of the reporter. Talk about style! He even changed the use of punctuation, employing lots of exclamation points !!! to indicate special excitement or surprise, and lots of colons :::::::::: to suggest pauses in the interior thoughts of his subjects. Wolfe used punctuation in a whole new way and expressed new moods and feelings with methods that had never been tried in traditional journalism.

Around the same time, Joan Didion made another significant breakaway from "totem journalism" by using her personal feelings and impressions to illuminate the lives of runaway kids in Haight Ashbury during the Summer of Love *(Slouching toward Bethlehem)*, the passions of murder and lust in middle-class California ("Some Dreamers of the Golden Dream"), and proving in subsequent reportage into the '90s that journalistic "objectivity" was a mask for distortion. She demonstrated that the first-person style, so scorned in traditional journalism, could provide authenticity and truth when practiced by an artist. She opened the way for a whole new way of seeing and describing the news of the day.

Both of these breakthroughs took courage, as well as talent and vision. Meeker souls might well have feared that styles and methods that broke the old rules would be rejected.

They might have felt trapped inside the image of themselves they and others had created. They would have held back, not wanting to alienate editors, even though they saw a different, fresher way of doing things. Courage is always an essential element of change—in art, as in life.

The abstract expressionist painters whose work brought the capital of art from Paris to New York devised new ways of using paint, and even used new tools as they "approached the canvas head-on, in direct, unpremeditated confrontation, and left it strewn with drips and splatters, accidental gestures and studio debris." Art historian April Kingsley, conveying in *The Turning Point* the fresh excitement of these innovators' work, goes on to explain that

> chance, gravity, and paint viscosity were, for the first time in the history of art, important factors in making a painting. New techniques of applying paint were exploited—dripping, throwing, squirting, squeegeeing and spattering—using crude, untraditional tools like unwieldy housepainters' brushes, sticks, basting syringes, and trowels. Cheap enamels substituted for tube colors. Yankee ingenuity replaced standard textbook studio practice for painter and sculptor alike.

Besides seeing themselves and their roles in new ways, creators employ old and new methods in startling combinations.

In mid-career, tenor saxophonist John Coltrane took up the soprano sax, a smaller instrument that hadn't been used in jazz since the '30s and '40s. Encouraged by Miles Davis, Coltrane found that by playing this new "old" instrument, "A new shape came out of the thing and patterns . . ." Mastering the soprano sax helped him develop his individual style, which became part of the New Thing movement that energized jazz in the '60s.

New eras, with new ways of living, call forth new ways of seeing and representing the world, through words, paint, music, film. Creators in every field find means of freshly communicating new experience, using what's never been used before, challenging taboos, boldly experimenting to break the old molds, giving us new ways to see, hear, and experience.

Art Is Not Limited to a Few

Professional artistic creators like musicians, painters, and writers are not the only ones who find new ways to refresh their work. Their innovations should not intimidate us, but remind us that creativity is available to all of us, whatever we do.

Dr. Dean Ornish overcame skepticism and denial from his own profession in order to create a new and successful approach to reversing heart disease without using drugs or surgery. He was rejected for funding by major foundations and medical institutions, as well as the National Institutes of Health, when he first applied for grants to study the effects of diet, exercise, and meditation on heart patients.

"It was discouraging," Ornish wrote in his best-selling book *Dr. Dean Ornish's Program for Reversing Heart Disease.* "It's impossible to reverse heart disease," medical authorities told him, and besides, "people won't change their lifestyles to that degree anyway." Dr. Ornish was asked by a leading cardiologist why he wanted to try something so "radical" as lifestyle changes, rather than "something more conventional," such as bypass surgery.

Ornish finally got the necessary funding to begin his study from Gerald D. Hines, a Houston real estate developer, who helped raise financial support from Houston-based individuals, corporations, and small foundations. (So much for the myth that businessmen are "not creative.") The results have been revolutionary, showing that heart disease can in fact be reversed by basic lifestyle changes, without resorting to drugs or surgery.

Yoga teacher Danielle Levi-Alvares broke out of what had become a stale routine by taking one of her classes outside to do a Zen walking meditation in a muddy yard. It awakened everyone. Danielle believes that "creativity is to take a fresh look at life, play with it."

The American painter and inspired art teacher Robert Henri believed that art "is simply a question of doing things, anything, well. It is not an outside, extra thing." In his wonderful book, *The Art Spirit,* Henri proclaims, "Art when really understood is the province of every human being."

The appreciation of art, and the creation of art, are not limited to a special few, an elite touched by a magic wand.

The appreciation of art, and the creation of art, are not limited to a special few, an elite touched by a magic wand. They are part of the splendor of being human, part of our common heritage, regardless of

CREATORS TALKING

"I'd heard since high school that drinking loosened you up, freed you in ways to get to the unconscious. But the myth doesn't ring true for me, though I do have guy friends who still romanticize the power of drinking as a way to get in touch with the muse. In comedy clubs you'll still hear men comics brag about drinking and then having the best gig of their lives. I'm like, 'Yeah, right, what have you been smoking?'"

—MARY BETH COUDAL, STAND-UP COMIC, WRITER

race, gender, color, background, language; regardless even of mental or physical handicaps.

All of us are endowed with spirit—which means that all of us are naturally creative. We wouldn't exist without the creative force, whose power is acknowledged and dramatized by the first story in the Bible, the creation story. These are the first words of the sacred texts of Judaism and Christianity: "In the beginning, God created the heavens and the earth."

In the story that follows, God creates humans, and these humans are also creators; in fact, their ability to create makes them human, distinguishes them from the animals. Animals may create—or, more strictly speaking, construct—nests or dams or hills or holes, but they are locked into their instinctual programming. They cannot think and act beyond that, cannot transcend their animalness, their sparrow- or hound- or horse-ness that restricts their movements and communication, confining them to their biological and geographic place in the universal order.

Humans have no such restrictions. We create stories and songs, pictures and sculptures, rockets that fly to the moon and beyond, machines and medicines that help heal the human body and mind, networks of instant communication and information that link the diverse peoples of the whole planet. Humans create new forms of society and economy and ways of being and living on the earth. We have free will, the power to create our own destiny, the very pattern and course of our lives. Such godlike powers are not dispensed to just a few geniuses and seers, but to all of us.

We fail to use our powers when we fail to think of our lives and our work, whatever it is, as creative—as potential art, or "life art." I don't mean this abstractly; I've seen people do it in all different kinds of situations. When a telephone operator sings her greeting as she answers the phone, that is art. When a chef adds the right ingredient to a soup at the crucial moment, that too is art. The masseuse's pressure on the right point in the shoulder, the businessman's observation of a child's shoe, the yoga teacher's guided meditation—all that is art and creation as much as the painter's brush stroke, the writer's choice of words, the sculptor's shaping of the clay, or the actor's intonation of a phrase.

One of the most awakening experiences for me in writing this book was to interview people from a wide variety of fields to learn how they used creativity in their own work. These are not just famous people, like singer and songwriter Judy Collins, or financially successful people, like businessman and benefactor Arnold Hiatt; nor are they only writers like Marcie Hershman and Gish Jen, or religious thinkers like Rabbi Harold Kushner and theologian Elaine Pagels. I learned about creativity in body work from masseuse Elizabeth Valentine, in cooking from chef Odette Bery, and in yoga from Danielle Levi-Alvares.

Creators see art not only in their professions, but also in the creation of daily life activity. There is art in the lighting of candles at breakfast. There is art in being mindful of the food we eat, in remembering to honor the light or soul or God within ourselves and every person we come in contact with throughout the day, whether friend, lover, family member, fellow worker, waiter, or stranger passing on the street. There is art in taking time to appreciate the clean wash of the mind's silence.

We fail to use our powers when we fail to think of our lives and our work, whatever it is, as creative—as potential art, or "life art."

One of the major blocks to experiencing creativity and creating experiences is the myth that we can enhance our creativity through the use of artificial stimulants, the ingestion of drugs and alcohol. I am not speaking as a moralist in exposing this myth, but as a truth-seeker.

I have written about this myth extensively because as a writer I was under its spell for a long time, as were many of my generation, and as many continue to be in new generations—from Dylan Thomas to Kurt Cobain, from Janis Joplin to River Phoenix. There are always new brands of booze and drugs that promise different magic transformations, new variations of the genie in the bottle. Old genies like LSD are revived, repackaged, and reglamorized for a fresh crop of exploring, curious, talented young people who are all too often captured by the myth that we can enhance our creativity by altering our state of consciousness. That myth, and others like it, are simply not true.

You Don't Have to Be a Mystic

Clarity of mind, body, and spirit is the key to creativity, to finding and producing the art in our work and our lives. No matter how deeply we may have sunk to some numbing addiction that stifles the creative spirit—whether drugs, alcohol, overindulgence in food, sleep, television, surfing the Web, or simply depression and malaise—there is always a road to recovery of our natural clarity.

I associate clarity with "spirit," in the broadest sense of the term, as defined by the Oxford English Dictionary: "the animating or vital principle in [humans] (and animals); that which gives life to the physical organism, in contrast to its purely material elements; the breath of life." For some, this may be a religious principle; for others, it is best signified by the broader term of *spirituality;* others may have another word for it.

You don't have to be a mystic, or be struck by a lightning bolt from the heavens, or hear supernatural voices to tap into what I mean by spirit. You only have to be clear, that is, unencumbered by rigid preconceptions, unbound from the chains of repeated patterns of negative behavior, unafraid of taking risks.

Robert Henri expresses my findings and my feelings in *The Art Spirit:*

When the artist is alive in any person, whatever his kind of work may be, he becomes an inventive, searching, daring, self-expressing creature. He becomes interesting to other people. He disturbs, upsets, enlightens, and he opens the way for a better understanding. Where those who are not artists are trying to close the book, he opens it, shows there are still more pages possible. . . . He does not have to be a painter or sculptor to be an artist. He can work in any medium. He simply has to find the gain in the work itself, not outside it.

Something in the world wants to destroy our hard-won clarity, some anti-spirit that tells us creation and art lead to madness and death. Those who promote the mythical glamour of the "doomed artist," psychoanalyzing art into an expression of neurosis, seldom, if ever, mention the central aspect of the creative experience: the incomparable joy of it—not the illusory bubble of fame, but what Robert Henri calls "the happiness that is in the making." As Molly Bloom puts it in the final, life-affirming lines of James Joyce's *Ulysses*: ". . . and yes I said yes I will Yes."

Life is a lot more fun and fulfilling when you see it as creation, and yourself as a co-creator of it (rather than a victim or passive passenger)—along with God, or fate, or the universe, however you understand the force that turns the world. True creativity never leads to despair; creativity leads out of despair.

If there is one word that embodies the true path to creativity, that serves as a key to the full use of our creative powers, it is clarity. To aid you in reaching an understanding of it, in a way that will enable you to use and enjoy both the idea and the condition of clarity, I have set up a kind of model of successive stages in this book, called Breaking the Myth, Emptying, Filling, and Creating. To achieve clarity you need only be in awe of the mystery of the universe, the life force and its power, and be willing to open to it.

You don't have to be a mystic, or be struck by a lightning bolt from the heavens, or hear supernatural voices to tap into what I mean by spirit.

On this journey, my model will serve as a road map for this fresh exploration of creation. We'll use exercises with drawing, listening to music, writing, and looking at nature to explore and unlock our own creative powers. We'll look at ways to use those powers to shape our daily lives, to give our moment-by-moment experience (which is where we always live) the grace and pleasure of art. This is what I mean by creating from the spirit.

2

The Creative Spirit

The consolation, the dignity, the joy of life are that discouragements and lapses, depressions and darknesses, come to one only as one stands without—I mean without the luminous paradise of art. As soon as I really re-enter it—cross the loved threshold—stand in the high chamber, and the gardens divine—the whole realm widens out again before me and around me—the air of life fills my lungs—the light of achievement flushes over all the place, and I believe, I see, I do.

A NOVELIST WROTE THOSE UPLIFTING WORDS AT A DIFFICULT TIME IN HIS LIFE and career, when even greater professional discouragement was just around the corner. With his novels selling poorly, the author was working on a play with all his might in hopes of restoring his financial as well as literary fortunes, both of which were in decline. The play on which he pinned his hopes turned out to be such a flop the audience hurled vegetables onto the London stage at the opening-night performance. Undaunted, the author wrote in his journal the next morning in exhortation to himself: "Produce; produce again; produce again better than ever and all will be well."

We usually don't associate Henry James—known as "The Master" of language and story—with failure, yet he suffered it as painfully as any other artist whose work is scorned. Since James is sometimes denigrated today as a privileged member of the literary and social elite of his time, it's enlightening (perhaps even inspiring) to note that he too suffered defeat, indifference, and hostility. He was pained by bad reviews (they don't get any worse than vegetables hurled on the stage!) and struggled to make enough money from his work to be able to live and continue writing. He once wrote that each of us, no matter what our situation or station in the world, has to deal with "the terrible algebra of your own existence." His fight against defeat, and his compassion for his characters, as well as the lyric power of his prose, have continued to inspire writers as diverse as James Baldwin and Cynthia Ozick.

The poet and teacher Martha Collins recently recalled, "I fell in love with literature because of reading *Portrait of a Lady*, a novel about a woman's mind, a woman's thinking, and James 'got it right.' Isabel Archer faced different problems than women do today, but the basic dilemma of her humanity is our own stuff, too." Collins, whose most recent book of poetry is *A History of Small Life on a Windy Planet*, said, "What I owe most to Henry James is he taught me I wanted to be a writer."

Perhaps James inspires so many because, for him, creating his novels, stories, and plays was an act of faith, a testimony to his belief in the achievement that brought a "flush of light" to his inner vista: "I believe, I see, I do." The world of his art is a "paradise," its gardens "divine," flushed by that light—all elements of the sort of transcendent experience his brother William wrote about in his own psychological masterpiece, *The Varieties of Religious Experience*.

The act of creation is one of the most powerful of those "varieties of religious experience," even for people, like Henry

> *The act of creation is one of the most powerful of those "varieties of religious experience," even for people, like Henry James, who are not formally religious.*

James, who are not formally religious. For some artists, the religious nature of their work is a given factor, the heart of the matter, even though the art itself may not overtly deal with religious themes. The painter and sculptor Norma Lewis, a member of the Unitarian Universalist Church of the Monterey Peninsula in Carmel, California, told the denomination's magazine, *The World*, "I see creativity as the ultimate religious act. My art and my religion are not only very connected; they are one and the same."

The sixty-four-year-old Russian composer Sofia Gubaidulina told a *New York Times* interviewer that she writes music to serve God. "I can't think of any way to explain the existence of art other than as a means to express something greater than ourselves," she said. "I can't reach a single musical decision except with the goal of making a connection to God. If I separated the religious goal from the musical one, music would have no meaning for me."

Musicians on a Quest

Playing and composing his innovative music became a religious quest for the great jazz saxophone player and composer John Coltrane. He had a spiritual revelation while kicking his drug habit in 1957 and said years later, "My goal is to live the truly religious life, and express it through my music. If you live it, when you play there's no problem because the music is part of the whole thing. . . . My music is the spiritual expression of what I am, my faith, my knowledge, my being."

Ridiculed by some critics for his innovative sounds, and for his search for God through his music, Coltrane was even blasted in an obituary by the English poet and sometime jazz critic Philip Larkin, who called Coltrane's music "enormously boring" and said his death "leaves in jazz a vast, blessed silence."

Coltrane himself addressed such harsh—and inevitable—criticism in a letter to a friend:

> It seems history shows (and it's the same way today) that
> the innovator is more often than not met with some degree

of condemnation; usually according to the degree of departure from the prevailing modes of expression or what have you. Change is always so hard to accept. We also see that these innovators always seek to revitalize, extend, and reconstruct the status quo in their given fields, whatever is needed. Quite often they are the rejects, outcasts, subcitizens, etc., of the very societies to which they bring so much sustenance. Often they are people who endure great personal tragedy in their lives. Whatever the case, whether accepted or rejected, rich or poor, they are forever guided by that great and eternal constant—the creative urge. Let us cherish it and give all praise to God.

In his sensitive book *Ascension: John Coltrane and His Quest*, Eric Nisenson, jazz editor and author of *'Round About Midnight*, writes that Coltrane's remarkable composition "A Love Supreme" has been described as a prayer, a work of devotion, and a psalm, but in fact is more than that: "a searingly confessional, frankly personal piece based on Coltrane's quest to reach and find God through seeking within." A few years before his death from cancer at age forty-one, Coltrane said he wanted to "become a saint."

His vision was realized in the St. John's African Orthodox Church in San Francisco, a storefront proclaiming "St. John Will I-Am Coltrane" as its own patron saint. The church played an hour of inspired improvisational jazz based on his music at every Sunday service, and provided hot meals and clothes to the homeless, as well as free counseling services and even music lessons!

I felt the living legacy of Coltrane as I joined one Sunday morning with the worshipers—old and young, black and white, male and female; some in clerical robes and others in T-shirts; some playing their own musical instruments along with the regular jazz group of tenor and soprano sax, guitars, drums, and piano, others just singing or swaying to the music; everyone welcome and welcoming, joined in spirit. All of us were there out of respect for Coltrane's music, faith, and vision.

> ## CREATORS TALKING
>
> "When I want to be more creative in my teaching, I stimulate myself through other people in the same field. I rent a yoga video to see how others do it differently—or I sit with my boredom to see what's behind it, what it's able to teach me. I try to be patient with it, and use meditation to come up with ideas."
>
> —DANIELLE LEVI-ALVARES, YOGA TEACHER

After his religious conversion, Coltrane thought of his music as prayer—which it continues to be for listeners around the world. Coltrane saw the inseparability—the unity—of his creativity and his religious faith.

Duke Ellington is another jazz great who turned to religion in the later part of his career, blending belief with music as he created "Sacred Concerts," which Eric Nisenson described as "large-scale efforts to explore the idea of God through jazz."

In a new generation, Fleetwood Mac guitarist Lindsey Buckingham told an interviewer that creativity serves the same purpose for him as attending religious services: "One of the reasons I enjoy working alone—and that's when things will often come out well—is because it's very much akin to a religious [experience]. There is some tie between religion and art; I think there's a lot of crossover."

Jenny Boyd, a psychologist, lecturer, and the ex-wife of Mick Fleetwood, interviewed Buckingham and seventy-four other contemporary musicians about the creative process for an absorbing book she co-authored with Holly George-Warren, *Musicians in Tune*. They learned that for a number of well-known rock and pop musical artists, "the act of creating often verges on the spiritual." Indian sitarist Ravi Shankar told Boyd that performing music was part of his own spiritual practice. Bass player Robert Warren said, "I believe there is a transcendent power, and you can get to it through the creative act."

In his own book, *Drumming at the Edge of Magic*, Mickey Hart, formerly of the Grateful Dead, speaks of "the spirit side of the drum" and how the drum took him "on a mythic quest."

Spiritual inspiration came to the rap group Run DMC after the veteran rappers Joseph Simmons, Darryl McDaniels, and Jason Mizzell, who were childhood friends in Hollis, Queens, returned to church and overcame drug and alcohol problems. Their comeback album, *Down with the King,* refers to their own religious reawakening. In a *New York Times* story of their recovery and subsequent comeback on the charts, Simmons told reporter Amy Linden that when people asked him how he could be a born-again Christian and a rapper, "That's like asking how can you be a singer and a Christian. I'm only using my mouth to talk. It's not that rap stands for violence; it doesn't stand for anything. It's poetry. It's an art form."

We All Have a Poem

The iconoclastic comic Bill Hicks told an interviewer: "We are facilitators of our creative evolution. We can ignite our brains with light." Hicks is an African American born in Texas who has found an enthusiastic following in London, where he draws record-breaking crowds for what a critic described as "acid home truths about the U.S.A." (Hicks calls it "the United States of Advertising.") A high school friend says Hicks was the first person he'd ever met whose goal was enlightenment.

Theater critic John Lahr wrote in *The New Yorker* that Hicks's comedy "takes an audience on a journey to places in the heart where it can't or won't go without him. Through laughter, Hicks makes unacceptable ideas irresistible. He is particularly lethal because he persuades not with reason but with joy."

When Hicks left Lahr's house after an interview, he turned and said in parting, "I believe everyone has this fuckin' poem in his heart."

However stated in this most cynically sophisticated era, the belief in the "poem in the heart"—another way of describing spirit—keeps popping up from the new creators and artists, even those angry at the Establishment.

In that defiant, iconoclastic spirit of laughter at self and society to get to the heart of things, actress Claudia Shear created the one-woman show *Blown Sideways through Life,* which opened in a small off-Broadway theater to rave reviews. It's the drama of her own "failure"—the plight of an overweight, no-longer-young woman trying to survive in New York in the '90s, having left or been fired from forty-five jobs, ranging from short-order cook to receptionist at a midtown house of prostitution.

Out of this dismal, all-too familiar saga of rejection and discrimination, Ms. Shear created a funny, wise, provocative satire capped with a joyous, triumphant dance that brings a surge of new life and hope to the audience. At least it did to me, and from the faces I saw around me that night and the ovation I joined, I was not alone.

There is no doubt that Claudia Shear has that poem in the heart—the spirit, the breath of life that brings meaning to existence and enables us to create.

Unexpected Spirit

For some, that "poem" comes out literally as poetry, for others as a dance or play or comedy routine; still others manifest it in work that we often fail to appreciate as creative because it doesn't fit the usual categories. Yet it calls on that same spirit, no matter what labor or activity is involved, from salesmanship to surgery.

Even science. A cliche that persists is that of the scientist as antireligious and anti-artistic, enemy of spiritual truth and beauty. The Nobel Prize-winning physicist Richard Feynman challenged that view in his memoir *What Do You Care What Other People Think?*, disputing the argument of a painter friend who held up a flower and said that he as an artist could appreciate its beauty, "but you, as a scientist, take it all apart and it becomes dull."

Feynman responded that the fascination arising from a knowledge of science "only adds to the excitement and mystery and awe of a flower. It only adds. I don't understand how it subtracts." Feynman recalls standing at the seashore and looking at the ocean as a scientist, and being inspired to write a free-verse poem about the wonder of the universe, and himself in it, all made up of atoms. He adds that "the same thrill, the same awe and mystery, comes again and again when we look at any question deeply enough." He describes that feeling of awe and mystery as "a religious experience."

Faith in Poetry

You don't have to be formally religious to have a peak experience while creating. When the Pulitzer Prize-winning poet Maxine Kumin was asked in an interview if her poetry was in some way "a fulfillment of some sort of spiritual need," she answered,

> I call myself an agnostic. I do not really have any faith, any coherent religious faith, and yet the one thing in my life that I feel passionate and evangelical about is poetry. I want to contribute to its well-being and to its future. And I suppose that speaking about the way poems occur is, if you read William James, something like the quality of a religious experience for me.

Her words reminded me of an experience in my own early struggle to write, when I was not simply an agnostic who didn't know if there was a God, but a newly minted Columbia College atheist, emboldened by discovering Nietzsche, Freud, and Hemingway's *"nada,"* or nothingness. I knew there was not a God and was proudly condescending to those who still believed, like my parents and most of my friends back home in Indiana.

In this smugly enlightened state, I returned to my dorm room one evening to struggle with a short story I was trying to write. A few hours after I had plunged into it again the story seemed to come alive, to take over, with a force of its own, carrying me along as page after page came out of my typewriter, scenes and dialogue and descriptions proceeding in some natural way, as if I were simply transcribing them. I lost all sense of time. When I finally came to the end of the

You don't have to be formally religious to have a peak experience while creating.

story, I looked up and saw that it was light outside. I felt tears welling up in my eyes, not of sadness but joy, and without thinking, but following some natural impulse, I sank to the floor on my knees and uttered a prayer of thanks for having finally "created" what seemed to be a real story—or, as it felt like, for having been the transcriber, the vessel through which the story came.

To whom did I offer this prayer of thanks? The God I no longer believed in? I didn't know or care; the impulse was deeper than intellect, beyond reason or argument.

Not just writers experience the spiritual nature of creation. The ceiling of the Sistine Chapel, with Michelangelo's unforgettable depiction of the finger of God reaching out to Adam—one of the basic images of Western culture and civilization—is perhaps the most eloquent testimony we have of the painter as transmitter of the sacred. It's a tradition that began with the earliest drawings in caves, flowered in the inspired paintings of biblical scenes and figures by the masters, and continues in the painting of contemporary artists like Agnes Martin, whose luminous new works have been likened to prayer by the art and literary historian Benita Eisler.

Creative artists in many fields find inspiration in one another's works, an interaction vividly described by the nineteenth-century French poet Charles Baudelaire, who found "new energies" from looking at paintings. Baudelaire believed that all the arts inspire one another, that a piece of music as well as a painting or a poem "throws open immense vistas to the most adventurous imaginations." So passionately did Baudelaire relate to painting that he began to write about it, and became one of the leading art critics of his time.

Rembrandt's classic painting of the *Prodigal Son* inspired a devotional book by the writer-priest Father Henri Nouwen. Jazz musician John Coltrane wrote to a friend,

> I was reading a book on the life of van Gogh today, and I had to pause and think of that wonderful and persistent force—the creative urge. The creative urge was in this

man who found himself so much at odds with the world he lived in, and in spite of all the adversity, frustrations, rejections, and so forth—beautiful and living art came forth abundantly.

Teachers as Guides

We learn and are inspired—awakened—by the other arts and sciences through the grace and wisdom of teachers. In my Spiritual Autobiography workshop, there is an exercise in which people write about a friend, mentor, or guide who has helped them move forward on their own journey. The people most often remembered in this honored category are schoolteachers.

I can't imagine my own life journey without them—I don't mean just for the facts and dates and numbers they taught me, I mean for the richness of spirit they evoked in me, opened to me, through gentle and wise introductions to the work of great creators. I remember sitting spellbound in a classroom at Shortridge High School, listening to a scratchy record player render the voice of Carl Sandburg reading his poem "The People, Yes." I went home to read more of those American midwestern poems about Chicago, and Lincoln, and the longings of the heart, and something stirred in me, deeply.

CREATORS TALKING

"Creativity is a synonym for inspiration. One of the most profound religious experiences I have is to find myself in possession of an idea and not know where it came from. I'll be trying to convey some difficult material in my writing and suddenly it comes clear to me what I need to say and how to say it. I feel awe when this happens; it's an inspiring experience. I don't know where it comes from—I'm tempted to say from God. For me this is an experience of divine self-disclosure—it's the intellectual version of a person having to do something that's very hard and suddenly finding she has the qualities of soul to enable her to do it that she never had before."

—RABBI HAROLD KUSHNER, AUTHOR OF *WHEN BAD THINGS HAPPEN TO GOOD PEOPLE*

It wasn't a poetry class but a history class, and Sandburg wasn't part of the curriculum but was added to enrich our understanding and appreciation by the teacher—not a poet or literary person, but the freshman track, football, and basketball coach, Roy V. "Abie" Aberson, one of the many dedicated teachers who blessed my life and nurtured as well as educated me—along with several other generations of fortunate students.

The most undervalued and underpaid professionals in our society, who not only create but give us our own basic tools for creating, are teachers. Teachers must not only know their subject but constantly keep pace with the rapidly changing world in order to help their students understand it. How creatively they do that was illustrated when the Department of Education, during President Bill Clinton's first term, brought two hundred outstanding teachers to Washington to give their views on education reform. One of those, voted Teacher of the Year in her state, was Vicki Matthews Burwell of Caldwell, Iowa. She wrote of what goes on in her classroom at the New Plymouth Elementary School:

> Today our fifth-grade class stood on a model of a Tenochtitlán causeway and fended off the enemy, we touched three-million-year-old stromatolites and mammoth-toothed fossils and we composed e-mail for a school in Pennsylvania. Through videos, we visited the Anasazi ruins in Chaco Canyon, had the magicians Penn and Teller introduce us to David Hockney's surreal look at a chair and were mesmerized by Gary Paulsen's passionate writing about the Alaskan Iditarod.
>
> We fell through the day like Alice in Wonderland, soaking up ideas, experimenting with and stretching our talents. We were civil engineers, archaeologists, detectives, paleontologists, art critics, computer nerds, teachers and community planners. We used technology, bright construction paper, dog-eared books, parents. We used our imagination, our background knowledge, and our intuition. We

went home exhausted and satisfied. Tomorrow we'll be back for print making and teamwork in long division. And Corey says he has a few card tricks to show us. Steven Spielberg never had it so good.

Is There Spirit in Selling Cosmetics?

Well, of course teaching is creative, but what about business? Isn't that the last endeavor we associate with creativity, much less spirituality? Business still carries the old '50s stigma of "the rat race," the "Organization Man," the "Hucksters"—updated by even more crass and cutthroat practices and anti-ethics that made the '80s a byword for greed and corruption. Certainly, many businesses still operate in that paradigm, but it doesn't have to be that way. The possibilities of business being created from the spirit open wide when listening to Anita Roddick, founder (creator) of The Body Shop, an international natural cosmetics firm with more than nine hundred shops trading in nineteen different languages in forty-two countries around the world, from the Arctic Circle to Bondi Beach.

"I see business as a Renaissance concept, where the human spirit comes into play," Ms. Roddick says in her book, *Body and Soul.*

> It does not have to be drudgery; it does not have to be the science of making money. It can be something that people genuinely feel good about, but only if it remains a human enterprise.
>
> How do you ennoble the spirit when you are selling something as inconsequential as a cosmetic cream? You do it by creating a sense of holism, of spiritual development, of feeling connected to the workplace, the environment and relationships with one another. It's how to make Monday to Friday a sense of being alive rather than a slow death. How do you give people a chance to do a good job? By making them feel

How do you ennoble the spirit when you are selling something as inconsequential as a cosmetic cream?

good about what they are doing. The spirit soars when you are satisfying your own basic material needs in such a way that you are also serving the needs of others honorably and humanely. Under these circumstances, I can even feel good about a moisturizer.

The idea of work as spiritual experience comes up in places we don't expect—because we've narrowed our view of the concept, trying to domesticate spirituality by restricting it to places of formal religious worship. Deanna Teifenthal, who took one of my workshops, wrote me later about her unexpected discovery of creativity and spirituality on a tour of the SkyDome, the baseball stadium of the Toronto Blue Jays.

> Before we started, they showed us a wonderful video on the building of the dome and its retractable roof. If you expected to hear about the mechanics of how it worked, you were disappointed. What it was, was a smattering of the spiritual journeys the workers and architects had! Guiding the steel beams into place with just a touch of the hand. Carefully choosing a partner you could trust your life with high above ground. Struggling to feel with your frozen fingers when the bolts slipped into place to join the beams. Soaring through the air at the end of a rising beam. Feeling the wind in your ears while working high in the air. Being one of a team of 5,000 to dust the seats and spruce up the SkyDome before the first game.
>
> The architect defined creativity as "just discovering what's already there," as he got the idea for the retractable dome roof from observing, among other things, a lobster shell.

Navajo Healing

The idea of work as a holistic endeavor rather than an isolated part of life, walled off from any spiritual source or practice, is rarely associated with mainstream, AMA medicine. It is present, though, in the world and work of Dr. Lori Cupp, a staff general surgeon at the Indian Medical

Center of Gallup, New Mexico. The first Navajo woman to become a surgeon, she views surgery as a powerful spiritual experience.

"In the Navajo religion and culture, there is an emphasis on how you relate to everything around you," Dr. Cupp explained in an interview with Elizabeth Cohen of the *New York Times*. "Everything has to be measured, weighed, and harmonious. We call it *nizhoni*—walking in beauty—and I believe what I do as a surgeon fits into this philosophy. I know my actions directly alter the course of people's lives."

Dr. Cupp has drawn on her own heritage to creatively devise methods of making her Navajo patients feel more comfortable: "Now I know how to gauge a person's discomfort by asking a few questions at a time and asking them to only uncover that part of their body I need to see." She has proposed that the hospital use a medicine man for healing ceremonies and has requested that when a new medical center is built, it include a traditional Navajo round room for such ceremonies, called "sings."

Dr. Cupp said that for many illnesses—depression, for instance—a ceremonial sing may be the best treatment. "But if I had a breast mass, I would want it surgically removed for a biopsy," she added.

"What an amazing and rare thing it is to actually work inside another human being," Dr. Cupp said. "At the time, I may be stressed or scared, but I also feel an unbelievable link to something larger—call it God or whatever, a universal spiritual connectedness."

The Breath of Life

Whether we are surgeons or stand-up comics, Pulitzer Prize-winning poets or "Sunday painters," jazz musicians or business leaders, for most of us the process of creation is—if not specifically religious (which implies a specific creed or denomination)—a spiritual experience in the broad sense of the term. I use the Oxford English Dictionary definition of spirit: "The animating or vital principle in [humans] (and animals); that which gives

By confining creativity to fenced-off, predefined areas, our society has tamed its power.

life to the physical organism, in contrast to its purely material elements; the breath of life."

Henry James echoes this definition of spirit when he writes that while in the realm of his art, "the air of life fills my lungs." Dylan Thomas described it in his poetry: "The force that through the green fuse drives the flower/Drives my green age."

Spirit is "something larger than the self," writes the author, critic, and Harvard lecturer Lewis Hyde in "Alcohol and Poetry"; it has

> the power to change you. It alters your Gestalt, your whole mode of perception and action. Both alcohol and the Holy Ghost can do this. But a spirit does more than just give you new eyes: it is the mover. . . . Spiritual thirst is the thirst of the self to feel that it is part of something large, and in its positive aspect, it is the thirst to grow, to ripen.

As King Lear put it, "Ripeness is all."

To reach a ripeness in our personal growth, to tap into our inherent creativity and spirit, we need to dispel some popular illusions. By confining creativity to fenced-off, predefined areas, our society has tamed its power; our accumulated cultural myths have limited and sometimes hidden our access to this power. A good way to break through to a new understanding of creativity and find ways of claiming it for ourselves is to expose some of the mythology that has grown up around the subject like crabgrass, obscuring it from view, choking off our access to it, keeping us distanced from its full use and enjoyment.

Let's look at some of the myths about creativity that are commonly accepted in our own culture.

3

Myths of Creativity

Myth Number 1: Creativity Is Only for the Artistic Elite

This myth tells us that a few special people have been blessed with the mysterious gift of creativity, and everyone else was passed over when God was giving out these valuable prizes! While everyone may not be a master or a Pulitzer Prize winner, everyone does possess creative power, a force that may be articulated in many different ways, from cooking and gardening to painting—and writing.

Another part of the myth is that creativity is only for the social and financial elite, a frivolous pastime. Ann Morrissey, a participant in a workshop I gave at the Unitarian Universalist Conference Center at Ferry Beach, Maine, wrote,

> Creativity isn't a big topic in a working-class neighbor-hood—if anything it was laughed at. I think that the assumption was that creativity was for people who didn't have to work for a living. The sons and daughters of the rich could afford the luxury of spending years exploring their creativity.
>
> By definition, therefore, anything done well by neigh-bors or family members was a skill. Baking well, sewing well, singing, etc., were skills where practice was needed. I don't remember them being seen as creative.

Creative ability is found in all sections of the country and the globe, without regard to race, color, religion, background, age, or wealth.

In my definition, those skills are no less creative than composing music, painting a picture, or writing a novel. Many creative artists come from working-class neighborhoods; some left those neighborhoods because their creative work was laughed at there.

Creative ability is found in all sections of the country and the globe, without regard to race, color, religion, background, age, or wealth. Talent isn't for sale—except through development of skills by love and work.

Being creative is part of being human, and one of the key elements of humanity is the creative gift of storytelling. It is basic. Joan Didion wrote, "We tell stories in order to live." My great-grandmother, who never finished high school and sold women's corsets door-to-door during the Depression to feed her family, told me marvelous stories of growing up in Georgia, of seeing the flames of Sherman's march to the sea when she was six years old. When I was a child, my mother created stories for me of animals' picnics, using all the elements I most loved—bears, deviled eggs, and trains. My pharmacist father told me stories of Kentucky, his birthplace, and of pioneers, like my ancestor Daniel Boone, chopping their way through the wilderness. I gulped these stories like lemonade and was thrilled to be able to tell them myself.

Whatever our work or talents or inclinations, we all possess, I believe, a gift of storytelling. Sometimes it is untapped or untried because we have been told, or have come to assume, that if we aren't professionals, we aren't gifted with the capacity to express ourselves in this way. After leading workshops in Spiritual Autobiography for five years at churches and adult education centers across the country, I've had firsthand confirmation of the natural ability of people of different ages, backgrounds, and occupations to create fascinating stories from their own experience.

CREATORS TALKING

"Yes, I think writing and music are spiritual disciplines. Absolutely. It's a very important entering point. I realized this many years ago. I'm a devotee of Yogananda. For thirteen years I've meditated consistently—for the past eight or nine years once a day, and for the past three or four years twice a day. It's part of that continuity, all part of the same thing. It's essential to keep in the flow of that."

—JUDY COLLINS, SINGER, SONGWRITER, NOVELIST

THE DEMOCRATIZATION OF WRITING

The playwright and journalist Barbara Graham came to one of my workshops to write an article on it for the magazine *New Choices*, published by Reader's Digest, and she made the insightful observation that this sort of activity represented a new phenomenon. She called it "the democratization of writing"—the recent popularity of opportunities for "ordinary people" (those who are not professionals) to enjoy the creative pleasures of writing.

The upsurge of this democratization has also led to a kind of backlash among professional writers themselves, some of whom scorn any processes that provide such openings to "amateurs." I heard about one such literary pro who expressed this disdain with the comment, "Everything that's wrong with contemporary society can be summed up in one word: *workshop.*" I think there's a protective response among some of the pros who fear their thunder will be stolen by these upstart amateurs! The mere notion that literate but untrained and unpublished neophytes can spend a weekend writing stories that please and enlighten and entertain not only themselves but their fellow participants—that writing stories of our lives is available to most of us—seems to demystify and thus somehow lessen the godlike aura of the professional storytellers.

I think there's a protective response among some of the pros who fear their thunder will be stolen by these upstart amateurs!

I don't mean to suggest that anyone who takes a weekend work-shop and writes entertaining stories can then quit her job and become the next Toni Morrison or Kurt Vonnegut. What I mean is that people who can write their names and high school theme papers can also tap into a creative source that enables them to tell their own stories, through drawing as well as writing.

No one was more shocked and pleased than I, who always con-sidered myself "artistically illiterate" because I couldn't draw a human shape (today it might be called "pictorially challenged"), to find that through a simple exercise with crayons I was able to portray a part of my past. I was even able to draw a shape and form that resembled a human being, beyond my usual rendering of a stick figure, and this primitive crayon sketch seemed such a miracle to me I had it framed and hung it above my writing desk. Pleased as I was by my crayon pic-tures, I did not harbor any illusions that I could whip up some pastels or portraits to show and sell at a New York art gallery, or rival the work of Franz Kline or Willem de Kooning! I was simply enjoying my own ability to use a dormant part of my creative powers for my own plea-sure and enlightenment.

Commitment to a professional path in the arts is a whole other order of experience than learning to call up and exercise one's cre-ative powers for personal pleasure and insight. The discipline (much less extraordinary talent) required for that kind of work—what Henry James called "steadily driving the pen"—is enormous, rigor-ous, and psychically as well as mentally challenging. That doesn't mean you shouldn't try it, but be aware of the wholly different demands of this path.

Myth Number 2: You Have to Suffer to Be Creative

The world seems to love the story of the suffering artist. Is it some kind of revenge on those who are artistic, that in popular mythology one of the components of successful creativity is personal agony and pain? The American writer who has had the most books written about his life is Edgar Allan Poe. Yes, he was a creative genius, and yes, he did suffer the torments of alcohol and drug addiction. The irony is, though, that he is almost alone among the great American writers of the nineteenth century who fell prey to those diseases! The giants of our literature in that century—Hawthorne, Melville, Thoreau, Emerson, Dickinson, Whitman, Twain—were not alcoholics or drug addicts, nor was their human suffering probably any more or less severe than that of the mass of men and women of their time. But it is Poe, the doomed, whose life remains the most popular story.

We love the image of the artist as wild and kooky, but as Robert Henri writes, "Art tends toward balance, order, judgment of relative values, the laws of growth, the economy of living—very good things for anyone to be interested in." This is the testimony of most working artists, as opposed to psychologists or sociologists generalizing about them. The prize-winning novelist Reynolds Price notes that "most productive writers live calmer lives than winkles."

That will never sell. Despite our society's outward changes in attitude about the destructive nature of alcohol and drugs, the phony glamour of the stoned, smashed, self-destructive artist still has tremendous appeal. Witness the astounding fact that among current American writers, one of the most common subjects of biography is none other than Hunter S. Thompson, the self-proclaimed "gonzo journalist" whose "fame attended his decline as a writer," as Christopher Lehmann-Haupt noted in his *New York Times* review of *Hunter: The Strange and Savage Life of Hunter S. Thompson* by E. Jean Carroll. Two other biographies of this author, who has become more famous for his "out-of-control, drug-abusing self" than his writing, were soon to come: *When the Going Gets Weird: The Twisted Life and Times of Hunter S. Thompson,* by Peter O. Whitmer, and *Fear and Loathing* by Paul Perry.

This American folk hero, who earns a good part of his living now speaking to college audiences while he glugs from a bottle of bourbon, began by working hard at reading and writing, producing his first and best book, *Hell's Angels,* in 1966, and then, as Lehmann-Haupt reports, dissipated himself once his career began to gather steam. This hurt his marriage, which was never idyllic to begin with: Mr. Thompson seems to have believed that while it was all right for him to sleep around, any suspected disloyalty on his wife's part deserved a beating. So the great scourge of public hypocrisy turns out to be something of a hypocrite in private. His intemperance also seems to have hurt his writing, as many of his editors can and do tell.

THE DOWNHILL PATH

It is true that many creative people drink too much, just as it's true that many creative people suffer from anxiety and depression. It is also true that people from all segments of the population suffer from a variety of neurotic disorders and drink too much! It does not follow, however—as the myth would have us believe—that suffering and/or drinking are necessary for creativity. Rather, as in the case of Mr. Thompson and almost every other artist who hits the booze-and-drugs trail, that path leads them and their work downhill, on a journey of diminishing health and creative production.

The book *Touched with Fire* dusts off some of the old cliches about writers and suffering, buttressing them with new statistics. Yet the author, Kay Redfield Jamison, a psychologist at the Johns Hopkins University School of Medicine, explained to an interviewer, "It's very safe to say there is a greatly increased rate of depression and manic depression in artists and writers, but that's not the same as saying you have to have depression or manic depression to be an artist or writer."

In fact, a number of writers and artists interviewed by *Newsday* reporter Fred Bruning challenged even the first premise of Jamison's theory about the "greatly increased" rate of depression and mental illness among creators. Author Geoffrey Wolff scoffed at the notion that excellence results from instability and chaos: "The idea of driving yourself nuts to be a good writer is crazy and adolescent," he said. "There's a snobbishness about it—that people who have lives of equilibrium can't be interesting. That is a child's notion of art. . . . Writing isn't like other work, but it isn't more dangerous or more painful. I'd be the last to cry, 'Woe is me, how hard for the writer.' Some do, and I always nod off."

An eloquent response to Jamison's premise came from Erica Jong, author of *Fear of Flying*, who said, "As a young person I suffered over tiny things and then found ways to use the hypersensitivity in my work. I could take the pain and put it somewhere. We heal ourselves by writing and, at the highest level, we heal other people, too."

Novelist and newspaper columnist Pete Hamill, whose memoir, *A Drinking Life*, won critical praise (he gave up the booze twenty years ago), said, "I don't buy the whole line that somehow art comes from neurosis and you should do nothing or you'll damage the art. My sense is you have to remain healthy physically and mentally. That doesn't mean surrendering knowledge of the darker impulses, just understanding them better."

The most succinct refutation of the Jamison theory (how glamorous it sounds, to be "touched with fire"!) is the insight of Oregon University professor Robert Grudin, who writes on the subject of artistic suffering in his brilliant book *The Grace of Great Things: Creativity and Innovation*:

> The Romantics saw the creative individual as a kind of Faust or an aesthetic Flying Dutchman, doomed by talent to torment and alienation. A more modern version of this myth, common among recent generations, is that inspiration lies somewhere between intoxication and psychosis, that it can result only from some physiological or psychological distortion of one's humanity. While these theories have some value in consoling the uninspired, they do not hold up in history. Creative individuals, even those whom society misprizes, do not necessarily face mental disorders or other woes.
>
> They more generally do, however, face temporary but severe pains in the nature of their work. Their pains are

symptomatic of many typical phases in the creative process: the failure of experiments, the refutation of hypotheses, the shock of criticism, the endurance of contradictions or anomalies, the reorganization or trashing of one's own material, and the mere awareness that such experiences necessarily await one.

Another misconception about creativity is that it is dangerous, that it may undo you, lead to your mental imbalance, drive you to kill yourself. The suicides of many creators are cited as proof of this damaging effect of creation. More often, the mental disturbances and suicides of creators have been stoked by alcohol and drugs, while creative acts have sustained them, kept them alive much longer than they might have lived without that positive force.

Anne Sexton was a friend of mine, and I say it was booze, not poetry, that deepened her depressions and hastened her death. She began writing poetry at the suggestion of her psychiatrist, who felt it would be therapeutic for a bored suburban housewife in the '50s suffering from anxiety and depression. Anne took a poetry course at the Boston Center for Adult Education, where she met and befriended other budding poets like Maxine Kumin and George Starbuck. Her work was almost immediately recognized as powerful and unique. Her first book, *To Bedlam and Part Way Back,* established her at once as a major poet with a fresh new voice. Her poetry was called "confessional"; yet I felt it "confessed" for all of us, by bringing out the dark thoughts of the psyche we're afraid to confront and holding them up to the light. Her poetry sometimes laughed, sometimes cried—it was a cathartic experience for me as a reader, and I think for most of her many devoted fans.

Another misconception about creativity is that it is dangerous, that it may undo you, lead to your mental imbalance, drive you to kill yourself.

Anne continued to write and work despite periods in mental hospitals and attempted suicides. When she finally died from an overdose of pills at the age of forty-two, her death was ascribed by some to poetry, as a manifestation of madness.

Yet Anne told friends in talks and in letters, "The poetry keeps me alive." For many artists, creation is salvation. To create is to live, and to want to live. The alcohol, I believe, killed her.

PUBLIC DEFEAT

I've never seen mentioned another important element that helps explain in a very mundane, practical way the mood swings of writers and artists. I once had lunch with a writer friend in my neighborhood when a local politician who had just lost an election came in. We expressed our sympathy, saying we had voted for him. My writer friend observed that perhaps politicians were the only people who went through the same kinds of public defeats that we endured as authors. When you get a bad review in the hometown paper or the *New York Times* or a national magazine, all the neighbors know. The world knows. Our equivalent experience with the politician who lost an election was getting bad reviews and having the neighbors come up and sympathize, saying they had bought the books anyway (a way of "voting" in our favor). And, like the politician's, our defeat would not merely be a blow to the ego, as in a popularity contest, but also to the income, as in paying the rent and putting food on the table.

If a doctor loses a patient, or a lawyer loses an important case, it's usually known only in their professional circles; rarely do friends and neighbors hear about it, much less read about it in the Sunday paper! Yet no writer with a new book, or artist with a new show, is immune

---

CREATORS TALKING

"I have a community of support, a lot of writer friends. Now I'm learning to let people read things. I used to be so anal about my work, no one saw it before I thought it was perfect. Now I let two or three people read the stuff in progress and talk to them on a regular basis. I need the encouragement of my friends."

—MARK MATOUSEK, JOURNALIST, EDITOR, COLUMNIST,
AUTHOR OF THE MEMOIR *SEX DEATH ENLIGHTENMENT*

Powerful art raises passions, from love to outrage, and in a sense the reviewer is expressing the public's emotional as well as intellectual response to the work.

to public disdain and ridicule. Reviewers of both art and literature can be vicious. I once had an otherwise successful novel (*Starting Over,* which later became a movie starring Burt Reynolds and Candice Bergen) described in a review in the *Washington Post* as "despicable." It went downhill from there. My friends in D.C. called to express their condolences. It felt as if I'd died, at least in D.C.; in fact, my book did, killed by that review, though it did well almost everywhere else. Not even the most successful, garlanded writers are immune to such put-downs; one of John Updike's novels was demeaned by one reviewer as "ugly."

Powerful art raises passions, from love to outrage, and in a sense the reviewer is expressing the public's emotional as well as intellectual response to the work. The anger stirred by innovative plays, symphonies, paintings, and sculpture has even caused audience rebellions and governmental bannings.

Then there are the times when reviews glow, but sales falter. One talented writer friend seemed never to recover from having his first novel highly praised, shipped by the publisher with a good advance order that indicated a modest success, only to be told a few months later that half the books had been returned, unbought, and he would not even earn back his modest advance against royalties. The double demons of money and artistic standing (which rises and falls like the stock market gone mad) remain a constant concern in the career of every writer, actor, painter, musician, director. As they say in Hollywood, the bottom line is, you're only as good as your last picture. That pressure alone is enough to drive anyone to dramatic swings of mood.

Looked at from this perspective, one could argue that creative artists must be mentally and emotionally tougher than people in most other professions, especially those who earn a steady income. Virginia Woolf called for "a room of one's own" and a small monthly stipend for women writers in the early part of the century. Most writers I know today, of all genders, races, and creeds, long for the basic physical and financial security of that modest underpinning. Except for screenwriters, who are members of the Writers Guild of America, writers do not receive the "benefits" common to most Americans, such as health care and retirement funds. Is it any wonder writers get anxious or depressed? Sweating over the rent, or worrying about how to pay the doctor or hospital bill, are not stimulants to creativity.

Yet such practical, down-to-earth pressures are rarely mentioned in discussions of the psychology of writers; they are not glamorous enough to suit the myth. More popular is the topic of a conference held at the 92nd Street Y in New York City in 1994 called "Wanting to Die: Suicide and American Literature." The *New York Times* reported that the daylong conference "explored the links between depression, creativity, and suicide."

One of the famous writers discussed at the conference was Ernest Hemingway, who committed suicide after a lifetime of alcohol abuse had led to failing health and paranoid delusions. Was it the alcohol, or the creativity, that led to his suicide? Or was it genetics, or environment? Those are especially pertinent questions in the case of Hemingway, whose father, brother, and sister also committed suicide, though not one of them was a writer. His father was a doctor.

Have you heard about any conferences on the links between practicing medicine and committing suicide? As far as I know, this is not generally acknowledged as a dangerous phenomenon; but perhaps it should be. Dr. Dean Ornish, the heart specialist and best-selling author, pointed out in *Reversing Heart Disease*, "As a profession, we [doctors] have among the highest rates of drug addiction and divorce of any identifiable group, and the average physician dies ten years prematurely. Each year, enough physicians commit suicide to equal a large medical school's entire graduating class. And that's just the known suicides."

What about the links between law enforcement officers and suicide? In a recent year, twelve New York City policemen committed

Love was a creative potion for George Eliot, who started writing the novels that would make her world-famous (Silas Marner, The Mill on the Floss, Middle-march) *when she found domestic happiness.*

suicide. I don't believe as many writers in New York City committed suicide in any recent year, despite bad reviews, manuscript rejections, falling income, lack of health plan or pension benefits, or any other stress-related circumstance common to the life of the writer.

My favorite story to counter the suffering-is-necessary-to-create myth is the true-life experience of the great English novelist George Eliot. Eliot was a plain and rather miserable young woman grinding out reviews for an intellectual magazine until she met a man with whom she fell madly in love. He was married to a woman who had continually betrayed him and even bore the child of his best friend, but in the England of that day, he was unable to divorce her. In love with Eliot, he went off with her to the Continent, where they lived happily "in sin," as some of their old friends back home in England huffed in pious recrimination at them across the Channel. George's friends even wrote her to break it off and come back, claiming they were worried about her welfare. She wrote back, asking why they hadn't been worried about her when she was lonely and miserable!

Love was a creative potion for George Eliot, who started writing the novels that would make her world-famous (*Silas Marner, The Mill on the Floss, Middlemarch*) when she found domestic happiness. As a lonely person longing for love, she felt lucky to eke out a living with her reviews of other people's creative works; as a woman living with the man she loved, she created great works of fiction that live today.

TESTIMONY OF A HAPPY NOVELIST

Novelist and poet Rosellen Brown, author of the highly praised best-seller *Before and After,* is a contemporary writer who doesn't buy the myth that you have to suffer and lead a miserable life to be creative. "I had a happy childhood, loved my parents and my two brothers, who I'm still very close to," she told me recently. "I don't think you have to be unhappy to create. John Irving said having a happy child-hood was good for him as a writer because he had no axes to grind, and I feel the same."

"I've been married to the same man for thirty-one years," she continued,

> and he's more delightful every day, and we have two terrific daughters. I've had the most ordinary life—boring, no great traumas. When people ask me where I get these painful stories for my books I say that's not my experience, those are my nightmares—I put them on the page to work them out. I do think most of us artists and writers have at some time or other felt like outsiders—but I don't think you have to suffer personally to write or paint, you just have to keep your eyes open, look around you.

So much for the idea that suffering is necessary to create.

Myth Number 3: Only the Arts Are Creative

Some people throughout history who have proved this rule wrong are: Marie Curie, Wilbur and Orville Wright, Joan of Arc, Albert Einstein, Jonas Salk, Eleanor Roosevelt and Franklin D. Roosevelt, Bill Clinton and Hillary Rodham Clinton, Mahatma Gandhi, Winston Churchill, Golda Meir, Martin Luther King, Jr.—to name but a few.

According to this well-worn myth, sometimes science qualifies as creative (surely Einstein can be counted!), but business is still often regarded as plodding, pedestrian, unimaginative—even running a profit-making corporation. When I called Arnold Hiatt, the innovative entrepreneur who pioneered some of the most advanced employee and community relations in recent American business as head of the Stride Rite Corporation and now director of its foundation, he said he'd be glad to talk with me about creativity but explained he was not himself "a creative person."

I disagreed. Hadn't he created a day-care center, a nonsmoking workplace, and a gym for employees, and captured new markets for his company when he anticipated the changing taste of consumers? Wasn't all that creative? Not by our usual definitions.

LOOKING FOR DETAIL

I learned in talking to Hiatt that his observation of detail, like that of a novelist, led to some of his greatest business successes. As treasurer of the Eugene McCarthy campaign in '68, he noticed the college kids were wearing work boots, and he bought a company that produced them. In the next decade he noticed Harvard students wearing boat shoes that could only be purchased in marinas, and he bought a company that made them and put them on the national market.

Business people often use their creative imaginations to turn obstacles into assets. California restaurateur Larry Mindel told Bill Citara, an interviewer for *Bay Food* magazine, how two of his successful San Francisco restaurants benefited when he saw a problem in a different light and turned it to an advantage.

> Ciao did exhibition pasta because it was such a tiny restaurant we didn't have enough room in the kitchen to make pasta. So I said, let's make it out here, what's the difference? The same thing happened at Prego on Union Street. In the middle of the bar area was a fireplace. And we didn't have any place to make pizza. So, I said, why don't we make pizza where the fireplace is? Then we don't have to put in another flue. So we did the first exhibition pizza thing at Prego.

Like The Body Shop founder Anita Roddick, Mindel emphasizes the importance of creating a good working atmosphere, being in business with people you like, and loving what you do. For his popular Il Fornaio restaurants he uses all Italian ingredients and recipes, and hires Italian chefs "who do it out of love, not just for a job."

My old friend and mentor, the Reverend Norman Eddy, began his creative ministry with the East Harlem Protestant Parish and still works and counsels in that neighborhood, where he has lived for more than forty years, making tremendous contributions in political action, aid for narcotics addicts, and ownership of housing by neighborhood residents. He gained a new understanding of creativity when he was a young man searching for his own spiritual path. He went to "a theosophist who read auras," he recalled, and what she told him "shook him up."

"She said I was an administrator, an activist. This hadn't crossed my mind. When she said it, I saw I'd often taken a leadership role in situations, although I thought of myself as sensitive, shy, and intuitive—an 'artistic' type. Yet these qualities were leading me to a life of action!"

Norm's career has proved that being an administrator and activist can be highly creative. Wasn't Martin Luther King, Jr., a creative person, and his own idol, Gandhi? King and Gandhi may not have written any novels or painted any pictures, but look how they have recreated the society and world we live in today!

"ZENNING OUT" WITH THE KIDS

Like many women, April Smith has managed to juggle motherhood and family life with a career—in her case, a highly prolific and successful writing career, primarily in network television. It's the toughest market there is, one in which writers (like me) are traditionally ground up and spit out like cannon fodder. April has carved out a distinguished record. She came to Hollywood to write a script for the series I created, *James at 15,* moved on to become a staff writer and producer for *Lou Grant,* and then wrote and produced high-quality television movies, picking up three Emmy nominations along the way. What is even more remarkable, she has pulled off what every TV writer swears they intend to do but so rarely do: she took a year off from the big bucks of TV to gamble on writing a novel.

April won the bet with her fast-moving, incisive tale of the social strata of Los Angeles, *North of Montana,* bought by Knopf for an advance of $750,000 and tagged as a major book for its list. She rents an office in the business section of her neighborhood, not far from her

April said parenting was not only a help to her creativity as a writer, but also a creative act in itself.

house, and goes there every morning to do her writing, whether it is of scripts or a novel. She has a household helper during the day, and her husband also takes part in the child-rearing. Still, I wondered how she did it—the professional writing combined with being a wife and the mother of an eight-year-old boy and a two-year-old girl.

April said parenting was not only a help to her creativity as a writer, but also a creative act in itself.

Part of the creativity of being a parent is being able to live in the moment, because the children's whole lives are in the present. Watching the way they grow is miraculous, the way they learn and change. It's awesome, and it makes you value the moment, when you see how it passes so quickly. It makes you grateful in a spiritual way. They really add a spiritual aspect to my life.

You're always problem-solving with kids, and often the solution is to create a distraction. If the kid is upset you want to get them out of their own distress. Rather than have a deep encounter with their subconscious it's better to get out the Barney coloring book, or make an origami airplane.

You have to be creative about sibling rivalry. When I'm alone with the kids they fight—my solution is to do a project together. Yesterday we cooked together—it wasn't anything great, just the old tuna-noodle casserole, but Emma got to stir and Ben got to chop, so they were busy doing something and forgot to hate each other.

What you do doesn't have to be glamorous. I think a lot of women feel intimidated if they're not being creative like the magazines tell you to do, whipping up cookies or art projects, but sometimes you just stall out and let them watch TV. Sometimes you can really "Zen out." Yesterday morning it was raining and the three of us did watercolors together; I was just pulling the brush across the page. It was almost like meditation, you can just be. It doesn't have to be work.

Luckily, the writing I do during the day uses a different part of the brain—I'm intellectual during the day, then I come home, and with kids it's all on the gut level. It does deplete your energy, but you get a lot back. The kids help the creativity I need in my work—absorbing their spontaneity, seeing the way they think is refreshing. It loosens up a lot of structures that are calcified.

Many male writers also find creativity in their role as fathers. Novelist Ivan Gold says, "Raising a son is the most creative thing I've ever done—in the back of my mind, of course, it's always a possible subject for fiction."

Rosellen Brown, a writing wife and mother who also teaches creative writing at the University of Houston, agrees:

> Raising children takes great creativity and I think it feeds into your work. There are many women writers today who have children, and their writing benefits from it—Margaret Drabble, Alice Hoffman, Anne Tyler. Tyler said her children dragged the world of pop culture over the doorstep into the house, or she never would have known about it. I could say the same.
>
> I believe people raising children are doing the most creative activity possible. You're keeping them healthy, fed, getting them to school—it's very much in bits and pieces, a mosaic of little acts of loving kindness, and it seems mundane but it's not. When you pull back and look at it, you see it's extraordinary.

It's extraordinary, too, how mothers can foster—and even shape—the creative spirit of their children. When master architect Frank Lloyd Wright was a baby, his mother,

Many male writers also find creativity in their role as fathers.

Journalist Jill Nelson was twenty years old and single when her daughter was born, and she had to figure out a way to write and take care of her baby at the same time.

Anna, hung prints of Gothic cathedrals around his crib, according to Meryle Secrest, author of *Frank Lloyd Wright: A Biography*. Wright's mother believed (and obviously helped determine) that he would grow up to become a great architect.

Rosellen Brown's "mosaic" of small acts made me think of a story I heard from Alice Olsen Mann, the head of the appeals department of a major law firm in Boston and a nationally known expert in her legal field. She mentioned once that when raising her son she developed different strategies for getting him to eat his vegetables, making broccoli more alluring by telling him the broccoli stalks were like "little trees." It was much more fun to eat "little trees" than plain old boring broccoli.

Mrs. Mann's story reminded me of how my own mother got me to eat Brussels sprouts by calling them "little boy cabbages." The formerly dull vegetables took on a new meaning and interest—they were specially made for me, it seemed! Knowing that, they didn't taste so bad after all.

Isn't the ability to see broccoli as "little trees," or to rename Brussels sprouts in a way that is appealing to a little boy, the same sort of creative activity as finding the right metaphor for a poem? That kind of creativity is part of the daily work of any mother. Who can doubt the creative imagination and energy it takes to be a wife and mother—or, for that matter, a single mother, one without any outside assistance from family or hired helpers?

Journalist Jill Nelson was twenty years old and single when her daughter was born, and she had to figure out a way to write and take care of her baby at the same time. She learned to sit on the floor with her typewriter on top of a box while a toddler crawled nearby, and then a two-year-old ran around. "I was creating what you do in that situation," she told me. A twenty-four-hour record of any such role would surely involve as much creativity as Van Gogh put into a day at the easel or Henry James used when "steadily driving" his pen.

Still, in some circles of our society, women are called upon to defend or justify their roles as wives and mothers. According to an article in the *New York Times,* when poet and musician Patti Smith transformed herself "from the belligerent Bohemian punk poet of the '70s who galvanized the New York underground to the loving wife and mother of the '80s," she "shocked her fans by disappearing to the Detroit suburb of St. Clair Shores." When Smith returned to the concert circuit on a tour with Bob Dylan at the end of 1995, some of her fans "snidely" said that she "withdrew from the music world in order to be a housewife," the *Times* reported.

Ms. Smith responded,

> There's no job harder than being a wife and a mother. It's a position that should be respected and honored, not looked upon as some sappy alternative. It's much more demanding, and required much more nobility than the other work that I did. Hopefully, I can inject some of the things that I learned from that experience into the work that I'm doing now.

Myth Number 4: Creativity Is Not Manly

When I was a freshman in college at Bloomington, Indiana, one of my jock fraternity brothers spotted me carrying a novel by F. Scott Fitzgerald—a book that was not a requirement for any class—and plucked it from my hand. He held it up with a grimace, as if examining a dirty sock.

"You like this stuff?" he asked, with not so much curiosity as contempt.

"Yeah," I said, in my best mock-thug voice. I was trying to sound macho, for I knew what was being questioned was not my literary taste, but my manliness. It was understood, like an unwritten rule of life, at least in the American Midwest in the mid '50s, that real men don't read novels—or write poems; paint (or look at) pictures; play or listen to classical music; write, act in, or go to the theater (with the possible exception of a college variety show sponsored by the right fraternity);

or show any sort of interest in or appreciation of the arts, which included anything that might be called creative, a word which in that time and place carried a nuance of femininity, or at least un-masculinity.

Nor was this attitude just a phenomenon of the heartland; Reverend Norman Eddy found it in New York City, in the mean streets of East Harlem, among the young gang members and those who fell prey to the lure of dope.

"On the street, to be creative is not macho," Norm reflected recently, "so there's no outlet for creativity, except in athletics, with the body."

> My eyes opened when I saw heroin addicts who were unable to express their creativity, and when I visited Riverside Hospital to see them in recovery I discovered that many of those young addicts had poems tucked under their pillow. I asked if they had shown them to their therapist and they said of course not—they wouldn't dare show them to anyone. I was an exception because I was a minister, so I was supposed to understand such things.
>
> Even today, the body is the only accepted way—or macho way—of being creative, on the street. That's a perfectly fine way, of course, but it's a shame to think of it as the only one. The body, mind, soul, feelings are all areas in which we can be creative. When Jesus says to worship him with all your heart, mind, soul, and strength, that's what he means. All of us are part of creation—one of our deepest desires is to create the beautiful.

"And, of course, everyone really is creative," Norm added with a smile. "Even the nineteenth-century robber barons who created the railroads and shipping lines had a kind of creative zeal."

Yes! But of course we don't think of them that way. They are seen as macho or practical or hardheaded—which in our culture are thought of almost in opposition to creativity.

Our society is more sophisticated now, yet those old strictures still hold to our thinking. Such obsolete concepts are probably among the factors behind the national ratio of 70 percent women to 30 percent men taking adult education courses. That is also the usual ratio for the workshops I lead in creativity or Spiritual Autobiography; yet the men who do participate enjoy and benefit from the experience as fully and actively as the women. In fact, they show signs of being just as creative as their wives and sisters!

A NEW MESSENGER ARRIVES

Perhaps the greatest breakthrough in attitudes in our time is the acknowledgment of gay men and lesbians as major cultural contributors who need not hide their sexual orientation. Despite the prejudice that still exists in the society at large, at least in the arts the old stigma and fear of homosexuality has been largely replaced by gay pride. Where once a man's "artistic leanings" were regarded as a shameful indication of homosexuality (hence the effort to prove oneself super-macho), our respected male novelists now include openly gay authors writing frankly on homosexual themes, like David Leavitt, Armistead Maupin (both of whom have had their work dramatized for PBS miniseries), Paul Monette, and Edmund White.

The most exciting and significant theatrical event of the decade is the winner of the 1993 Pulitzer Prize for drama, *Angels in America*, subtitled *A Gay Fantasia on American Themes*. Rather than hopelessly

CREATORS TALKING

"I keep a journal; even in the lean years I kept it. Even when the book is going well I keep it. I segue from the events of my day to the aesthetic task. Since I write autobiographically anyway, I make entries to get the memory down. Also, I like to stop work when it's going well. It's like stopping eating while you're still hungry—sort of like Hemingway is said to have stopped work every day in the middle of a sentence."

—IVAN GOLD, NOVELIST, TEACHER, AUTHOR OF *NICKEL MISERIES*, *SICK FRIENDS*, AND *SAMS IN A DRY SEASON* lamenting the victims of AIDS, the scourge of our time, *Angels*, by playwright Tony Kushner, builds to a stunning finale of courage and mystical power, with an angel descending to the hospital room of Prior Walter, the AIDS-afflicted patient, announcing: "The great work begins. The messenger arrives."

Rarely has art in our time created—by an act of imaginative will—such a life-affirming message of hope from the very theme and throes of death.

Myth Number 5: Women's Work Is Not as Creative as Men's

Women's struggle for equal pay and opportunity in the business world is necessary in the world of the arts as well. Example: A painting by Jasper Johns recently sold for $17.7 million. For that same amount of money, you could buy "an anthology of all the women artists in history"—a piece by about fifty women artists—including work by such luminaries as Georgia O'Keeffe and Frida Kahlo.

This eye-opening (and hopefully mind-opening) information comes from the Guerrilla Girls, an anonymous group of activist women artists formed in 1984 to combat "the underrepresentation of women in the arts." The inequality was made glaringly obvious when the Museum of Modern Art opened that year with an international painting and sculpture show of work by 166 people, and only sixteen were women—slightly less than 10 percent.

Both older and younger feminists combined to form the group that spells its name "guerrilla" like the freedom fighters, but whose members wear gorilla masks in public appearances and on posters as an image of their anger. Romaine Brooks, an identified member of the Guerrilla Girls, said in an interview with author Suzi Gablik in *Art in America* magazine:

Women's struggle for equal pay and opportunity in the business world is necessary in the world of the arts as well.

Today, when we visited the Roanoke [Virginia] Museum, there was a painting by Thomas Eakins's wife. I guess the only reason her painting was in the museum is that her family comes from around here—that's what we were told. It reminded me of a show of . . . artist wives of famous artists, and they were all extremely gifted and talented. In one case, the woman had destroyed most of her work at the end of her life because she felt it would be a burden to her children— nobody paid any attention to her the whole time she was making the work, so only a few pieces were left. Milton Avery's wife, Sally Avery, was in the show. It turned out she'd supported him for 25 years, and when the woman curator went over there to get a few pieces for the show, all of Milton Avery's work was on the walls, and her work was in a pile on the floor. So the curator said, "Why is your work on the floor?" And she answered, "Well, Milton gets the walls and I get the floor." And that is a crippling atti- tude. And even though it's now 1993 and things should be different, I think it's still an attitude that one encounters.

Things are different in some ways, however, at least partly due to the protests of the Guerrilla Girls.

Romaine Brooks explained in the same interview,

We did a critique of the Whitney Biennial a number of years ago, at the Clocktower in New York, where we gave all these statistics revealing how sexist and racist all the Whitney Biennials have been. Well, the most recent Whitney Biennial is 40 percent women, and it's probably 35 percent artists of color, and I'd say we really take full credit for this. Things that we've been pounding on and talking about for years are finally bearing some fruit.

I saw a documentary movie on the life and work of New York painter Joan Mitchell, who tells of going to a gallery owner in the '50s who looked at her paintings and declined to take her on. He shook his head, saying wistfully that he loved her work and knew it would sell, "if you were only male, French—and dead."

MEN EARN TWICE AS MUCH

Rebecca Blunk, director of performing arts for the New England Foundation for the Arts, told me that in arts management

> very few women in the presenting field [professional impresario] make over $50,000, but many men do. Art is generally undervalued in our society, so it is safe to put women in charge of it at paltry salaries. Once an organization requires big budgets and new buildings, salaries go up and men are more likely to be in the top spots. A 1994 survey in the TAB newspapers in Boston listed the top ten salaries for people in management positions in culture and the arts in the city; the only woman on the list was Ann Hawley, director of the Isabella Stewart Gardner Museum, and she was at the bottom, or tenth place, with an annual salary of $104,865. Number one on the list was Kenneth Haas, general manager of the Boston Symphony, at $275,600.

Ms. Blunk also pointed out that many women are still regarded as earning a secondary household income, and many start out in the arts as volunteers and cannot overcome that image.

I know of a case in which a married woman and a single man formed a company in the entertainment field in the '60s, and he told her she should take a lesser salary because she was married and had a second income, while he did not. She accepted this, although she did at least an equal part of the work. This was typical for that time, and probably occurs today, although surely it is no longer taken for granted, as it was so recently.

In the world of writing and publishing, women are faring much better. Two of the biggest advances for first novels in recent years went to works by women. When I started out as a writer there were no women working as editors in chief or heads of publishing houses, except for the remarkable Helen Meyer, head of Dell, who was one of the giants of the industry. Now there are women in both positions throughout publishing.

Myth Number 6: You Have to Live in an Ivory Tower or by a Pond to Create

Many talented writers of the '50s were scorned by critics for going into academic life—"retreating to the ivory tower," it was called—yet some of our finest novelists of the era, like Saul Bellow, Bernard Malamud, Mary McCarthy, Harvey Swados, and Herbert Gold, supplemented their writing with teaching at universities, as did even more of the poets, including Maxine Kumin, Anne Sexton, Richard Wilbur, W. D. Snodgrass, and Robert Lowell, to name but a few who found nourishment for the muse as well as financial stability in college classroom teaching.

The "ivory tower" stigma has largely dissipated. Many of the new generation of writers come out of graduate writing programs, like two of my former students from the Iowa Writers Workshop—Tracy Kidder, whose *Soul of a New Machine* won a Pulitzer Prize for nonfiction, and Thom Jones, whose collection of stories, *The Pugilist at Rest*, was nominated for the National Book Award for Fiction in '93. Many graduate writing programs around the country have working writers on the faculty, from short-story writer Deborah Eisenberg and novelist Frank Conroy at Iowa, to novelist John Edgar Wideman at the University of Massachusetts and novelists Eileen Pollack and Jenefer Shute at Emerson.

On the other hand, many writers have found not only their subject matter but their creative spirit from living very much in—and as part of—the world. Louis Auchincloss worked at the prestigious New York law firm of Sullivan and Cromwell (one of its senior partners, John Foster Dulles, complained that the younger men in the office "wrote novels") while writing distinguished novels of New York society life in the tradition of Henry James and Edith Wharton. When one of his works, *The Rector of Justin,* became a critical success and a bestseller, Auchincloss left the law firm to devote himself full-time to writing. He soon found that without that structure of his other career, he couldn't write, so he formed his own law firm, working half-time on legal matters and devoting the rest of his time to writing (without any senior partners to complain.)

The best-selling Icelandic novelist Olaf Olafsson is also president of the Sony Electronic Publishing Company, a leading producer of video games like *Bram Stoker's Dracula, Cliffhanger,* and *Sewer Shark.* Running a business that racked up $150 million in sales in 1993 did not keep Olafsson from writing four hours every night during the week and six hours a day on weekends in his Upper East Side Manhattan apartment. An English translation of his novel *Absolution* was published in the United States in '94. Olafsson was described as "the most respected novelist in the most literate country in the world" by *New York* magazine, but his literary success didn't tempt him to leave his full-time job in the business world.

"So far, it has not been a hindrance to my writing," he told reporter Dinitia Smith, "though I've had less time in the past two years than I wanted to. When I'm so busy that I can't write, I do get frustrated."

But that frustration is balanced for Olafsson by the fact that, as he says, "When I write, I don't have to please anybody but myself. I don't have to write a particular story to pay the phone bills."

Writers who seem to find creative energy in the world include novelist Joan Didion, who in her role as reporter loves to explore new scenes and subjects. William F. Buckley, former host of the TV show *Firing Line,* turns out a syndicated newspaper column, and lectures and debates around the country and the world, told me, "I write my novels every afternoon between the hours of four and seven."

Anne Sexton formed a rock group, Anne Sexton and Her Kind, in the early '70s to back up her poetry readings—much to her own delight, but to the chagrin of the poetry establishment. Norman Mailer has always thrived on mixing it up out there in debates, boxing rings, prisons, and politics, not only covering elections as a journalist-observer but once jumping into the fray himself by running for mayor of New York (as did his longtime debating foe, Bill Buckley). The end of the Cold War even saw the emergence of the writer as national leader in the person of playwright Vaclav Havel, who rose from political prisoner to president of the former Czechoslovakia.

Artists and writers also find fulfillment in working for political causes. The San Francisco painter Mayumi Oda recently took a year off from her art to devote her efforts full-time to a project for pressuring governments around the world to destroy their stores of plutonium. She feels the cause is worth the sacrifice of a year of her own work, since plutonium weapons can destroy our civilization; no more people, no more art.

Creative people have traditionally given time to causes they believe in, joining in community action on behalf of oppressed peoples, human rights, animal rights, the preservation of the earth. James Baldwin devoted great energy and time to civil rights causes, as did his friend Kay Boyle, who never in her ninety-one years was without a cause for the betterment of the world and its inhabitants. Both drew sustenance from such activities, as demonstrated by their productivity as well as the high quality of their work (they both achieved the goal of what Baldwin called creating "a shelf of books" by the end of their lives). The musicians who put on Live Aid and Farm Aid, the activist actors who are often scoffed at for their genuine dedication and beliefs, are typical of the connection between creativity and contribution to the human community. Robert Redford has not only become involved in ecology, but has also given back to young people the support of a mentor with his extensive programs for development of films at the Sundance Institute. Paul Newman's foundation sponsors camps for disabled children and gives grants to community programs like Vera Gold's 96 Bay State Road writers group and magazine in Boston.

THOREAU'S DINNER AT HOME

Experiences as diverse as those just mentioned disprove the isolation myth, but I want to point out an infrequently mentioned aspect of the "lonely creation" phenomenon. Famous "loner" artists, like Thoreau, had significant and regular friends and colleagues in their lives. Thoreau helped perpetuate the isolation myth when he romanticized his own life at Walden Pond, but he omitted the crucial information that he went home for dinner every week and dropped in to talk with his friend and neighbor Mr. Emerson.

Thomas Merton felt pulled from his lone outpost at the hermitage on the grounds of Gethsemani and yearned to be at worldwide conferences of religious leaders in Europe and Asia. It was at such a meeting of Christian and Buddhist leaders and thinkers in Bangkok that he met his accidental death in 1969. I don't mean to dismiss or discredit either of these two great creators, Thoreau or Merton, yet their lives offer dramatic and even poignant illustration of the need to be nourished by community.

THE POWER OF GROUP ENERGY

I would have sworn as recently as five years ago that, at least in the actual act of writing, one has to be alone. That surely has nothing to do with community, and can only be stymied by it. Yet in leading my workshops, I have seen people stimulated by community while writing in the same room with the others. Participants report a kind of group energy that raises the level of their own creativity, as they come to know one another through their mutual stories. I have felt it and recognized it in the course of leading these exercises in creativity. Writing in a room while other people are writing, then reading what you have written aloud to the group, raises the level of the writing and stimulates release of the story within. The community experience of sharing gives it a new resonance, increasing the richness of the creative act.

Writers, painters, and musicians love to socialize, as well as work at artist colonies like Yaddo in Saratoga Springs, New York, and MacDowell in Peterborough, New Hampshire. A group of abstract expressionist painters of New York formed the Artists Club in a loft on Eighth Street in Greenwich Village for fellow painters, sculptors, and art dealers. The painter Jack Tworkov explained the club's appeal in his journal: "I'm consciously happy when I'm there. I enjoy the talk, the enthusiasm, the laughter. . . . There is a strong sense of identifi-

Famous "loner" artists, like Thoreau, had significant and regular friends and colleagues in their lives.

cation. I say to myself, these are the people I love, that I love to be with. Here I understand everybody, however inarticulate they are. Here I forgive everyone their vices, and I'm learning to admire their virtues."

Participants report a kind of group energy that raises the level of their own creativity, as they come to know one another through their mutual stories.

Maybe those in the creative arts were the first to discover the richness and support of community that is now sweeping the nation. In *Sharing the Journey: Support Groups and America's New Quest for Community,* Princeton sociologist Robert Wuthnow reports finding that 40 percent of nearly two thousand randomly selected Americans participated in support groups. These were not Twelve Step or therapy groups but Bible study, prayer, adult Sunday school, or adult education groups. Participants said the groups made them feel they were not alone and supplied encouragement and support when they were feeling down.

Even groups that form for weekend workshops create such bonds. People who take my Spiritual Autobiography seminars sometimes exchange addresses and continue to meet on their own for months or years. The most frequent response from the members of one such group, when asked what was most important to them in the course, was that they learned they weren't the only ones who went through "the dark side" on their journey. The valuable message, not just in words but in shared experience, was: You are not alone.

There are, however, times when you may want to be alone—not in the context of your life, but for a circumscribed period. Sometimes we feel an overload of social interaction, no matter how fulfilling and creative it may be, and we long for solitude. Canadian singer and songwriter Sarah McLachlan spent fourteen months touring, and then she visited impoverished areas of Thailand and Cambodia with the World Vision Charity. Afterward, she rented a secluded home in the woods outside Montreal.

"I stayed there for seven months by myself, except for my cats," she told *New York Times* reporter Sheila Rule. "I'd been on the road living in a bus with thirteen people. I had no sense of privacy or sense of self. I was in hibernation the first couple of months, but when spring came everything blossomed and opened up. My spirit decided to be set free and I started writing."

McLachlan, whose album written during that time was called *Fumbling Towards Ecstasy*, said that her creativity "has been aided by solitude."

Everyone must go by their own instinct in such matters, deciding what is right for their own spirit, without making a mythic "must" of any single choice.

Myth Number 7: Creativity Is a Full-Time Job

Examples of people who have proved this rule wrong: insurance executive and poet Wallace Stevens ("Money is a kind of poetry," he wrote); Sony Electronics Publishing president and novelist Olaf Olafsson; banker and poet T. S. Eliot; family doctor and poet Dr. William Carlos Williams; novelist, wife, and mother Sue Miller; novelist, wife, and mother Gish Jen; poet, housewife, mother, teacher, farmer, and horsewoman Maxine Kumin; novelist, journalist, wife, and mother Joan Didion; novelist, wife, mother, and teacher Lynn Sharon Schwartz; novelist, wife, and mother Jayne Ann Phillips; and every woman writer who is also a wife and mother, as well as those who are single mothers.

Women who are married with children or are single mothers simply have no choice but to find a time and place and way to do their writing. Those I've cited are only a few examples of the many who manage to do it all with no harm or loss to their creative work, and often feel that work is fed and nourished by their other roles. April Smith says, "Having children gives me perspective, it grounds me."

Rosellen Brown believes,

> Raising kids keeps you in the mainstream, the world you write out of. I feel like I'm writing out of my experience of ordinary American life, though it's slightly different to be a mother who's a writer. I'm not quite as available, but neither

would a woman lawyer be available to drive the car pool in the afternoon. You have to protect that time if you work at home. But it's a great and useful thing to me as a writer to go sit at an elementary school band concert, or a high school wrestling match. Children remind you that you live in the world and that world is what you want in your writing.

Many women take on these demanding multiple roles and find creative ways to make them all work. Historically it is mainly men who have moaned and whined over having other obligations that "interfere" with their creative activity, and even in our more liberated era, some men are keeping the tradition alive. Raymond Carver complained that having to share the duties of household and child raising forced him to be a short-story writer, since taking time out for chores like going to the laundromat precluded his sustaining the longer work of a novel. (He should have asked writers like Rosellen Brown, Alice Hoffman, and dozens of others how they managed to do it.)

Despite the dramatic gains by women toward equality as creators in the literary marketplace, it still seems surprisingly common for men to ask the women they live with as wives or lovers to support their creative habit, so that they—these sensitive men—can remain "pure" in their creativity, courting their elusive muse with full attention while the woman attends to such mundane matters as paying the rent or mortgage, taking care of the kids, and not only "bringing home the bacon" but cooking it up and washing the greasy skillet afterward.

Myth Number 8: Creative People Don't Have Good Relationships

This is often a cop-out used by creative people themselves. I know, because I've used it myself as an excuse for my own poor record of broken relationships, and I even conned myself into believing it for a while. It's similar to saying, "I'm creative, so I have to drink a lot." You may not maintain relationships, and you may drink, but the same is true of many people whose work has nothing to do with the arts or

Creativity doesn't necessarily need to take anything away from you. Odds are, it will only expand your experience.

creativity. Throwing in creativity as an excuse for other unsatisfactory behavior is simply a way of avoiding—for yourself as well as the world—the real issues.

According to this myth, all of one's emotion goes into creative work, so nothing is left over. Hemingway even believed that this applied to sex—that creative energy was the same stuff, or came from the same source, as sexual energy. He thought that when he was really working hard on his writing, any sexual activity would drain his creative energy. This is the male artist's version of "I can't tonight, dear, I have a headache!"

This is one of the Hemingway myths I had bought myself, largely abstaining from sex in the final creative burst that comes in the last few months of finishing a book. Then one summer I went off to the seashore with a wonderful woman I was living with, assuming that the concentrated writing I would have to do to finish the book would sap my sexual energies. My lovely lover showed me what a sap I was! Having not read or paid much heed to Hemingway's weirdo-macho philosophy, she simply proceeded on her own desires and assumptions, taking me with her, and I had the most fulfilling summer of my life as I finished writing the novel *Home Free*.

Creativity doesn't necessarily need to take anything away from you. Odds are, it will only expand your experience.

Myth Number 9: Creative People Are Children and Aren't Responsible

This is a favorite of landlords who don't want to rent to writers and artists, parents who don't want their daughters or sons to marry one, and personnel executives who don't want to hire one. It's also used by some creators who like to perpetrate the myth as an excuse for their own irresponsibility: "I can't help it, I'm too sensitive and artistic to (a) pay the rent, (b) show up on time, (c) clean the apartment, (d) go grocery shopping, cook, or wash the dishes, (e) _____ through (z) _____"; you can fill in the blanks yourself!

I asked people in my workshop to write down what they had heard growing up about creative artists. These are some typical responses, which I think reflect the general attitude of our society: "aimless, shiftless, and poor," "radicals, hippies, beyond the pale," "into deviant lifestyles," "usually people with sad hearts."

Creative workers sometimes bring an image of irresponsibility on themselves, a glaring example being the refusal of some writers to join organizations acting on their behalf, such as the National Writers Union. They argue that creative people are somehow harmed by being in groups. According to this myth, their delicate sensibility is mysteriously upset by acting in concert with their fellow artists; and to think about such mundane issues as money, rights, benefits, and fair contractual agreements for all is somehow crass. This is indeed a childish opinion. Publishers are adults who correctly act in their own best interests; writers must have the maturity to do the same. In the movie industry they have done it, and members of the Writers Guild of America enjoy health insurance and retirement benefits as a result.

Myth Number 10: The Older You Get, the Less Creative You Become

Oh, really? How about Marc Chagall painting in his nineties, Graham Greene turning out fine novels in his eighties, Katharine Hepburn acting on television at eighty-eight, Jason Robards performing in a Pinter play on Broadway at seventy-one, Martha Graham choreographing at ninety, Hume Cronin and Jessica Tandy performing on stage and screen in their eighties, May Sarton bringing out her collected works and writing new ones at eighty-two, Georgia O'Keeffe painting in her eighties, George Burns flicking his cigar as he celebrated his ninety-ninth birthday, Edward L. Bernays, the "Father of Public Relations," lecturing and writing two years past his hundredth birthday, Lena Horne singing in her seventies, *New York Times* reporter Harrison Salisbury retracing the Long March of Mao Tse-tung to write a new book about it at eighty-five, Elizabeth Layton of Wellington, Kansas, learning to draw in her seventies and exhibiting at the Smithsonian in her eighties, dancer-choreographer Katherine Dunham at eighty-five going on a hunger strike to call attention to the plight of the Haitian refugees?

Now that the baby boomers are getting gray, there are many signs that aging is becoming hip. The accomplishments of older citizens are being recognized and even—gasp!—discovered. A front-page headline in the *New York Times* toward the end of 1995 proclaimed "Older Writers Budding, Blossoming." The article reported that Bessie R. Doenges, who came to New York City at age nineteen to be a writer, had finally landed her first literary agent at age ninety-four.

Ms. Doenges wrote, at thirty dollars apiece, a column for two small weekly newspapers. It was read with pleasure by novelist Mary Morris, who recommended the author to her own agent, Timothy Seldes. Mr. Seldes said he was struck by "the amazing vitality and originality of the voice," and was enthusiastically submitting a collection of "Bessie Writes" columns to book publishers. Larry O'Connor, a Manhattanite who edits the *Chelsea News* and the *Westsider,* said of Ms. Doenges, "She's a classic case of a talent being discovered." That it happened when she was ninety-four, O'Connor said, only makes it "more dramatic." (That same week, *The New Yorker* "discovered" a woman poet in her eighties.)

A photograph showing Bessie lying on her living room couch as she wrote reminded me of the famous photo of the youthful Truman Capote lying on a hammock when his first book was published. Maybe now that old age is becoming fashionable, the work of people in their eighties and nineties will become as "hot" as the products of teenagers. That is good news for writers' groups like the one at the West Side YMCA in New York, where writers aged sixty-six to eighty-one gather weekday afternoons to read works in progress they hope to get published.

Now that the baby boomers are getting gray, there are many signs that aging is becoming hip.

A woman in one of my Spiritual Autobiography workshops read a piece to the group about how she wanted to be a painter but her husband didn't like her tak-

CREATORS TALKING

"I take my fear in my hands, sit down and deal with the resistance to it, which is sometimes enormous—and I'm resolved I'm going to sit there two to four hours and struggle, whether anything comes or not. The resistance is quite intense—but the resistance gets less as I continue the work. I'm working on it in dreams. Sometimes it emerges there."

—ELAINE PAGELS, PROFESSOR OF RELIGION AT PRINCETON UNIVERSITY, AUTHOR OF *THE GNOSTIC GOSPELS; ADAM, EVE, AND THE SERPENT;* AND *THE ORIGIN OF SATAN*

ing time out from the house and children. After the children left college, she got divorced in her fifties and started to paint full-time.

"But I didn't really get my life together until I was seventy-five," she reported. It was after that age that she found her real style as an artist and began doing her best work, some of which now hangs in museums in New York and Boston. When she finished reading, the workshop participants broke into spontaneous applause. A doctor in his forties told her, "You've given us all hope—that there's still time to 'get it together'!"

Indeed. Having recently crossed the line of sixty—an age that once seemed to me beyond imagination, a Methuselah-like period of life—I'm amazed at how different it is (thankfully!) from what I'd been led to believe by the myths of our culture. My own experience seems in some degree a reverse of the predicted path. I feel much better today at sixty-three than I did at thirty-five, because I don't wake up with a hangover anymore. I gave up drinking and took up the Exercycle, followed by t'ai chi and then yoga a decade ago. That was the first physical exercise I'd done since Boy Scout Camp in Indianapolis. Since '85 I've gone every year to Rancho La Puerta, a health spa in Mexico just below the border, for an all-around, weeklong workout that begins every day with a mountain hike at six-thirty in the morning. It feels great, and so do I.

In the past decade I've written a novel, a made-for-TV movie, three nonfiction books, and dozens of magazine articles; taught college

"But I didn't really get my life together until I was seventy-five," she reported.

and graduate courses; lectured; and created and led workshops in Spiritual Autobiography and creativity in churches, adult education centers, and prisons throughout the country. I look forward to doing more, as much as I can, as long as I can. I feel lucky to be a writer, since I can't imagine ever not wanting to write. Nor is this unusual.

When novelist Irwin Shaw was asked by a reporter on his eighty-fifth birthday when he planned to retire, he looked shocked, then answered, "Writers don't retire!" The same is true for musicians, actors, directors, painters—any creative people. Marc Chagall was painting in his nineties. The writers of my own generation, now in our sixties, continue to produce new and good work, and I can't imagine any of them stopping as long as they're breathing. Most of them have gray hair, as I do, and few are mistaken for graduate students; but none of them act or think or work like the "old codgers" we were taught to believe was the norm for the sixth decade. Of course, we're blessed to be living at a time when life expectancy is longer than ever in history, and more is known about how to keep healthy.

Another happy revelation: What you heard about sex and aging is a myth, too.

Living healthy, without booze, it's better than ever.

Myth Number 11: The Biggest Myth of All— Booze and the Muse

The deadly idea of alcohol and drugs as glamorous keys to creativity runs through our whole society, affecting people not only in literature and the arts, but in all fields, from business and industry, to science and sports.

In reality, alcohol and drugs are destructive not only to creativity, but to health, well-being, and successful functioning. Alcohol is more popular than drugs because it's legal and socially approved—and as if that weren't enough, it's given an extra boost with millions of dollars of creative, psychologically researched advertising.

ALCOHOLIC ROLE MODELS

The fascination with artists self-damned and doomed with alcohol and/or drugs continues. Author John Cheever, who broke the cycle of alcohol addiction, wrote: "If you are an artist, self-destruction is quite expected of you. . . . The thrill of staring into the abyss is exciting."

John Berryman, the poet who died an alcoholic suicide, wrote of the poet in his autobiographical novel, *Recovery,* that he "really thought, off and on for twenty years, that it was his duty to drink, namely to sacrifice himself."

In no other professions aside from the arts are drunkards and drug addicts held up as heroes or role models to young people starting out. Imagine a young intern being told nostalgic tales about great drunken doctors, or a first-year law student regaled with stories of alcoholic lawyers whose "collapse came a few staggering steps" from the front door of the courthouse!

The most eloquent testimony to the rewards of sobriety for the working artist comes from Raymond Carver in a poem based on his own experience. It was published in *The New Yorker* after his death from cancer:

GRAVY

No other word will do. For that's what it was. Gravy.
Gravy these past ten years.
Alive, sober, working, loving and
being loved by a good woman. Eleven years
ago he was told he had six months to live
at the rate he was going. And he was going
nowhere but down. So he changed his ways
somehow. He quit drinking! And the rest?
After that it was all gravy, every minute
of it, up to and including when he was told about,
well, some things that were breaking down and
building up inside his head. "Don't weep for me,"
he said to his friends. "I'm a lucky man.
I've had ten years longer than I or anyone
expected. Pure gravy. And don't forget it."

What Is Your Creative Myth?

Examine your reason for not creating what you want to create, and see if it's a myth you have bought or constructed for yourself. What would it mean if you saw it as myth, rather than fact? What could you create? When can you start? (Now?)

Old Myths of Creativity
TO BE CREATIVE YOU MUST BE:

1. A member of an elite group
2. Born with an artistic gift
3. Neurotic, bordering on suicidal
4. A lonely introvert
5. Effeminate or female
6. A man
7. A full-time artist
8. A big boozer
9. Stoned on drugs
10. Immature and irresponsible
11. Young
12. Single and childless, living alone in a garret, cave, or mountaintop
13. Self-absorbed
14. Born wealthy, or doomed to poverty and deprivation
15. Reckless and neglectful of your physical well-being

New Truths of Creating from the Spirit
CREATIVE PEOPLE:

1. Come from every walk of life and work in every field and occupation
2. Lead rich lives and share themselves with others
3. Find nourishment in community
4. Cultivate their natural senses to stimulate their creativity
5. Develop clarity as the source of creativity
6. Take responsibility for their lives and work
7. Use their creative gifts in all areas of their lives
8. Regard age as an opportunity to apply the wisdom of experience to their art, and share it with others
9. See obstacles as an opportunity to create new solutions, techniques, and skills
10. Recognize the body/mind/spirit connection
11. Find surprising new ways to perform routine tasks
12. Use their dreams as a source of ideas and knowledge
13. Feel connected to the whole of humanity and the universe
14. Practice silence and make room for it in their daily lives
15. Appreciate their time on the planet and express their gratitude for it

PART 2

The **K**eys to **C**reation

4

Evoking the Spirit: The Power of Clarity

A BARRAGE OF DISTRACTING AND DEADENING FORCES FROM BOTH OUTSIDE AND inside constantly assaults us, in a way that disturbs and even destroys our clarity of mind, body, and soul: the abuse of alcohol or drugs; food, when overconsumed to the point of discomfort or vomited out in bulimia, or underconsumed in the way that leads to anorexia; sex, when used as a kind of anesthesia, or performed in compulsive, love-less repetition in anxious pursuit of new partners; even relationships, when they become a kind of addictive distraction. Television, too, is a narcotic when automatically turned on for the comfort of noise, words, pictures, regardless of what is being shown. We use these things to numb our senses—and our sense itself.

Don't worry: I'm not advocating that you give up all these things and become a saint. I wouldn't know how to tell you to do it, or want to do it myself, even if I could! What I want is to provide some clues for tapping into your creativity by first "clearing" yourself of the accumulated debris of substances and practices that clutter and deaden the mind and the senses.

To me, the most powerful key to accessing creativity is clarity. Clarity is the compass that orients you, the lens that focuses, the "sword in the stone." Retreats at Buddhist or Christian monasteries,

To me, the most powerful key to accessing creativity is clarity. Clarity is the compass that orients you, the lens that focuses, the "sword in the stone."

yoga centers or ashrams, meditative weekends sponsored by synagogues or churches or adult education programs, classes in meditative disciplines such as t'ai chi or yoga, all can provide a space in our experience out of the rush and jangle of everyday life. Such "time-outs" interrupt our rote behaviors and provide the chance to get in touch with our deeper levels of consciousness. They open a clearing in which to create.

All these experiences have opened up my life in the past decade and a half—experiences that once would have put me off, even frightened me. I wouldn't have admitted the fear to anyone. I joked about such activities and made fun of people who engaged in them. Silence can scare the wits out of people who've kept their minds stuffed for a long time.

Many people think practices like t'ai chi or silent retreats are only for monks and yogis. But let me tell you my honest belief that if I can do them, anyone can do them! I have an easily distracted mind in a nonathletic body, and I'm trying (like most people I know) to live in a fulfilling way and make the most of my brief time on earth. I've been blessed with some happy accidents and a lot of what I can only call grace to be here, feeling better than I ever have in my life at age sixty-three, after abusing my body and mind for many years with booze until my own "turning," when I was forty-eight years old.

The Road Back

My crash came in Hollywood, where I'd gone to work on the NBC-TV series I had created, *James at 15*. I stayed two and a half years, pouring down increasing amounts of wine every day to numb the growing anxiety of trying to "pitch" myself and my work to the buyers of filmland, watching projects collapse around me, and finding my own work harder to do as my "resting pulse" raced to 120, roughly twice what it ought to be. Finally I split for Boston, also splitting the longest relationship of my life with a woman I thought I would be with for-ever; then I went to my father's funeral, and then my mother's six months later.

I found solace by the pond in the Boston Public Garden, where the words of the Twenty-third Psalm seemed to have led me: "He maketh me to lie down in green pastures; he leadeth me beside the still waters. He restoreth my soul." I was also restoring my body in a pro-gram of diet and exercise guided by Dr. Howard Hartley. I lost twenty pounds and reduced my pulse to eighty, dried out for a month without booze and reduced my pulse to sixty, then turned toward a spiritual path that led me back to church.

Meditation or Prayer Is the Key

Since spirit and spirituality are part of the subject of this book, I want to make clear that it is not my intention, ever, to impose my own faith on you.

As a baby I was baptized with a sprinkling of water in a Presby-terian church. I attended a Presbyterian Sunday school near my father's drugstore in Indianapolis until about the age of nine or ten, when I went with a friend to a Baptist Bible-study class. I was so drawn to the vigorous hymns ("Throw out the lifeline, throw out the lifeline, someone is drifting away!") and the powerful stories of Moses and Jesus that I asked at age eleven to be baptized by full immersion. In college I turned away from the church and became an aggressive intellectual atheist, a position I more or less adhered to until 1980, when my life started coming apart and I returned to church. I joined King's Chapel in Boston, where I've been a member ever since. King's Chapel is an anomaly, a Christian church in the Unitarian Universalist Association, whose membership is largely humanist. I like the combi-nation, for my roots are Christian, and the Unitarian outlook is open to a great variety of beliefs, requiring no rigid dogma, and emphasiz-ing "the interconnected web of the universe."

During my years outside the church, my antireligious feelings were most inflamed by proselytizers who tried to impose their own

I think of spirit as in "spirited," always as a life force and a blessing, never as a damper.

beliefs on me and others. The people who kept my respect for religion and spirituality, even during the times I was most hostile to it, were those who never tried to recruit me to their faith but simply lived it— people like Reverend Norman Eddy of the East Harlem Protestant Parish, and Dorothy Day, whose Catholic Worker movement in the Bowery fed the hungry and gave shelter to the homeless in the midst of an affluent, indifferent society.

When I recently talked about creativity and the spirit with Reverend Eddy he said, "Meditation or prayer is the key. It doesn't have to be through Christ or Buddha or the Sufis. It's finding the way to the core of our being, to become a co-creator with God. As the years go by, I feel one needs a guide. Jesus is the guide for me, while others find it in Buddha, or Mohammed. All religions embody the spirit in different forms."

I would go even further to say the spirit is also embodied outside formal religions, sometimes in mentors of the far or even recent past, men and women of the spirit whose lives and work enlighten and inspire our own. They could be creators of art, literature, or music, who touch the deepest part of our soul, our longing and aspiration.

I think of spirit as in "spirited," always as a life force and a blessing, never as a damper. Some people put a restrictive connotation on "spiritual," as if it means "taking the veil," retreating from life, putting a protective screen between you and the world. I think of it in the opposite sense, as bringing you into the world in a full, joyous way, opening your eyes and ears and mind and heart to the wonders of creation, in all their glorious presence; the power of being present to our senses, our natural perceptions and powers.

Life with Nothing Added

I had cut down on my drinking on my doctor's advice, and was measuring the number of glasses I could consume in a night (one, or two at most) without my pulse rising, but it was a constant struggle, a battle of will against a habit based on a lust for the old numbing. I felt I had it under control, though I noticed the glasses I drank from tended to get larger, growing into fishbowl size, which I still counted as one glass. I slipped periodically, then renewed my efforts at abstinence, all of which consumed a lot of energy, but I consoled myself that at least I didn't get drunk anymore.

In the spring of 1981 I took Erhard Seminars Training, or est, that controversial program for personal growth often panned in the media. (The one fact about est that stuck in the public mind was that participants weren't allowed to go to the bathroom. The discipline of not being able to leave the room during sessions was an effort to hold people's attention. It later was dropped, though not until it was immortalized as a joke in the movie *Semi-Tough*.) Despite the bad press, I listened to some friends I respected who told me how valuable the est training had been for them, and I plunged in as part of my own search for growth. Before signing up, I wondered if this work would in any way be counter to spiritual growth, and I was assured by a Trappist monk who had done the program that "whatever genuine spirituality you bring to this will be deepened by it."

That was my experience. The program opened me and freed me up in many ways, resolving troubled feelings and fears left over from an old, destructive experience in Freudian psychoanalysis. I came away with a new sense of energy, excitement, and possibility. I took a follow-up seminar called Be Here Now, whose purpose was to teach people to "live life with nothing added." I realized for me that would mean not "adding" alcohol. What followed this realization was a lifting of the desire to drink. The lust for it was gone.

I didn't make a pledge not to ever have a drink again. I just didn't want to drink. A few times in the next few years I had a glass of wine or champagne at a wedding or birthday party, but it made me nauseated. I felt I'd become allergic to alcohol, and a doctor told me that was possible, that sometimes pregnant women develop such an allergy, as their bodies "know" it is bad for them.

I don't know of anyone else who had this particular result from est. All I know is, that's what happened to me. Frankly, I wish it had happened somewhere else, somewhere less controversial, like a church basement or the YMCA. But it happened where it happened and I can't deny it—though editors have sometimes excised (censored) mention of it from magazine articles I've written. The stigma associated with programs like est is that they are cultlike, that they brainwash people. That was simply not my experience with the est training. I did not come out of it believing anything different than I had before. In fact, I found my basic beliefs reactivated and strengthened, and I returned to my church and community with renewed commitment and enthusiasm.

One of the goals people have in taking such seminars, and perhaps the greatest benefit from taking them, is to see ourselves from a fresh point of view; to experience a process powerful enough to thrust us out of the confusion that grows up around our lives so we can see through the underbrush of excuses, dilemmas, stories, stuck-ness, repetitions, and addictions that blind our vision and clog our action. One reason people return to such programs or do new similar work is because inevitably the confusion grows up again, like jungle vegetation.

For me, living life with nothing added enabled me to eliminate alcohol. A friend was able to stop "adding" new wives! He had been divorced once, remarried a younger woman, and was about to begin a new affair with a still younger woman. When he took the seminar about living life with nothing added, he saw that if he started the new affair he would simply keep repeating this behavior in cyclical fashion for the rest of his life, "adding" new wives and children every seven years. When he saw this (or, in a deeper way, "got it," in the jargon of the est program), he did not proceed with the new affair. He persuaded his wife to do the same program, both recommitted to their marriage, and they are still together twenty years later.

Does It Call to You?

Transformational programs are not for everyone. Some people are traumatized or offended by such processes, though others are inspired by them. Every method of change involves risk—not only programs like est, or the less confrontational version that replaced it, called The

CREATORS TALKING

"When I'm working I have a schizophrenic need to be away from every-body—and then alternately to be back with the people I'm working with. I'm stimulated by the reaction of others—but then I have to have com-plete isolation.

"When you put up ideas to an audience of five people, something won-derful happens. I'm suddenly mentally putting myself in their shoes, seeing the building from their eyes. I'm no longer myself, I'm everybody else in the room. Interesting things pop out at me I hadn't seen myself."

—EVANS WOOLLEN, ARCHITECT

Forum—but even Freudian psychoanalysis, which in my own case was harmful, while for others may be healing.

A good subjective test was suggested by Werner Erhard himself, founder of est, when he was still active in the program. (After a controversial *60 Minutes* exposé-attack on him in 1991, Erhard left the country and sold his firm to the program leaders, who formed Landmark Education to present The Forum and other seminars.) Before a packed house at the Armory in Boston in 1988, Erhard said after making his pitch, "The work I've just described may 'call' to some of you—it may sound like something you want to engage in. If that's the case you should do it. There are others who simply don't feel any response, or you just didn't like what you heard—it didn't 'call to you.' In that case you should not do it."

This is a good rule for any course of action, from personal relationships to deciding on a job, a school, or a place to live. Remember as well that when your senses are numbed, it's hard to hear any kind of "call." Being clear is the optimal way to be attuned to what really does call to you, in a positive, life-giving way.

I wish I'd abided by the rule of responding to what called to me—and rejecting what did not—back in the 1950s when I was about to go into years of psychoanalysis. I asked the psychoanalyst if it mattered that I didn't like him. No, it didn't matter at all, he said—that's something "we can work with." My entire instinct told me this was wrong, that this man would not be able to help me, but I looked at his professional degrees and certificates on the wall and feared that I was only "resisting" this crucial treatment. Surely the doctor, like Father, knew best. I have come to believe since then that there is no way to get help from someone you don't like and trust. I have also learned time and again to trust my own deepest gut instincts; when I've forced my will against them—and I sometimes have, even after I was clear of drugs and alcohol—I've met with disaster.

From time to time I have gone back and done personal growth seminars. While none have had the impact of my initial experience with est, most of them have been valuable in providing new ways of seeing problems, renewing commitments, clarifying vision, and getting new methodologies to use in my search for growth. I have also enjoyed the people I've met in this work—doctors and waiters, lawyers and truck drivers, ministers and secretaries, black and white, gay and straight, all committed to looking for further personal growth, to finding ways of being more effective in their lives and work, to breaking up old patterns and seeing new possibilities.

I've also had crucial, creative recharging from church retreats, Bible study, prayer and meditation groups, a weekend of "sitting" at a Zen monastery, t'ai chi lessons, yoga classes, a week at a health spa, and other such programs.

Again, what path you follow, what voice you listen to, ought to be those that call to you. You may hear a message a hundred times and have it seem irrelevant, then hear it again in different words by someone else in another setting, and it may come alive for you. Books act on us in a similar way, as novelist Elizabeth Bowen observed: "Certain books come to meet one, as people do."

Reverend Joan Gattuso, minister of the Unity Church of Greater Cleveland, had that experience when the spiritual text *A Course in Miracles* "came to meet" her. Though she had heard its messages in many forms before, somehow this reached her in a way that nothing else had. She wrote in her own powerful book, *A Course in Love,* that after encountering *A Course in Miracles,* "I stepped upon a new path that led me into a number of trainings, teachings, and spiritual adventures. My life began to radically transform, and I began to view all life from a different point of view, seeing relationships radically different from the way society and psychologists do." This path led her to her own "soulmate" and husband, and a rich new way of counseling others on relationships.

No Burlap Necessary

Though my own path has led me to a release from the alcohol that I consumed as daily fuel for more than a quarter century ("You use it like a car uses gasoline," one therapist told me in my hard-drinking days), I'm not a modern male incarnation of Carry Nation, taking an axe to the bars and preaching damnation of all who drink. Many of my friends have found relief and an increase in energy and appreciation of life in giving up alcohol altogether. I also have many friends who enjoy wine and spirits in moderation, including my own minister, as well as colleagues in the arts who do their work without the sort of overindulgence that would cloud their creative clarity. I have no desire to reform them or urge them to give up a part of life that is pleasant and nondestructive for them.

When I gave one of my first workshops in Creating with the Spirit, a participant spoke up with some anxiety when I asked for a discussion of views on alcohol and creativity. This man said he'd read an article that quoted Joan Didion as saying one of her favorite times of the working day was in the late afternoon when she read over what she had written while drinking a glass of white wine.

"So what do you think about that?" the man asked me in a challenging voice, as he leaned forward like a prosecuting attorney.

"I think it's just fine," I said.

I meant it. I know and respect Joan Didion and her work, and I know her artistic integrity would never allow her to lose her own sense of clarity, which is one of the hallmarks of her powerfully lucid style. If she enjoys a glass of wine while she reads over her day's writing, I'm

To find your own clarity and creativity, you don't have to put on a burlap shroud and exist on a diet of boiled locusts and beet greens.

glad. What bothered me about the man's question was the tone of worry and challenge, fear that I was going to deprive him of something that he couldn't do without. That's the danger signal of addiction.

I'm making an assumption about that man because of his attitude, and my own experience as a former drinker who also would have jumped to the challenge if anyone suggested taking away any of my booze habits. I may be wrong, though, and the only one who knows that is the man himself. If he is "in denial," the people who love and live and work with him will know, though even those closest to the one with the problem may be reluctant to tell him.

To find your own clarity and creativity, you don't have to put on a burlap shroud and exist on a diet of boiled locusts and beet greens. Part of being creative in one's daily life is to savor the natural pleasures of it, the awakening of the senses—rather than crushing them with so much overload they go numb. There is, or ought to be, real pleasure in tasting one's food—even preparing it—whether your diet is nouvelle cuisine or middle-American meat and potatoes or New Age vegetarian. You can ruin any taste by overindulgence, or heighten it by savoring.

One of my favorite magazines is *Gourmet,* because of the loving, appreciative way its writers and photographers approach that wonderful subject—food! *Gourmet* is not just about fancy, expensive meals, but the deep pleasures of simple, basic tastes and their comfort and fulfillment in different seasons. The late Laurie Colwin, a talented novelist who wrote marvelous essays for the magazine, once did a piece on her passion for tomatoes, along with a few of her own favorite recipes thrown in as a bonus. Here was a person who was making the fullest use of her sense of taste, and her genuine appreciation of one of the "ordinary" gifts of our abundant life, one we take for granted, like background music—the common tomato that can grow in your own backyard:

One of the joys of summer is to go roaming through the garden, pulling ripe tomatoes off the vine and biting in. Juice and seeds drip all over your nice white shirt, but who cares? . . . On one of the great days of my life, a friend with an enormous garden invited me and a pal to wander through his tomato patch and take as many plump specimens as we wanted; it was the end of the summer, and he had over-planted. I felt like the person in the Andrew Marvell poem "The Garden," about whose head ripe apples fall, except that these were tomatoes—in this case sharp, ripe, juicy cherry tomatoes.

In this world of uncertainty and woe, one thing remains unchanged: Fresh, canned, pureed, dried, salted, sliced and served with sugar and cream, or pressed into juice, the tomato is reliable, friendly, and delicious. We would be nothing without it.

As I read Colwin's paean to tomatoes, an old memory rushed to my mind: My cousin Junior, just before he went off to serve in the Air Force in World War II, walked with me through our backyard Victory Garden, plucking the biggest, fattest tomatoes, shaking salt on them, and eating them right there on the spot, urging me to do the same. I did, enjoying this wild way of eating tomatoes—not in the tame confines of the family kitchen, all sliced and served with a meal (much less packaged in contemporary supermarket cellophane!), but plucked from the vine, from nature itself, straight to my mouth, almost like a forbidden fruit, and tasting all the more glorious for it.

Finding Our Own Balance

Don't deny yourself the natural pleasures given us as part of the human condition—don't take the simple, sensuous pleasures for granted, but rather, savor the hot bath, the cold shower, the scent of wood smoke, the comfort of blankets, the sweet taste of honey, the soothing sound of string quartets or early morning birdsong, the sudden flesh-to-flesh thrill of a kiss. This galaxy of wonders we take for granted is given to each of us, yet we often ignore it.

The smarter you are, the easier it is to think up ingenious ways to excuse your addiction.

Become aware of your senses, "try them out" consciously, experiencing the clarity that comes from attention. In this state of awareness, eat a peach, listen to a piece of music you like, feel the bark of a tree, smell a rose, look at your own hand. You'll taste, hear, touch, smell, and see things in a way you haven't before, or maybe in a way you've lost since childhood. "Be with" your senses as an exercise. It's one of the accessible keys to clarity, available to all of us.

Don't let the enjoyment of your senses fade into a neutral background of nonexperience. Nor should you overindulge in their pleasure until it turns to need, and the need grows into an out-of-control addiction. Every so often, to continue enjoying our pleasures, we need to make a reality check to see that they haven't got out of balance, haven't tilted our behavior off course into a mindless and sense-numbing consumption of booze, or sugar, or television, or indiscriminate sex. I am not suggesting abstinence, but balance—the kind of balance that allows you to enjoy and appreciate the use of your mind and body for creating a meaningful life. Unless your habits get so out of hand that your loved ones or colleagues are brave enough and caring enough (as well as fed up and frightened enough) to challenge you, then you are the only judge of your own balance. And it's easy to fool yourself. The smarter you are, the easier it is to think up ingenious ways to excuse your addiction.

My denial was much like the experience journalist Pete Hamill describes in his memoir:

> I never thought of myself as a drunk. I was, I thought, like many others, a drinker. I certainly didn't think of myself as an alcoholic. But I was already having trouble in the morning after remembering the details of the night before. It didn't seem to matter; everybody else was doing the same thing. We made little jokes about having a great time last night—I think. And we'd begun to reach for the hair of the dog.

It is rare that even friends and loved ones dare speak the truth to someone about overindulgence or addiction. It takes tremendous courage and "tough love" to confront a person who is falling into dependence, for defenses are sometimes impregnable, and responses of people who feel themselves challenged or accused can be angry, and even violent. It is safer to flow with the status quo, even when someone is harming himself and others.

We depend on friends, and they on us, for the accuracy of our sense perceptions. There is clarity in the truth, hard as it may be to hear the warnings or challenges of friends who care about us. It's important to have some friends whose senses are alert and clear, whom you can depend on for an accurate reading of your own condition. If our friends' perceptions are dimmed by drugs and alcohol, however, we can't depend on them in such matters—or perhaps we depend on them to confirm us in our addictions, knowing they would be the last to know, and the last to want us to turn from the habits they join us in.

At one point in my heavy drinking days I became aware enough of my own drink-inspired troubles, from sick hangovers to booze-fueled arguments, to ask several friends if they thought I was an alcoholic, or needed to do something about my drinking. I was (falsely) assured that there was nothing wrong, that "everyone" drinks, especially writers, and there was nothing to worry about.

Only one person spoke the truth to me.

The late John Ciardi, a marvelous poet, powerful lecturer, and dedicated director of the Bread Loaf Writers' Conference for many

---

CREATORS TALKING

"One of the myths I believed about creativity was that you had to be in an altered state—I thought it was an irrational process over which you had no control. With fiction writing, it's surprising how analytical a lot of it is. You control it a lot more than I thought—though when you're waiting for it to be there, it's not there."

—GISH JEN, NOVELIST, AUTHOR OF *TYPICAL AMERICAN* AND *MONA IN THE PROMISED LAND* years, wrote me in 1972 to explain that the reason he hadn't invited me back to serve on the staff of Bread Loaf, as I had every alternate year since 1962, was that in 1970 my drinking had become so out of control that it was affecting my lectures, which had become "fuzzy" on the mornings after my furious consumption of vodka. (I had taken to carrying a half-gallon jug around with me from one party to another, so as never to be out of booze.) As director, John felt he had to be "faithful to the ghosts" of the writers like Robert Frost who had founded the conference and its traditions, to see that only the highest quality of performance was offered by those on the staff. My drinking had disqualified me. I was shocked at the time and offended; yet I later came to appreciate Ciardi's honesty and courage. It stuck like a burr in my consciousness, one of the first promptings in my own head that the time was coming when I had to stop if I wanted to continue to work—indeed, to live.

I count myself lucky to have had such a friend as Ciardi who was willing to speak the truth to me. (I'm happy to say I returned to teach at Bread Loaf again when I'd given up alcohol, and experienced the conference sober for the first time!)

Editing Out the World

If you're getting out of control and you have a friend as wise and tough as John Ciardi to tell you so, you're lucky, but you can't count on such outside influences. The most you can hope is that a clear-headed friend, if asked, will tell you the truth. But you can't depend on anyone else to take responsibility for your own behavior and performance, personally or professionally. After getting opinions from people you trust, in the end you are the one who must finally determine whether you are working and living at your peak condition, in the optimal state to achieve the greatest clarity when you want to create.

The Reverend Norman Eddy said recently, "I see marvelous people, moved by the spirit, unconscious of it, trying to see what it means, and if they would just look within, the best in them is telling them what to do!"

You always know, though, of course, you can always deny the truth.

It's easy to fool yourself. Like other writers and artists, Pete Hamill justified his drinking with a favorite refrain that my fellow boozers and I used to croon with great self-righteousness: "If I was able to function, to get the work done, there was no reason to worry about drinking. It was part of living, one of the rewards."

Growing up Irish in Brooklyn in the '40s, Hamill learned that "part of being a man was to drink," and started guzzling beer in grammar school. He recalls that even then, "It was as if the beer were editing out the world, eliminating other elements, such as weather, light, form and beauty."

He drank through his early years as a star reporter for the *New York Post* in the '50s and '60s, but in 1972, he began to notice little signs of deterioration in his work:

> Typing a column or a script I would misspell simple words, not just once, but eight or nine times. Sometimes my fingers felt like gloves filled with water and typing was a plodding effort of physical labor.
>
> My hands trembled too, and there were little odd twitches in my legs, little spasms of protest, or I'd wake up with no feeling in my legs. I shook off most of these signals. I was just getting older, I told myself.

He was thirty-seven.

That New Year's Eve he watched his hands trembling in the mirror of a bar as he tried to light a cigarette. Later in the evening he looked down at the vodka-soaked lime at the bottom of his glass and he said to himself: "I'm never going to do this again."

He began a new era of sober and successful productivity of novels, movie scripts, and nonfiction books. In *A Drinking Life,* Hamill reports that after a while the temptation grew weaker, and one day he

Just as numbing ourselves can be a habit, so keeping ourselves awake and clear can be a habit as well.

gratefully realized that "somehow, I'd replaced the habit of drinking with the habit of nondrinking."

Just as numbing ourselves can be a habit, so keeping ourselves awake and clear can be a habit as well. The choice is always there to set on one path or another. We can pick up a bottle or tune in to some mindless television and get in the habit of blanking ourselves out, or we can wake up one morning, take a deep breath, and set on a new, fresh course that will bring our senses and spirit back to life. The choice is ours.

Finding the "Mississippi of Fresh Spirit"

Everything in our society seems arrayed against us in the search for clarity and creativity. Everything is done for us, prepackaged before we can create it, from entertainment to food, so we are separated from our natural creativity, the way it showed up for people in daily life routines up until the second half of the century. Back in the '50s my old mentor and professor at Columbia, the sociologist C. Wright Mills, struck a nerve of public pain and response in his book *White Collar*, when he illuminated the plight of the new middle class of office workers, men and women who no longer created or consumed the fruits of their own labors, but became anonymous functionaries cut off from the meaning of their work.

Rebelling against that restricted, increasingly robotized kind of life himself, not only intellectually but experientially, Mills used to roar in to Columbia on the BMW motorcycle whose motor he learned to repair himself. He built his own house in Rockland County with his own design and his own hands, and enthusiastically learned to cook, taking special pride and pleasure in baking his own bread. Pacing the classroom like a restless prophet, he foresaw the communal spirit of the '60s when he urged a return to the land, to small communities where people would learn to use their own tools and talents to grow their own food, create their own arts and crafts, and make their own forms of community.

In Mills's class I wrote a paper on the new mass society that was forming the kind of future predicted in W. H. Auden's great poem "September 1, 1939": "faces along the bar / cling to their average day / the lights must never go out / the music must always play." That was in the pre-television era. Now with the installment of the tube as a kind of psychic life-support system for the public, an all-pervasive tranquilizer, numbing night and day, providing its own glimmering light, its never-ending babble of noise, its faster flashing images and ten-second "sound bites," its increasing violence, Auden's vision has been not only realized but surpassed.

We must consciously fight for our clarity and reclaim our creativity. What for? To be human, to enjoy and experience the sights, sounds, tastes, touches, smells, and emotions given us as part of our humanity. Giving up the habits that blot out those senses is not a loss but a recovery. We recover feeling, and we see with more than the eyes. In this kind of clarity I see much more powerfully the role that friends play in my life and enjoy a much greater appreciation of the gifts that other people are in my own journey. What a desert it would be without them!

Clarity enables you to blink and see how much you have, how rich are your resources, no matter what your station in life or position in the economy. The substances that temporarily numb our pain also

---

CREATORS TALKING

"The more you read, the more you're motivated to write. I remember being released by reading *The Catcher in the Rye*, realizing you don't have to follow all the rules imposed by an educational process. It gives you the courage to try something of your own. Reading J. P. Donleavy's *The Ginger Man*, I realized you didn't have to have a subject and a predicate. In legal writing I've been something of a novelist and gotten away with it. I don't follow the 'whereas' forms, I just tell the story."

—ALAN NOLAN, ATTORNEY, NOVELIST, CIVIL WAR HISTORIAN, AUTHOR OF *AS SOUNDING BRASS*, *THE IRON BRIGADE*, AND *LEE CONSIDERED*

The Buddhists talk of the need to "empty" ourselves to gain enlightenment. This kind of emptiness can lead to filling up.

numb our pleasure, and for a much longer time. The novelist Donald Newlove, in his powerful and myth-breaking book *Those Drinking Days,* conveys a sense of joy in the kind of clarity I am talking about: "Yesterday I had a day I couldn't buy for a million. I didn't drink. Today I have today: a Mississippi of fresh spirit flowing through me moment by moment from my first waking second."

So do I. As I write this book I'm looking out a window onto San Francisco Bay. I've been working here all summer at the home of a friend, writing in the mornings, and biking every afternoon to the Golden Gate Bridge. The wind blows clean and cool off the water as my wheels crunch over the gravel path, and I take my hands off the handlebars, feeling I'm floating, like I did as a kid. Last night we had dinner at a small Vietnamese restaurant in the neighborhood and the food was great—light and delicate. I tasted every bite. Tonight we're going to a yoga class, and I'll awaken muscles I didn't even know I had a few years ago. I wake in the morning to have a bowl of fruit and cereal, whose flavor I savor as I look at the papers, then set to work.

Or is it play? When I sit down at this keyboard of my laptop computer I feel true pleasure in calling up the file, tapping out the words, "hearing" them in my mind, reworking sentences to get the rhythm right, expressing thoughts through a medium I've loved and created in since I was six years old. I am blessed. And I am grateful. I still make mistakes, wrong choices, have aches and pains, doubts and worries, lapse into sloth, and drag myself back to awareness again. One thing I know: working and living clear sure beats the old way.

I also see how creativity is not restricted to words I put on the page. After giving my workshop on Spiritual Autobiography for several years, I was asked by the Paulist Center in Boston to present a daylong program that might be useful for people recovering from alcohol dependence. I devised (created) some exercises that became the beginning of a whole new workshop, one that broadened beyond alcohol to all forms of creativity. In working "clear," ideas seem to sprout naturally, and there's a flow that leads from one idea to the next. When you're "in the flow" you seem to meet the people you need to help you carry on the next project, and the currents of your work take you to the next right place to develop it.

I think this flow is part of the feeling Donald Newlove was describing when he spoke of the "Mississippi of fresh spirit." It's available to all of us, all the time, if we take the trouble to seek it—or as Huck Finn would say, to "light out for it." You can't find your way if your head isn't clear, if your senses are not alert. Having emptied ourselves of alcohol and drugs, and the myths that promote them, as the key to creativity, we've cleared ourselves to find what Mark Twain called, in another context, "the territory ahead."

Having cleared ourselves, we find in some sense that we are empty. It's a shock, and it can be frightening. What will we do without our old crutches and supports? How will we get through the day—much less the night? But emptiness is only temporary; Spinoza reminds us that "nature abhors a vacuum." Jesus tells a parable of a man who cleans his house of demons, and seven worse ones come to take up residence. Emptiness can be dangerous—but it can also be powerful.

The Buddhists talk of the need to "empty" ourselves to gain enlightenment. This kind of emptiness can lead to filling up. I'm not speaking of gas tanks or energy, but movements of the spirit, the force of creation.

5

Emptying

AN OFTEN-REPEATED ZEN STORY TELLS OF A LEARNED PROFESSOR WHO GOES
to visit an old monk, famous for his wisdom. The monk welcomes the
professor, invites him inside his temple, and offers him a comfortable
seat on a cushion. The professor says he wants to learn from the monk,
to gain some of his wisdom; before the monk can say anything, the
professor launches into a long and proud account of his own accomplishments, his own theories, his own knowledge. The monk listens
quietly, then asks politely, "Would you like some tea?"

The professor nods and smiles, continuing to spout his ideas, and
the monk hands him a teacup. The monk takes a large pot and pours
tea into the cup held by the professor. The tea rises almost to the very
lip of the cup, and the monk placidly continues pouring—as the professor continues chattering. Only when the tea overflows and the monk
continues to pour does the professor finally notice and stop his monologue. He leaps to his feet and demands, "What are you doing? What's
going on?" The monk replies, "This cup is like your mind. It can't take
in anything new because it's already full."

The story is a dramatization of the idea that "being full" (in this
case, full of yourself) is not always desirable, and that "emptiness" can
be a valuable, even essential condition, a state in which we can receive

much that is of value. If our cup is already full, nothing can be added—it simply spills over and is wasted, like the tea poured in the story.

"Emptying" is a crucial process on the spiritual path, the path to creativity and wholeness that the Navajos refer to as being "on the gleaming way." This kind of emptying is part of the process described at the beginning of the book: the model of successive stages that lead to a new discovery of our creativity: Breaking the Myth, Emptying, Filling, and Creating.

There are different kinds of emptying. Some are very destructive to the mind and body, and one must be careful to discern what acts are really in the service of the spirit, the creative force. Bulimics, who force themselves to vomit their food, are, strictly speaking, emptying, but obviously not in any life-enhancing way, nor are anorexics, who keep themselves empty of needed nourishment. Couch potatoes remain empty of knowledge and experience by vegetating in front of the TV.

One of the keys to emptying is awakening our senses, as described in the chapter on clarity. If we are overstuffed with food, booze, drugs, television, ear-blasting music, telephone chatter-gossip, continuous computer games, or any other sense deadener, we need to empty in order to receive—ideas, inspiration, information, experience, knowledge, love.

At first the very idea of becoming empty sounds unappealing, even frightening, or perhaps painful. Isn't that the opposite of what everybody wants? Don't we all really want to have everything, be full, and therefore satisfied? Yet we all know times when emptying our minds through meditation, or our bodies through a healthy, regulated diet or fasting, can be refreshing, awakening us to heightened perception and aliveness. When we are in good shape, sharp, and clear is when we feel most alive, when we're open to experiencing the natural highs of life.

The Joy of Spinach

Emptying doesn't necessarily mean, as we usually are quick to assume, loss or deprivation. Emptying can bring a fuller appreciation, even fuller sensation, an expanding of the senses. I unexpectedly experienced this in a small way when I started to cut down on fat in my diet. I steamed vegetables for the first time, eating them without any butter or sauce. I assumed this would make them tasteless or bland, but to my amazement, when I ate my first steamed vegetables I felt I was actually tasting them for the first time. No wonder I had never liked spinach—I had never really tasted it! The butter and sauces I was accustomed to having vegetables drowned in by restaurants and popular recipes had blotted out their true taste. The steaming brought out their natural flavor, enabled me to really know it for the first time. This simple experience opened up a whole new area of enjoyment for me. Less was more, what seemed like deprivation was enhancement, discovery of new pleasure.

Depriving ourselves—emptying—can sometimes be a method of bringing a spiritual sense to our experience. This intriguing subject has been illuminated by Rabbi Harold Kushner. In his book *To Life: A Celebration of Jewish Being and Thinking,* Rabbi Kushner explains that the real significance of the Law in Judaism is that it teaches "how to take the ordinary and make it holy."

Writing of the often misunderstood dietary laws of Judaism, Rabbi Kushner says that we "sanctify the act of eating" by keeping kosher. Rabbi Kushner views the rules for cooking and eating kosher as a means of celebrating, not being deprived or punished. When he has lunch with a non-Jewish friend in a restaurant, he doesn't feel sorry for himself and think about a horrible God who wants to deny him the pleasure of eating pork products. Instead, he is thankful that there is a God who, despite all the other concerns he has about his creation, cares about what the rabbi is having for lunch.

Emptying doesn't necessarily mean, as we usually are quick to assume, loss or deprivation. Emptying can bring a fuller appreciation, even fuller sensation, an expanding of the senses.

Illuminating the idea of freedom being achieved by restriction, Kushner points out that the Torah—even with all its rules and regulations—"is a source of freedom." For instance, if he dines at a restaurant with a non-Jewish friend, his companion has far more choices than Rabbi Kushner, whose choices are limited by observing the Jewish dietary laws. How can it be, then, that the observant Jew is more free than his friend? Rabbi Kushner compares the freedom the Law offers to the freedom athletes feel in disciplining their bodies, enabling them to perform physically in a way that many people can never experience. It is the freedom of being "the master of the appetite rather than the slave."

By eliminating from his diet the foods proscribed by his religion, Rabbi Kushner is adding a sense of the sacred to his every meal, and increasing his own self-discipline, his own power to control his appetite.

The idea of emptiness is a paradox, and sometimes we have to embrace it, to understand different aspects of it, before we're able to enjoy a sense of fullness of spirit. Before we can even look for the spiritual path, we need to first empty ourselves of the substances and habits that numb us to our own deepest feelings.

A Spiritual Impulse

Like many other people, my own interest in anything spiritual didn't begin until I stopped drinking for a long enough period to really be sober, not just recovering from a hangover. I had gone for about three weeks without a drink—the longest time without alcohol in my adult life—when I overheard a man say he wanted to go to church on Christmas Eve. I suddenly had an impulse to do that too. This urge came as a shock to me, since I hadn't been inside a church for more than a quarter of a century—roughly the same period of time during which I'd made alcohol part of my daily diet.

A woman I met on a book tour told me how she and her husband quit drinking after going to the edge of physical abuse and realizing the danger they were courting, the road they were heading down. It was her custom to make a big breakfast on Saturday when they both had hangovers, and one Saturday, after they'd both been clear and sober for several weeks, her husband came to help—something he'd never done before. When they sat down to eat he said what a beautiful morning it was, and she agreed, and then they both looked out the window and started laughing. It was rainy, stormy, and dark—outside. Inside, in their new lives, it was a beautiful day. Others have told me similar stories. It makes sense. When you're drinking, as I was, to numb yourself on a regular basis, to blot out the psychic pain of life, you are also blotting out the natural instinct for any sort of spiritual experience. By "spiritual," I emphasize again, I don't just mean going to church or synagogue or adopting any particular faith.

Whatever our creed or spiritual practice may be, one of the most common ways we numb ourselves to the spirit is through noise, outer and inner. The outer noise is the daily rush and bustle of getting up, radio, talk, traffic, work, meetings, discussion, phone, lunch, business, Muzak, shopping, dinner, TV. Hopefully, there are many more loving and satisfying pauses and interruptions in the day, but it is rare that the noise ever stops, the everlasting distraction.

Giving Up Noise

In one of his midweek sermons at King's Chapel just before Lent one year, Reverand Carl Scovel suggested that instead of sacrificing sweets, or undergoing any such customary deprivation of food or drink during the coming season, we give up—noise. Turn off the TV. We smiled. A shocking idea. Original, though. And maybe not too hard. Just think, we could stuff ourselves during Lent, but in silence; yes, that's what Carl was recommending we expose ourselves to—silence. Of course, we'd be able to hear ourselves chewing as we smugly ate all that fudge and those cookies and even the Valentine candy, or double-rich ice cream. Was that the idea—we'd hear ourselves eating, and be embarrassed? We'd be aware, we'd realize what and how much we were eating because there wouldn't be any TV to take our mind off what we were doing. Another one of his tricks, no doubt. No TV? Insidious. Radical.

Still, I decided to give it a try. There weren't any programs I was dying to watch anyway. So what was the big deal? It ought to be a snap, and evidently would look good on my record (with God, in that enormous account book God keeps). The first night I came in and started to flip on the tube like I always do, no reason, just to see what's on—or maybe not even to see what's on. Maybe just to have something on—anything. Why did I do it? I always did, I'd gotten in the habit of it during the past—how many years? I wasn't sure.

I began to ask myself questions. Why was I turning on the tube when I wasn't even watching it? Voices? Maybe. I was living by myself, maybe the voices were a kind of company. Welcome, too. Keeping me from my own company, my own thoughts. Resisting the urge to turn it on wasn't easy. I was used to turning it on automatically—another addiction. But harmless, surely? Or was it? Anyway, I kept my pledge, left the screen blank. I lay down on my bed and read for a while. I noticed how quiet it was. Wow. Kind of peaceful. Restful. Not bad. In fact, a relief.

After that, when I came home I would get out a book and lie down on the bed to read, instead of clicking on the TV. I began to look forward to the silence. Even after Lent, I was comforted by knowing that silence was there, a kind of haven, or mental meadow, or pasture of the soul. I entered it gratefully, thinking sometimes of the psalm: "He maketh me to lie down in green pastures. He restoreth my soul."

Billie Holiday Kicks TV

A few months after I gave up TV, I found myself turning the tube back on in that automatic way, sinking back into the habit, the numbing. Like all other addictions, this one isn't beat just because you conquer it once. It creeps right back into your life and takes over. It's a serious drug, a narcotic of mind and soul. No one articulated this better than Billie Holiday, in her autobiography, *Lady Sings the Blues*. She is speaking at a period when she has again kicked her heroin habit, and reflects:

> This time, the doctors have told me, with any kind of luck,
> I should be able to stay straight for two whole years. . . .
> But no doctor can tell you anything your own bones don't
> know. And I can let the doctors in on something. I knew I'd

really licked it one morning when I couldn't stand television any more. When I was high and wanted to stay that way, I could watch TV by the hour and loved it. Who can tell what detours are ahead? Another trial? Sure. Another jail? Maybe. But if you've beat the habit again and kicked TV, no jail on earth can worry you too much.

Does this mean we must hock our TVs if we want to be spiritual people? I don't think so. TV can be beneficial when used thoughtfully, to watch a program we know we'll be interested in, even a regular weekly show. The challenge is to not be pulled under the steady influence of the tube as a companion, as a mental and spiritual narcotic that we can't do without. The gift of silence, with all its refreshment, can be forgotten, lost, if we return to the easier numbing of available noise.

Support for Silence

It's hard to stay alert to our habits, to battle the addictive, noncreative ones on our own. That's why community is so crucial to the spiritual path. One of the benefits of being part of a spiritual community is that it supplies you with other ways of getting back on the track, of coming awake again, of practicing your discipline.

Sometimes at King's Chapel we had a Silent Day at the Parish House, on a Saturday, beginning at around nine in the morning and lasting till three or four in the afternoon. There would be books of spiritual readings around, or you could bring a book yourself, or a notebook to write your thoughts in, or just sit and look out the window, or simply close your eyes and rest. We had lunch in silence, too, eating together around the table, smiling perhaps, or exchanging glances or silent greetings, but not talking. There was something extra in this, in being silent with other people, as if the others' silence gave a greater weight and meaning to your own, as if your own could be shared and mixed in with these others, as they too

The gift of silence, with all its refreshment, can be forgotten, lost, if we return to the easier numbing of available noise.

chose to be with fellow seekers, in community, in a common experience of respect, contemplation, prayer. I would leave those occasions feeling closer to the others who were there, as if I knew them better, in some deeper way than discussion would have given us. I always left feeling refreshed, too, as if I'd taken a dip in a fresh spring.

If you are part of a church, synagogue, or any kind of faith community, suggest your own kind of Silent Day if there is no equivalent in your program. If you aren't part of a faith community, try it with whatever kind of community you are part of, or want to organize—a Twelve Step program, a writer's group, or even people you get to know at work. Perhaps they too feel a need for respite from the sound assault of the workplace. You might even suggest it to your boss—a day, or even a morning or an afternoon, set aside for people who wish to sit in silence, with reading available of a meditative nature, or whatever each person wishes to bring to share, for anyone to choose from. I know, it sounds impractical, yet perceptive administrators know that any exercise that lowers stress and brings a sense of calm to people will eventually enhance their work.

Silence can even enhance performance in team sports, according to Phil Jackson, former coach of the Chicago Bulls, in the powerful book he wrote with Hugh Delahanty, *Sacred Hoops: Spiritual Lessons of a Hardwood Warrior.* Coach Jackson is a Zen practitioner who teaches meditation and Buddhist techniques to his team, and he has found that

> the experience of sitting silently together as a group tends to bring about a subtle shift in consciousness that strengthens the team bond. Sometimes we extend mindfulness to the court and conduct whole practices in silence. The deep level of concentration and nonverbal communication that arises when we do this never fails to astonish me.

Another way to experience silence with a group is to invite a few friends to your own house or apartment for a day or a morning on the weekend. Unplug the phone, radio, and TV, provide some of your own favorite books or articles that inspire contemplation, set those out, along with tea or coffee and perhaps some fruit, and share some hours of silence together.

Giving ourselves the gift of silence sometimes solves problems, leads to new insights or understandings. Business leader Arnold Hiatt told me that when he was a student at Harvard he was torn about whether to study medicine like his brother. One afternoon he was walking along the Charles River and noticed the monastery of the Cowley Fathers on Memorial Drive. "I went in," he recalled, "and I sat down, and it was very peaceful and calm. It was like 'hearing silence.' I decided I wasn't going to pursue this course I was on, that I really didn't want to do it. I went out very relieved."

Our great nineteenth-century novelist Herman Melville wrote, "All profound things and emotions of things are preceded and attended by silence," a thought that affirms Hiatt's experience. Melville went on to say, "Silence is the consecration of the universe. Silence is the invisible laying on of the Divine Pontiff's hands upon the world. Silence is the only voice of our God."

The silence of the Quakers is their way of worship. In an essay titled "The Eloquent Sounds of Silence" in *Time* magazine, the Indian-born author Pico Ayer wrote, "Silence is an ecumenical state, beyond the doctrines and divisions created by the mind. If everyone has a spiritual story to tell of his life, everyone has a spiritual silence preserve."

Nights at a Monastery

Besides one's own spiritual community—which may be a church, a synagogue, a Quaker meeting, a Twelve Step group, a support group born out of any number of empowerment or adult education programs—spiritual resources exist in the larger community around you which can be of tremendous value on your own journey, in staying on the path and strengthening your commitment to creativity and wholeness. The religious education committee of my church once undertook

Giving ourselves the gift of silence sometimes solves problems, leads to new insights or understandings.

the project of compiling a pamphlet of resources in our own community. We asked everyone to contribute ideas to the list—places, people, and events that they had found to be enriching. It's a useful kind of guide to have for any group. One of the first places we put down was Glastonbury Abbey, a Benedictine monastery in Hingham, Massachusetts, about forty-five minutes from us in Boston.

Experiencing the silence and peace of a night in a monastery can provide a marvelous deepening of spiritual enrichment. Inhabiting the sacred space of any religion or spiritual discipline helps us empty our minds of the worldly concerns of accumulating, achieving, competing, conquering, climbing (socially and/or professionally). It offers rest for a while in the peace that lies beyond all that, in the realm of the spirit where none of that earthly struggle counts, but is seen as fleeting, ephemeral.

You needn't be a Catholic or even a Christian to spend an evening or a weekend at a Benedictine monastery, nor do you need to be a Buddhist to spend such quiet time at Zen Mountain Monastery in Mount Tremper, New York, or other places like it. You needn't be rich or privileged, either. Monasteries usually ask for a contribution in the range of $20 to $25 for a day and night, including three meals and all

CREATORS TALKING

"Of course I get stuck. There are times when putting a menu together is a nightmare. Sometimes I'm blocked. I sit home, go through book after book of recipes looking for inspiration. I also get inspired and unstuck by seeing other chefs working in the kitchen. I encourage them to be part of the menu planning. We change the menu every month because I personally can't cook the same item for a month. As difficult as the first day of doing a new menu is, by the end of the month we're ready for a change. A chef who worked for me said that one of the pleasures of working here is that you leave with five hundred ideas."

—ODETTE BERY, CHEF, ANOTHER SEASON RESTAURANT, BOSTON;
AUTHOR OF ANOTHER SEASON COOKBOOK

services and facilities, but if you can't afford that, and feel a sincere need for this kind of experience, they will accept whatever you are able to contribute.

In the early 1980s the religious education committee was looking for new places to hold our semiannual retreats in spring and fall. Two of the "scouts" reported back favorably about Glastonbury, with one concern. "There are crosses all over the place, a cross is in every room, and this might be disturbing to some of our Humanist members who are good Unitarians but aren't Christians."

The attributes of the place were so great that we decided to take the risk. We explained to people clearly that it was a Roman Catholic monastery and the cross and Christian symbols were naturally prominent throughout the place. As it turned out, no one who stayed at Glastonbury was bothered at all by the Christian symbolism. There was no pressure to take part in any ritual or state any belief; the place was simply at the disposal of guests to take what parts of it they wished to enjoy according to their own beliefs and inclinations. All were impressed by the gracious hospitality of the community, and we weren't surprised to learn that hospitality is the "specialty," or mission, of the Benedictines, as teaching is of the Jesuits.

Glastonbury became a favorite place for our retreats. We came to know some of the resident community, who always welcomed us and made us feel at home. Some of us have even gone there for individual retreats, to spend a night or two in the quiet, peaceful atmosphere of a monastery, a place of prayer. We were welcome to join the monks in the chapel at their offices of prayer, held at regular intervals throughout the day and evening, as they chanted and sang the psalms and prayers of their devotions. Glastonbury is not a "silent" monastery, as some are, and there is conversation at meals, but the place itself is, of course, one of quiet and contemplation.

Thomas Merton wrote in *The Seven Storey Mountain* that when he saw some of the monasteries of Europe as a young man, he thought them a kind of oddity, relics from the past. Later, when he turned to his own spiritual path, eventually joining the Trappist Monastery of

Gethsemani in Kentucky, he began to appreciate monasteries as focal points of powerful prayer. He came to believe that monasteries, rather than being superfluous, are essential to the world; that perhaps the concentrated prayer from these places, like a kind of spiritual atomic power, is what keeps the earth going around, what keeps the whole human enterprise continuing.

The ability to be silent is—like every other ability— strengthened by practice and discipline. The ability to be silent is like a muscle that needs to be exercised.

I find that after spending quiet time at a monastery, it is easier to practice silence at home.

The ability to be silent is—like every other ability—strengthened by practice and discipline. The ability to be silent is like a muscle that needs to be exercised.

The Challenge of Silence

Silence is a challenge, and it can be disturbing for some people. On one of our church's retreats at Glastonbury, part of the program was to have the midday meal without speaking, with music playing in the background. One man, a professor, looked nervously around the room, then picked up a carton of orange juice that was on the table and began to read the wording on the sides of it. He read those words over and over, studied them, dwelt on them, in a desperate effort to fill up his mind, to avoid the emptiness of silence, or the simple, wordless message of the music. A woman who looked increasingly disgruntled during the meal expressed her anger to one of the retreat leaders afterward about being subjected to this experience. She said she "hadn't come here for that," and was so disturbed that she left, escaping even the memory of less than an hour of silence.

In my own pursuit of spiritual growth, I went on a personal silent retreat for five days under the guidance of a spiritual director. A spiritual director is usually a priest, nun, or minister who is trained to lead lay people into a deeper experience of prayer, meditation, and awareness of God, meeting with them once or twice a month, engaging in discussion about these matters, and offering suggestions for developing that dimension of life. The process might be thought of as a therapy of the soul.

My own spiritual director at that time was a member of the Society of St. John the Evangelist, an Episcopal order of monks. My director had explained at the outset that he asked those he met with to do a personal silent retreat once a year at the order's retreat house in Newbury, Massachusetts.

I went on this retreat eagerly, yet with apprehension. I wondered if I'd get bored, or anxious, or depressed; though I hoped I'd be relaxed, comforted, calmed, perhaps even inspired. I took lots of books, a notebook to write in, and plenty of pens. I stayed in a new retreat house by myself, took my evening meal with the brothers in their large farmhouse, and talked to no one except the spiritual director, whom I met with for an hour each day.

It was one of the loudest times in my life. With other noise shut out, it was as if my own head grew more raucous, with contending interior voices yelling for attention. It was fascinating, never dull, and, in fact, pretty tiring! I felt I had gotten in touch with a whole aspect of myself that had been drowned out, or shut up, and it felt healthy to experience all the complexity of my own mind when given free rein. The once-a-day meetings with the spiritual director were a kind of anchor, or focal point, and he always recommended psalms or texts to read and meditate on, which I did, engaging them much more vigorously in this state of silence, with only my own voices going at it, than when I was speaking with others in a group.

Though it was sometimes exhausting, it was invigorating too. I felt like Jacob wrestling with the angel. That is, in fact, what the five days seemed most like in retrospect—a kind of extended wrestling match, with different parts of myself, and God. It also seemed a relieving process—an emptying—of all those voices that rose up in my mind when I exposed myself to a state of extended silence.

The Art of Emptying

Monasteries, of course, aren't the only places for finding silence, meditation, and contemplation. There are a number of ashrams in this country now, open to people of all faiths who want to experience with other seekers a break from daily life. Removing ourselves from that routine temporarily can be a relief, a kind of healing, a process of emptying ourselves of habitual patterns of thought and behavior.

Living in Boston, I had heard about the Kripalu Center in Lenox, Massachusetts, in the Berkshires, and I had seen its catalogues in coffeehouses and stores on Charles Street on Beacon Hill. The catalogues always showed healthy men and women doing yoga or climbing mountains or splashing in a lake, smiling and obviously enjoying themselves in a lovely natural setting. I decided to go for a weekend and drove over with a friend who was also curious about the place.

The building and grounds of Kripalu were originally a Roman Catholic retirement home for Jesuit priests, known as Shadowbrook, and were bought in the late '60s by Amrit Desai, known to his followers as Gurudev ("beloved teacher"). Desai came from India to teach yoga, developed a following at his first ashram in Pennsylvania, and established this larger center in the Berkshires.

In 1995, Desai was ousted from the institution when he admitted sexual relationships with followers that he had previously denied. Kripalu survived the ensuing crisis, and the resident staff, who live and work there year-round and run all aspects of the operation, have continued the programs and work of the center.

During my four visits to Kripalu, the resident staff was hospitable and friendly but never tried to impose their beliefs on the guests. I felt perfectly comfortable there and was never pressured, even to attend the program or classes I had signed up to take. I enjoyed the abundant and tasty vegetarian food, the sessions in yoga and meditation, and special programs for empowerment in particular areas. Friends who have been there in the post-Gurudev era tell me it's operating well.

Kripalu is one of those places that provide a context for "emptying," for breaking free of destructive habits you haven't been able to shake. A woman I know was sent there by a friend who was worried about her drinking and smoking and increasing depression. There is no alcohol, tobacco, or caffeine at Kripalu, so going there automatically means emptying those substances from your body. Like most people, I got a headache from caffeine withdrawal the first time I went.

My friend at first rebelled, laughing at the staff and calling them escapists, but they just smiled, and by the end of the week she felt better than she had in a long time. She decided to go again for the three-week yoga teacher training, gave up alcohol and cigarettes, and became a popular yoga teacher herself! That's how powerful an exposure to a new way can be.

Yoga in Paradise

For months I had studied with fascination a full-page ad with photographs on the back cover of the *Yoga Journal* for an ashram in the Bahamas. The pictures looked too good to be true, and the price also seemed too good to be true for what looked like a beautiful beachside resort. I didn't go until I discovered a friend who had actually been to the place.

"It's like spiritual boot camp," Cheryl told me. She said if I didn't mind getting up at five-thirty in the morning for the early meditation, and going to two meditations and two yoga sessions every day (attendance is required, to ward off people who just want to take advantage of the great beach location at a low price). I'd probably enjoy the experience.

The Sivananda Ashram Yoga Retreat on Paradise Island turned out to be as good as it looked in the pictures. Doing yoga postures on a platform on the beach, with the spray of ocean waves wafting over you and the warm sun beaming down, is hard to beat. When the surf gets too loud, class is transferred to a platform on the bay side of the island, an idyllic spot itself, with gentle waves lapping and cruise ships passing by.

Attending the two-hour meditation sessions in the morning, sitting on pillows on the concrete floor of the temple, with chanting and singing in Sanskrit, facing candles and framed photographs of gurus, would not be everyone's idea of a vacation. If you let yourself sink into it, though, using the time to relax, clear the mind, and empty yourself of the usual worries, fears, and concerns, it can be a beautiful way to begin the day.

After that mental emptying, followed by emptying the body of soreness and fatigue in morning yoga, you can fill your body with fresh breads and muffins, hot and cold cereals, fresh fruit and salads, tea, and milk, at an abundant brunch at ten o'clock. The ashram asks people to volunteer for taking turns at cleanup, dishwashing, and food preparation, but aside from those alternating minor duties you are free then to enjoy the beach or go into town until the afternoon yoga session at four o'clock. Dinner is at six, followed by evening meditation, which is usually lighter than the morning chanting, like a meditation walk, a bonfire on the beach, or reading stories aloud from the Hindu tradition.

To emphasize their welcoming and respect for other faiths, the residents and teachers at the ashram encourage visitors to sing or lead hymns from their own religious tradition during walks or evening get-togethers. Never when I was there was there a hint of any attempt at conversion, or that most dreaded of all things we fear when we have to go to a place whose traditions are foreign and mysterious to us— brainwashing.

My fellow retreatants were an interesting and congenial group of people ranging in age from twenty-something to seventy-something, from the United States, Canada, Germany, England, Australia, with varied backgrounds, from a retired entertainment lawyer to a United Nations guide, a Soho painter to a Washington, D.C., housewife. I stayed a week and left invigorated.

While it's great to go to the Caribbean, it isn't necessary to go to an exotic place to do yoga. I took my first classes at the Boston Center for Adult Education, and the benefits to mind, body, and spirit were just as great. Most adult education centers, as well as Young Men's and Young Women's Christian Associations, and Young Men's and Young

Women's Hebrew Associations in most cities, offer classes at modest prices. If you can't find any classes in your area, the *Yoga Journal* lists teachers from every state in the back of the magazine, and even if one isn't in your own city or town, calling or writing them is likely to lead you to the nearest yoga class.

Nor do you need to go to ashrams or monasteries to find silence. Reverand Carl Scovel loves to hike in the White Mountains of New Hampshire, especially enjoying the silence of it, the natural meditation that goes with the experience. He most enjoys going by himself, and doesn't encourage conversation when he leads hikes for parishioners and friends.

Sometimes wordless times come as a surprise and relief. The writer and stand-up comedian Mary Beth Coudal told me she was taken to a dance recital recently, and what she most enjoyed was the spectacle of this kind of dramatic art without words. Words are her stock in trade, yet sometimes they seemed to overwhelm, clutter, and distract; this experience of watching a different kind of artistic performance, with no words at all, was especially restful to her.

"There wasn't any 'blah, blah, blah,' and it was great!" she explained.

Centering with Meditation

When we shut down the outer noise of the world—the traffic, boom boxes, televisions, radios, stereos, speeches, discussions, songs, conversations—then we are left with another kind of noise, the nonstop chatter of the mind.

> *When we shut down the outer noise of the world—the traffic, boom boxes, televisions, radios, stereos, speeches, discussions, songs, conversations—then we are left with another kind of noise, the nonstop chatter of the mind.*

This constant, clamorous inner voice reminds us of what to regret, what we ought to do, didn't do, what might be done, what has to be done, what was done to us twenty years ago, what we should have said to the person who did it and what we could say to anyone who tries it again—I have even caught myself talking out loud walking down the street as I play out some of these dialogues of the mind. I have heard this constant noise described as sounding like a foreign radio station whose rat-a-tat messages are meaningless if we don't know the language, or like the chatter of a horde of monkeys at the top of a banana tree, or a personal Tower of Babel.

Everyone agrees this interior babble is annoying, exasperating, crazy (and human)—all right, but how do we turn it off? How do we get some relief from it? Maybe that's why we turn on all that outer noise—to drown out the noise inside our own head. Maybe that's also a reason we drink, do drugs, overeat, oversleep, overwork, oversex— engage in anything that distracts us, anything that takes our mind off—our mind!

The other way to try to silence it is meditation—the conscious effort to empty the mind of all that detritus.

Humans have attempted for centuries to devise methods to still the mind, to try to remove ourselves from the chaos of the long-running record inside it. Today we are not discovering new and better ones but rather continuing or rediscovering the oldest ones. In this area there is no scientific advance, there is only the discipline of the ancient techniques.

Concentrating on a still point, a light, a candle flame, is one of the ways of focusing the mind for meditation. Mantras—words with sacred connotations or with no connotations at all—are repeated to focus the attention, and to "bring the mind back" to a point of concentration, nondistraction. Transcendental Meditation, brought to this country by Maharishi Mahesh Yogi and his followers in the '60s, uses a mantra to keep coming back to, usually a Sanskrit word of one or two syllables. Some yoga meditations suggest simply concentrating on the breath as it passes in and out of the nose. A Japanese technique counts to ten backwards, and then repeats it over and over.

Centering prayer, a kind of Christian version similar to TM, begins by asking God or Jesus to be present, and then uses a mantra such as God, Peace, Love, or Jesus. Instead of repeating the mantra, the

CREATORS TALKING

"I didn't have a vision, I wasn't a visionary. I knew I couldn't be a sharp businessman. If the company was to succeed with me at the helm, it would have to succeed in a different way. We had to be responsive to the consumer. You learn to listen carefully—your hearing becomes acute. You learn to pick up messages out there—in the market—and in the workplace. I learned that at this small company which I started."

—ARNOLD HIATT, FORMER CHAIRMAN OF THE STRIDE RITE CORPORATION, DIRECTOR OF THE STRIDE RITE CHARITABLE FOUNDATION

meditator lets it go, and uses it again only when thoughts wander off to bring the mind back to the focus, the still point. Father M. Basil Pennington, a Trappist monk, has been instrumental in spreading the practice, and illuminates the process in his key book, *Centering Prayer*.

Many meditation practices, from centering prayer to yoga, emphasize the importance of breathing. In fact, one of the systems of yoga, called *Pranayama*, studies the link between breathing and consciousness and gives exercises to balance mind, body, and spirit through breathing. Michelle Hebert, an outstanding yoga teacher in southern California, wrote on "The Breath of Life" in *IDEA Today* that we have the ability to control our breathing patterns, "to quicken our breathing or slow it down," and that "breath can change energy levels from low to high, from sluggish to revitalized. . . . When a person is in a state of anxiety, fear, or stress, his or her breathing is often shallow or uneven." Breathing exercises can shift those conditions to "a calmer, more balanced state."

Health pioneer Dr. Herbert Benson of Massachusetts General Hospital explains in *The Relaxation Response* that the body cannot be in a state of stress and relaxation at the same time. By controlling the breath and focusing the mind on a single point, anyone can create physical relaxation. Dr. Dean Ornish, author of *Reversing Heart Disease*, found that such relaxation techniques can reduce both blood pressure and cholesterol levels.

What's the big deal? Don't we all breathe automatically? Isn't that one thing I don't have to learn? Well, you do, if you want to have some influence over it, and over your body and mind. Left to its own devices, the breath, like the mind, simply whirls out of control. Breathing techniques can be learned at any yoga class, or through a number of instructional tape cassettes.

The Wandering Mind

The mind always goes wandering off. One meditation technique is to watch it wander off, to be the observer of your own mind, separated from the gabble of it. But the gabble always rises up, just as powerfully for people today as it did for Abba Isaac of the Desert Fathers, who wrote in his instructions on this way of prayerful meditation:

> Perhaps wandering thoughts surge about my soul like boiling water, and I cannot control them, nor can I offer prayer without its being interrupted by silly images. I feel so dry that I am incapable of spiritual feelings, and many sighs and groans cannot save me from dreariness. I must needs say: "O God, come to my assistance; O Lord, make haste to help me."

As it was in the first century so it is today!

Geoffrey Wolff, in his article "Writers and Booze," speaks of the clamoring voices in the head as something peculiar to writers when he explains their temptation to drink:

> Writing is hard. I don't mean it's harder than everything, because it's not; I mean only that it's uphill work to write. And what's toughest is the din that echoes in a writer's ears after the day's work is done. A writer can't shut down the damned noise, his characters' voices, their competing complications. . . . Booze will send me to never-never land, dress me in thick wool, earmuff me against the voices, blink off the light, give rest and sleep and peace. Just what I must have wanted. Just what I don't want.

I would argue that it isn't only writers who "can't shut down the damned noise" in their heads, it is all human beings. I would bet that when Mr. Wolff is in between projects, he still can't shut down the damned noise without conscious effort. The lure of drink to "earmuff" a person against the interior voices is also why others turn to alcohol— businesspeople and homemakers and pole vaulters and auto mechanics, who also want to "blink off the light" and go to "never-never land."

It is much easier to pour a drink than to find a quiet spot, take a breath, and devote twenty minutes to trying to clear the mind through meditation. Meditation, meditative prayer, whatever the name we give to that effort to still and empty the mind, is extremely difficult and challenging. Doing it for twenty minutes twice a day, once in the morning and once in the evening (as TM and centering prayer recommend) is a major commitment, one I have had a hard time keeping. I followed a single twenty-minute prayer schedule every day for about five years, then stopped for a few years, and have started again with only ten minutes, hoping to flex this "muscle" of meditation and work my way back to twenty minutes.

Healing with Meditation

For most people, this kind of prayer or meditation is a struggle. The effort to empty is a challenge, yet it brings great benefits: a lessening of tension, a relaxation, greater ease in personal and business dealings. Few have had as dramatic results, though, in as short a time as Joan Borysenko, the author, lecturer, and cofounder of the Mind/Body Clinic at Massachusetts General Hospital.

In her best-selling book *Minding the Body, Mending the Mind,* Joan tells us that when she was twenty-four years old, working on her doctorate at Harvard Medical School, she was living on coffee and cigarettes, trying to cope with a troubled marriage and an infant son for whom she had "too little time." She goes on:

> I was also a physical wreck. Troubled by migraines all my life, I found in college that the intense competition had added crippling stomach pains and vomiting to my list of

psychosomatic illnesses. As a graduate student, I also came down with severe bronchitis four times in two years and had to study for my doctoral exams while my head spun in a fever. If this weren't enough, I also developed the high blood pressure that ran in my family.

My marriage fell apart during this year. I was now a single parent plagued with fainting and crippled by abdominal pains that were diagnosed as spastic colon. I was given antispasmodics, painkillers, and tranquilizers—all to no avail. Then a viral infection in the lining of my lungs created suffocating pain that took me to the emergency room of the nearest hospital.

There was no Mind/Body Clinic for me to go back to then, but there was a friend in the lab where I conducted my graduate research who was excited about his new hobby—meditation. He compared it to a mini-vacation in which he could switch off all his cares and concerns and come out refreshed and ready to tackle whatever came up. My first thought was that meditation was for ascetics who lived in caves. I was a hard-headed scientist, literally killing myself to master the ways of the medical establishment.

Nevertheless, I gave it a try—largely out of desperation—practicing each day. The test came a few weeks later while I was sitting at an electron microscope, trying to unlock the secrets of cancer cells. I felt the familiar stabbing behind my right eye, the light sensitivity and nausea that heralded a migraine. It was time for an experiment.

Retreating to my office, I pulled the shade and shut the door. I settled into a chair, relaxed my muscles from head to foot, shifted my breathing from tense chest breathing to relaxed diaphragmatic breathing, and began to meditate. In time the pain subsided. After the meditation was over, I was left with a feeling of having been washed clean, like the earth after a heavy rain. I ran around the laboratory announcing that I had performed the most important experiment of my life. It was the beginning of a great change in my life.

Another kind of meditation technique, one which Joan uses in working with people who are trying to attain a more calm lifestyle, is called "mindfulness," sometimes described as the "be here now" approach. It focuses on whatever you are doing at the moment, whether it is washing the dishes, eating a piece of bread, or crossing the street—being present to the experience, emptying yourself of all the distractions of the past and future.

Joan writes,

> During a full-day session that occurs at the midpoint of the Mind/Body Program, we take a long walk in a park by a river near the hospital. There is no "purpose" to the walk—nowhere to go and nothing to accomplish. The accomplishment is being present in the process of walking. Our patients are usually amazed at how incredible the commonplace is. They hear sounds and see sights with new ears and eyes, with the kind of enjoyment a child experiences.

Western Zen: Emptying and Embracing the Hollow

There are other simple techniques to experience the calming effect of silence. Singer Judy Collins told me, "I use exercise and breathing to center and clear my head. I like to run and swim—those are Western forms of Zen."

Running is one of the most popular contemporary ways of clearing the mind, and you don't have to be a marathon champion to have the experience. Oregon professor Robert Grudin tells in *The Grace of Great Things: Creativity and Innovation* how "a long jog, with its strong rhythm and sense of psychological expressiveness" is one of the everyday methods he uses for clearing his mind when he's blocked or confused, and adds, "Contrapuntal music works on me similarly, and sometimes a glance out of my office window, of the graceful Douglas firs that stand to the south, is enough to clear my head."

Swimming is a key practice for Constance H. Gemson, who took part in one of my Spiritual Autobiography workshops at the 92nd St. Y in New York. She published her first article in *New York Newsday* on her experience of swimming "to find serenity."

By swimming, I am creating and keeping the silence as I glide through the familiar water in a pool on West 86th Street in New York city. Each experience is the same, yet different. I go back and forth, back and forth, to finish this cycle sixty-six times, or half a mile. . . . I swim three times a week in my search for a clearer, calmer life. . . .

By swimming, I find my own rhythm and silence. In my crowded life, this is vital. In my secular city, I swim and I'm refreshed.

Kurt Vonnegut has suggested (in an introduction to a collection of stories by Budd Schulberg) that another Western form of meditation is simply reading short stories—in this process the pulse beat slows, the mind concentrates on the immediate word being read, the static of interior chitchat is turned off, and we experience the same benefits as those of the more rigorous exercises of "pure" meditation emphasized by the Eastern traditions.

When I started expounding the virtues I had found as a beginning yoga student to my old friend Ted "The Horse" Steeg, a great athlete who was a "little All-American" (an athlete from a small-enrollment school) at Wabash College, and a champion in all town sports from softball to basketball in Woodstock, New York, he began to laugh. At first I thought he was trying to joke away my enthusiasm for living in the moment and shutting off the noise that the yoga postures provided. But that wasn't it.

"You yo-yo! Why do you think I've been playing sports all these years?" he challenged. "That's what it does—puts you in the moment and shuts down the mental noise!"

"Oh, yeah—I guess it does," I sheepishly admitted, healthily shedding some of my false guru-ship.

Coach Phil Jackson affirms, "What makes basketball so exhilarating is the joy of losing yourself completely in the dance."

By emptying, we are preparing ourselves to be filled.

Whatever the process—from swimming to playing basketball, reading short stories to centering prayer, Quaker meetings, Zen sitting, and Transcendental Meditation—the stilling and focusing of the mind empties you of distractions, puts you in the present, a phenomenon described by Annie Dillard in *Pilgrim at Tinker Creek*: "Experiencing the present purely is being emptied and hollow; you catch grace as a man fills his cup under a waterfall."

By emptying, we are preparing ourselves to be filled.

The Wisdom of Bodyspirit

Some people in search of a spiritual dimension to their lives may start by taking a course in yoga or t'ai chi, the most meditative of the martial arts. Both of these physical practices help empty the mind of distraction, and at the same time tone and strengthen the body. Sometimes students come to these practices strictly in search of physical empowerment and in the process are awakened to the spirit.

All will discover that discipline of the body is also a way to discipline the mind, and that these practices themselves are a form of meditation. When you hold a yoga pose you are focused on your body holding the pose, rather than your ongoing mind-gabble. When you concentrate on performing the movements in t'ai chi, you are similarly freed from the interior babble stream.

The turn toward a spiritual path often—though not always, and not by some kind of hard-and-fast rule—involves an awareness of the body, an attention to one's physical condition that may not have been present before.

This, too, makes sense, and is illuminated by Nancy Roth, an Episcopal priest who writes in her book *A New Christian Yoga*, "In the Hebrew scriptures, human life is understood as one indivisible unity of body and spirit, which in Hebrew is expressed in the word *nefesh*. The closest equivalent we can manage in English is 'bodyspirit,' without the space between the words."

Bodyspirit. The two concepts were indeed joined in my own experience.

Though I'd gone to my first t'ai chi class purely, I thought, as a way of learning to use my body in a better way, when I slowly lifted my arms with palms upraised in the opening movement of "the form," as it's called, I sensed at once this was also prayer. ("The form" of t'ai chi is a series of flowing movements like a slow dance, which look like David Carradine's slow-motion movements in his *Kung Fu* television series.)

Roth explains that she began taking yoga classes because she wanted to make her body stronger and more supple in order to be a better dancer. She had found that "the absolute attentiveness" required in a strenuous ballet class "had a centering and calming effect that I could only describe as 'spiritual.'" When she enrolled in yoga class she had a similar experience, finding that "the exercise affected both my body and my spirit," and that the relaxation posture at the end of the class became for her "a doorway into prayer."

My Body, My Burden

This whole idea of "bodyspirit" seemed, suddenly and marvelously, a revelation to me, which was not surprising since I had gone for most of my life without seeing (and vehemently denying) any connection between the body and the mind, much less the spirit.

That the mind and body are connected seems, of course, the most obvious truism imaginable—after all, the mind isn't floating outside you somewhere, in a separate compartment! But still, that concept is difficult to grasp when you've been brought up in a culture that until the last few decades separated those spheres of being. Dr. Herbert Benson had to battle to get his theories of direct mind-body relationships—like meditation lowering the pulse and blood pressure—accepted by the medical profession, even after they were tested and proved.

It used to suit me just fine to believe that the mind and body had no connection, since my mind—or at least the imaginative part of it, the part that enabled me to write—had served me pretty well. My body, on the other hand, while it had all its parts in working order, in high school was not strong or big or agile enough to make me a good athlete (a circumstance that, happily, turned me from trying to play football, to what for me was the more natural occupation of writing about other people playing football).

From my teenage years onward, I simply regarded my body as a necessary if annoying adjunct to whatever I thought of as "me"—a sort of burden to be fed, clothed, and washed as cursorily as possible, with the least bother. From my early twenties until age forty-eight I abused my body with tobacco and alcohol to such an extent that when I finally paid attention to it by starting that exercise program and getting off booze, I was told that if I had waited another six months I would have done permanent damage to my heart.

Even so, at first I looked on my new attention to my body simply as a practical measure, to enable me to live longer to use my precious mind and imagination. It didn't dawn on me that a person's physical and mental capacities were connected, and influenced one another—and even had to do with the spirit, an element I had denied altogether all those years. I began to see the interconnection when I started taking the t'ai chi and yoga classes.

Putting the Parts Together

"The word 'yoga,'" Nancy Roth explains in *A New Christian Yoga*, "comes from the Sanskrit word yug, which means to 'yoke' or 'join together.' For Hindus, the various disciplines of yoga help to join together body and mind, the human being and the divine, and the self and the world."

After coming back from the ashram in the Bahamas, I wrote that

> waking to a tinkling bell in the dark at five thirty in the morning, with the sound of the surf outside, going to meditation in the chapel, and on to yoga on the platform by the beach, with the sun and sea spray blessing our bodies, I soon found I wasn't making any distinctions between the purely physical and the rest of my being. All of it felt comfortable, calmed, alive.

The resident swami at the ashram, Swami Shanmugananda, had told me,

> There is only one yoga. It is all for mystical union. Don't overemphasize the asanas [postures], that is a misunderstanding. People are attracted to Hatha yoga, taken by the physical postures, but what's behind it is mystical practice. The purpose of the postures is to facilitate the body to be steady during meditation. If the mind is not pure, then even if you're doing the most excellent postures, it's meaningless—it's like having a car in good condition, and the driver is drunk.

At the last yoga session I attended on the island, the instructor ended the session by quietly offering a prayer for "the asanas and what they teach us." They taught me in my bones as well as my mind what I should have known all along—that the body, spirit, and intellect can't be split into isolated compartments. What nurtures any part nurtures the whole.

In yoga, in joining together, I began to see—or rather, experience—the interconnections of all those elements of my life I had looked on and experienced as separate. This included, finally, the creative, which I held out longest of all as a separate realm, a sort of magic kingdom which the elect were privileged to enter and work in—the elect being people like myself who were "professional" creative people, those who made a living as writers, painters, sculptors, musicians. In yoga class, finally, what I experienced in a small but obvious way brought home to me the connection of creativity as part of the whole, a function of bodyspirit.

Ideas from Asanas

A few years ago I was commissioned to write a movie script based on my novel *Selling Out,* about a writer in Hollywood who was going to pieces as he used more booze and drugs to try to regain his creative powers, and brought himself instead to the brink of self-annihilation before turning away from that destructive course at the last minute. (Yes, it was autobiographical.) The day before I was supposed to send in a draft of the script, I realized that the endings of two scenes were all wrong. I needed to come up with some better dramatic resolutions before letting the producer and director see what I'd written.

I looked at my watch and saw it was nearly four o'clock in the afternoon—several hours later than I'd imagined. It was one of those times when I'd been staring at the word processor without any result for hours on end. I had a yoga class in Cambridge at five o'clock, and I really wanted to go, but I was afraid of leaving these scene endings unresolved, afraid I wouldn't have time enough to fix them if I took off the two hours it would require to put on my sweatpants, T-shirt, and gym shoes, catch the subway to Cambridge, take the class, and return. I sat for another five minutes or so staring blankly at the screen of my computer, feeling stale, numb, and sedentary. Then I suddenly jumped up and grabbed my yoga things, justifying this bolting from duty with the thought, What's the difference? I'm not getting anything done anyway. I hurried off to class.

I put the script and all its problems out of my mind and simply decided to enjoy the yoga experience. While I was doing the shoulder stand—one of the inverted poses—one of the scenes I was having trouble with came to my mind, and the idea for ending it followed immediately, an idea that seemed natural, right, and fitting. I smiled—upside down—and wondered if the key to getting ideas when you were stuck was to stand on your head, or at least your shoulders. Maybe turning the mind upside down had shaken out the right idea!

Later in the class I was doing the "triangle" pose, holding myself as steady as I could at "the edge" of my capacity to stay in the position. When the instructor told us to release, to "come back to center," the ending to the other troublesome scene in the script snapped into my mind, complete, as if freed by the release of the posture.

It felt as if the yoga positions had released the ideas, that stretching my body had somehow stretched open my mind to allow the scene endings to come out. If I had stayed home, glued to the computer screen, I would simply have logged more empty hours and brought myself further frustration—along with rising anxiety—without resolving the questions in the script.

The experience brought clearly to my mind what I'd been living—but not recognizing so specifically—for nearly a decade: that the mind, body, and spirit are inextricably connected, and that what we do to and with our body will influence our mind—including the imagination, and our creative powers.

Ever since I started on the path of bodyspirit in 1980, I have felt far better than I had since high school (waking without a hangover is in itself a plus), and I have enjoyed the actual process of writing more than before. But the direct relationship of the physical with the mental and spiritual—and creative—aspects of life didn't fully hit me until that yoga class.

I don't mean to trivialize the vast and profound significance of yoga in the world by passing it off as a gimmick to get ideas, but rather to suggest what happened in my minor experience was a metaphor that brought home to me some of the connections offered by the "yoke," the tying together, that yoga provides.

To illustrate how rich and varied is the whole concept of yoga, I again call on Nancy Roth, who explains,

> Some of these practices concern devotion (*bhakti* yoga), knowledge (*jnana* yoga), action (*karma* yoga), and inner concentration called the "royal way" (*raja* yoga). Hatha yoga is a branch of *raja* yoga and involves postures, meditations, breathing techniques, and concentration exercises, or meditation. The word *hatha* actually consists of two words, *ha*, which means "sun," and *tha*, which means "moon." The sun represents the expenditure or expression of energy; the moon, the acquiring or conservation of energy. The joining together of these principles through the exercises of Hatha yoga creates a balance like that of the cosmic rhythm of the sun and moon.

Since the human body does not vary according to religion, it is not surprising that exercises which originated in Hinduism can be readily incorporated into another theological context.

Yoga as Prayer

Before I had read Nancy Roth's thoughtful concept in *A New Christian Yoga,* I found it natural to think of my yoga practice as a spiritual or bodyspirit experience that in no way conflicted with my belief as a member of a Christian church. In fact, I knew the yoga supported and enriched my spiritual life, and, even more dramatically, at a crucial time of darkness was my primary spiritual connection.

Just as I naively was beginning to think I was "getting it all together" in following a spiritual path (always a time to be on guard, I now know), I took a turn in what I thought was good faith that brought pain to another person as well as myself. I made a commitment to a relationship with a woman that I couldn't keep, that I knew almost immediately was impossible for me. It was all the more painful because I had imagined I was doing this out of a spiritual motivation, as part of my own spiritual path. The shock of it turning out to be so clearly and devastatingly a mistake brought down a curtain of darkness in my mind and spirit. Prayers seemed hollow now, and phony. Weren't these the words I had used to justify this mistake as I was in the process of making it? The words now taunted me, and I couldn't speak them.

At this time, when prayer with words shut down for me, when even going to church was painful to me, the one thing that brought me a sense of peace and interior calm was going to yoga class. I realized this was my prayer now, the one kind I could engage in, because it was wordless. I knew it was no less prayer.

When prayer with words shut down for me, when even going to church was painful to me, the one thing that brought me a sense of peace and interior calm was going to yoga class.

Nor is "Zen sitting" any less a prayer, though it is without words. I have joined others in "sitting" at Zen Mountain Monastery

CREATORS TALKING

"There are times when I'll weep at the thought of having to write a sermon. Yet, when people come out of church the next day, and if I feel I've touched something significant in the lives of six of them, I'm rewarded. There has to be a willingness to pay the dues of hard work—there's no shortcut, no way around doing it. I've heard ministers preach who had insight but didn't want to do the work necessary to take it beyond the first quick insight. When I hear that, I get irritated or indifferent."

—Reverend Carl Scovel, minister, King's Chapel, Boston

in New York state, near Woodstock, and at the beautiful Zen Center at Green Gulch, outside of San Francisco, where services every Sunday morning begin with forty minutes of silent sitting, followed with a Dharma talk by one of the teachers, questions and discussions from the listeners, and then a community partaking of tea and homemade muffins baked by volunteers in the predawn hours that morning.

Return to the Form

Another sustaining concept that came to me, and kept me in the practice of going to church even when it was hard to do, was something I learned from David Zucker in t'ai chi class. Our classes were held in the beautiful, spacious ballroom of the Boston Center for Adult Education, a former merchant's mansion on Commonwealth Avenue, just off the Boston Public Garden. The setting was wonderful, except that there was a class in wine-tasting in a room next to us, and after our own class began it would inevitably be interrupted by men passing through, carrying cases of wine to the tasters, making a noisy rattling sound as they went, disturbing or breaking our quiet concentration.

My t'ai chi classmates and I got annoyed and broke our rhythm. David then told us that this interruption was a good thing, something we could make use of, since those kind of unwanted, unexpected interruptions that upset our concentration were part of the experience of daily life. "Let them come," he said. "Don't worry if you break your rhythm or even stop and start over again. The only thing to remember when it happens is: Return to the form."

The words rang deep in my consciousness. "Return to the form." It applied to my going back to church, in the routine I had been in before; it applied to going back to work on a book or a script or an essay or article when something had interrupted it, or taken me completely away from it. There was no use lamenting whatever it was that broke my concentration or yanked me physically or mentally or emotionally or spiritually out of a project. Just center again. Just take a deep breath and remember where you are. Return to the form.

The words have become a guide to me and come to mind in all different situations, giving me a way back. They are a way of dealing with interruptions, upsets, the million large and small crises that tug and tear at us through the course of a day, a year, a career, a lifetime. Return to the form.

Athletes Learn from the East

In t'ai chi or yoga or any other such discipline, the action of the body is not just exercise but meditation or prayer, a way of centering, calming, becoming aware. It is a powerful way of emptying, clearing the mind and the body at the same time, making them more alert and effective. The body and mind, working together in these disciplines, act as a living metaphor and expression of spirit, a manifestation of bodyspirit.

In the West we tend to think mainly of women engaged in these disciplines, and most yoga classes in America, as well as t'ai chi, are made up largely of women. Yet recently, prominent male athletes have made public their use of such disciplines to improve their own skills in professional sports—which also, not incidentally, require enormous creativity. An athlete, in performing, reacts, must "see" the field or court, becomes part of the flow of a game, and even directs the flow. Kareem Abdul-Jabbar is a student of yoga, and Robert "The Chief" Parish, legendary center of the Boston Celtics, started taking t'ai chi at age thirty to make himself more effective on the court.

One does not, however, need to be an athlete to engage in such practices, or get the full benefit of them creatively and spiritually. As athletes can use t'ai chi and yoga for their development, I can use it to support and enhance my creative life as a writer. The effects of such disciplines are not confined to the hours of actually doing them, or the space where one takes a class or performs the routine. Continuous practice affects other areas of life, as in the experience of t'ai chi teacher David Zucker, who is also an actor, mime, director, and playwright, and finds that "the form" inspires and informs all his creative work. For anyone who practices, the strengthening of the spiritual is a natural and inseparable part of the activity, the integration of bodyspirit.

Tilden Edwards of the Shalem Institute has written,

> Our bodies are gifts and vehicles of God, integral to our being. Much attention is paid to the body in contemporary Western culture. However, both in and out of the church the body tends to be approached in terms of physical fitness and beauty apart from a direct relation to God. One of the gifts of our greater knowledge of Asian religious practices in the last few decades has been the introduction of Hatha yoga, with all its care in revealing the integrality of body and spirit.

I don't mean to proclaim that since physical well-being and care of the body create conditions for the fuller flowering of creativity, one needs to become a body-built paragon of muscle like Arnold Schwarzenegger or an Olympic sprinter like Jackie Joyner-Kersee in order to create. If that were the case, I'd still be stuck on my last script, much less would I have gone on to produce the books, essays, and articles that followed it. Attention to the body, respect for it, the exercise of it to keep it in good working order, is one of the keys that can help unlock the creative as well as spiritual powers within us.

I take a class now in a form of yoga called *ashtanga*, which emphasizes continuous movement during the session so that the pulse

When you are being stripped, or emptied, you don't know if you'll ever be full again—in fact, it's hard to believe.

runs higher, as in aerobic exercise. The goal of "keeping the body heat up" (which is aided by turning up the room temperature) enables the muscles to move more freely, so we're able to stretch it into more positions. One of the results of the class is a lot of sweat, more sweat than I can ever remember pouring out of my body in any other form of exercise—pools of sweat, forming on the floor beneath me. This releases the toxins in the body, according to the teachers. At the end of the class I certainly feel cleaned out.

I originally assumed that at the end of such a rigorous class I'd be dead tired and starving. Instead, I am energized, and not very hungry at all. I think this phenomenon is another aspect of the unexpected rewards of emptying. By using our body till it seems empty of strength, we get new strength; by sweating profusely, the body not only eliminates toxins, but also eliminates the need for stuffing itself with food. It's almost as if by emptying, we are fed—or filled up, as in "made whole" again.

Emptying is part of the process of nature—the leaves fall, the flowers wilt, the skins of animals molt, and new buds, blooms, and pelts are grown in due season. The day is emptied of light, so night can come down, and out of the empty dark a new dawn rises. In the ageless lines of Ecclesiastes, "The sun also riseth and setteth in the west, and the rivers return from whence they have come."

Emptying.

Filling.

The process can sometimes be painful. Many people have recorded through the ages that part of the beginning of a spiritual journey is a stripping away of the old person before a new one can be born, the emptying before the filling. When you are being stripped, or emptied, you don't know if you'll ever be full again—in fact, it's hard to believe. In this weakened and frightening state you feel naked, alone, barren. Anyone who tries to reassure you at such a time that "things will get better" sounds like a phony, a Pollyanna, speaking the platitudes of Job's friends. You snarl back, like a cornered animal.

I did, anyway. In that 1980 flight from Hollywood, the year my parents died and my relationship split apart and I was broke and sick, someone called to tell me that a raunchy movie had been made, using—or partially using—the title of my most successful book, the novel *Going All the Way*. This trashy exploitation film was called *Goin' All the Way*, evidently trying to protect against any complaints of mine that it was exactly the same title by replacing the "g" in "Going" with an apostrophe. It seemed like the last straw. The movie played at a Boston theater near where I lived. I passed it on the way to church. Friends asked if it was mine. Ads ran in the local papers. I called my agent from a pay phone at La Guardia Airport and was told there was nothing I could do about it.

"I feel like I'm being stripped," I wailed.

There were tears in my eyes. I really felt stripped. At the time, I didn't know that the very words I used—"being stripped"—were part of any transformative process, spiritual or otherwise. I barked at anyone who told me things would get better. I was empty. Now I know I had to experience that, to be filled in a new kind of way. Now I see that emptying leaves you available for such a transformation. Then, I only knew I was empty.

I'd never have believed what follows: fullness.

6

Filling Up

TO EACH OF US, WHEN IT COMES, THE FEELING OF EMPTINESS SEEMS THE darkest of pits, the worst that anyone ever endured. Yet in most cases—certainly mine—our own "stripping" is peanuts compared to that of people who were stripped by accident or nature in some permanent way, and yet use the opportunity to "fill" with a different, greater power. Sometimes the kind of restrictions Rabbi Kushner speaks about, that bring greater discipline and command, are imposed by physical handicaps or ailments. A person may be "emptied" of some function, or many functions, by genetics, disease, or happenstance—yet the discipline required to overcome the losses may increase other powers, especially the creative.

Told in graduate school that he had Lou Gehrig's disease, a crippling illness, physicist Stephen Hawking went into a two-year depression (his own time of emptying). He holed up in his room playing Wagner records, reading science fiction, and "drinking a fair amount," letting his studies and his dissertation fall by the wayside.

In *Stephen Hawking's Universe*, John Boslough tells us that when Hawking's condition temporarily stabilized, he realized it would not affect his mind, and since it took no physical ability to do physics, he decided to start working again (filling up). He returned to writing his dissertation, got married, fathered two children, earned his doctorate, and began working on a formidable challenge—nothing less than the mathematical proof of the beginning of time.

Confined to a wheelchair, unable to speak except through a computerized voice box, Hawking has led the way as one of the most important scientists of our time, illuminating black holes, the "big bang" theory, and the "unified field" theory of what makes the universe tick. He provides a miraculous living example of the creative spirit working through a severely handicapped body, with incredible discipline.

Audiences all over the world have been inspired by Christy Brown, the Irish writer/hero of the book and movie *My Left Foot,* who managed to create against seemingly impossible odds, finding through heroic discipline a way to use his mostly disabled body to create. Such people also exemplify bodyspirit to me and illustrate through their lives and work how the creative spirit can triumph against all odds.

Sometimes the odds are physical, as in a paralyzed body. Sometimes people lack opportunities because of their socioeconomic status in a given society; yet that very deprivation, or emptiness, stirs them to find new ways to create.

I think of a marvelous documentary called *Style Wars* about minority kids from the blighted slum areas of New York City who painted what the world, or at any rate the city government, described and outlawed as "graffiti" on the sides of subways. I had thought graffiti meant scatological words and ugly scrawlings on bathroom walls. These paintings on the subways were bright, colorful, mural-like art done with spray paint by young people who stole into the yards where the cars were kept to express their yearning to create beauty in a grim, blasted world. They refer to one another as "painters," and call one of the masters of their form a "Picasso."

When you see one of the subway cars come up from underground in the film and move into the shattered, broken world through which it passes, brightly alive with colorful scenes, faces, and flowers and swirls of suns, stars, and planets of the imagination, it's like seeing the spirit break out. It's like a painted cry saying, "We're here—look at us, look at what we see, what we create, look at the beauty of it, you can't stomp us out, we will rise again some other way!"

The spray-painted subway cars reminded me of paintings I had seen from South America, shown by theologian Harvey Cox in a talk on Liberation theology. From countries emptied of hope by despotic, dictatorial suppression, where any sign of spirit was stamped out, there were paintings of Jesus lying on the ground with holes in his body, like bullet holes—and growing up through the holes were flowers, bursting toward the sun. They were saying, without words, "You can't stamp us out; you can kill us, but we will rise again, this spirit will rise again, through the holes of your bullets it will bloom, and nothing can destroy it, for it is the life force, the spirit."

No more powerful testimony to the spirit exists than the drawings and paintings done in the World War II concentration camps. In *Spiritual Resistance: Art from the Concentration Camps,* published by Union of American Hebrew Congregations, we see the work smuggled out of Nazi death camps, done by prisoners trapped in the ultimate hell of this century. We learn that

> the artists of the camps defied Nazi regulations on canvas, paper, tissue—in pen, or ink, or color wrung from tattered clothing—to demonstrate their transcendence of the horror of the moment. While many of these artists never stepped from the camps, the strength of their will survives.

The artists drew portraits of their fellow inmates and scenes of camp life, hiding their drawings in double walls or burying them. Some traded bread for paper or paint and used flour sacks and burlap bags as their canvases. On the doorstep of death, in affirmation of life, they created.

New Warriors

There is a concept around now, used in the dialogue of the New Age or personal growth or human potential movement, of the "warrior," originating perhaps from Carlos Castaneda in his Don Juan books. It doesn't mean the warrior as soldier in the traditional sense of a military man with a gun on a political mission for a nation-state, but rather an individual who has developed his own powers of bodyspirit through tremendous discipline; has developed himself and his senses to be able to perform at his peak or beyond it—not in service to some military aggressor but to the spirit, the life force of the universe. This kind of "warrior" is exemplified in the practice of t'ai chi, in which no blow is struck, yet a foe is deflected. David Zucker tells how this works, in one of the most illuminating explanations of the power of emptying:

> The basic premise is that you understand your own body's energy completely first, and then you understand the other person's, so if someone is aiming a blow, you're so totally not there you empty yourself completely, which is the meditative aspect, the religious aspect. You empty yourself so you have no ego about it, no fear of life or death, so you kind of become the other person. If I were trying to punch my own hand, I couldn't do it because I know exactly when I'm going to do it—so if I was in tune with you as you are yourself, you couldn't hit me because I would be able to sense that energy coming and just move. That's really the self-defense aspect.

I think of the disciplines of t'ai chi and yoga as practices to strengthen us to be that kind of warrior, to create, to serve as conveyors of the spirit. The kind of warrior I am speaking of may use her disciplined power not only for evading injury and deflecting anger, but in the service of healing, in all its manifold forms. Such warriors are in the tradition of the Flower Soldiers of the Native Americans, an ancient discipline of teachers and Medicine Men and Women described by Hyemeyohsts Storm in his wisdom-fiction narrative *Lightningbolt*.

The kind of warrior I am speaking of may use her disciplined power not only for evading injury and deflecting anger, but in the service of healing, in all its manifold forms.

Contemporary healing can come through the laying-on of hands. This does not promise an instant cure but brings about an easing of pain and eventual recovery through the practiced, educated use of bodywork techniques. One who employs such methods in such a spirit is Elizabeth Valentine, a masseuse in Boston, who explained she had worked with pregnant women in France, and with clients of a doctor who treated survivors of sexual abuse. "The idea of massage was to help heal the split between body and mind," she told me.

Other kinds of healing come through practice of the arts and sharing one's art with others. Singer Judy Collins speaks of healing through music:

> I've said that performing is healing, and so is writing, absolutely. I was just talking to my friend Erica Jong about our work, how it heals. It reaches me when the only thing that helps me is writing. I've always been a great believer in the self healing qualities of creativity.

Healing ourselves is one way we act as what Creation theologian Matthew Fox calls co-creators with God—a theology in which we are not helpless pawns who must plead our case to a distant deity, but rather serve as responsible partners in creating our lives and the world we live in. An early, inspirational co-creator was the visionary medieval nun Hildegard of Bingen, who "saw herself as the mouthpiece of the Lord, merely conveying his messages to her hearers and readers," according to biographer Sabina Flanagan in *Hildegard of Bingen: A Visionary Life*. That might be a way to explain her prodigious output—three massive works of theology, books on plants, animals, medicine, and healing, seventy songs, cycles of poetry, a musical play, more than three hundred letters—at the same time she was also a traveling preacher, abbess of a monastery, healer, exorcist, advisor, prophet, and seer.

The Voice That Says "Get Up!"

Learning the myths about alcohol, drugs, and creativity helps empty our mind of some of the dangerous misconceptions and distortions about the subject. There are also many other negative myths we need to rid ourselves of to reach our full creative potential: the myth of low self-esteem ("I'm not good enough"), fear of failure ("Now there's proof I'm no good!") or of success ("I don't deserve it"). Getting rid of these deep-seated personal myths can be a continuing process, but one that must be engaged in to reach more of our potential as creators and human beings.

Another powerful and debilitating myth is that we can "save" someone else. Many use that as an excuse to continue destructive relationships that for years on end drag us down. I have watched this painful process with a friend who lives with an alcoholic who has "bottomed out" many times. This drinker has been put in jail, lost the love and support of family, been fired from job after job, been taken to hospitals by the police after threatening suicide and/or murder—yet has never once made the decision to give up the bottle. During all this the partner has lost not only work and income but physical health, with a disease brought on by stress. Both deny that they need outside help, which would be a sign of weakness!

We all have negative voices in our consciousness, and cleaning them out is a lifelong process. Figure skater Nancy Kerrigan summed it up in a Nike ad, which showed her falling down and then getting up to skate again, saying there are always the voices that tell her to give up; the only voice she listens to is the one that says, "Get up!"

But what new voices or ideas do we put in place of the old ones after we have "cleaned house"? Emptiness is only a temporary condition; Spinoza reminds us that nature abhors a vacuum. Jesus tells a parable about a man who cleans his house of demons, and seven worse ones come to take up residence. An empty house is an invitation to intruders, demons who want to take over the place.

Some of those "demons" are fear of the new, fear of change, voices that, sirenlike, try to lure us back to our familiar old pain so we don't have to deal with the unknown. The emptiness that comes after giving up destructive old habits can be frightening, and in our panic we may turn to other ways of numbing ourselves.

We all have negative voices in our consciousness, and cleaning them out is a lifelong process.

I experienced this when I first gave up drinking. So terrified was I of the prospect of full consciousness that I began to smoke marijuana to replace the numbing sensation of alcohol. I rationalized that the marijuana was healthier because I didn't have hangovers, and besides, it wasn't damaging my liver. In a little over a year I realized I was smoking dope regularly—the dependence had crept up on me. This seemed especially ludicrous because I had also begun to go to church regularly and attend classes in Bible study. When I woke up to what I was doing I felt schizophrenic, and worse, hypocritical.

Realizing I couldn't go in both directions at once, I threw out my stash of marijuana and all the paraphernalia that went with smoking it. Of course, I was able to give it up, to rid myself of this very seductive and subtle demon of distraction, because I had something else to replace it with—the spiritual nurturing and prayer and church community that had become a significant part of my life. I am certain that without that sustenance I could never have given up the grass.

That's why I bristle at the simpleminded slogan, "Just say no to drugs!" You can't say no to something that powerful without having something powerful to replace it. I think that's what Jesus was warning us about when he spoke of the demons entering the empty house. I don't mean you have to run out and adopt a particular religious faith if you don't have one; I mean that trying to move in a spiritual direction is important, because the processes of that path are nurturing and strengthening, and the path going the other way leads toward numbing and oblivion.

Another popular route is the path of least resistance, which is not only boring and dull, but dangerous, for it can easily veer off into the direction of oblivion. Laziness and fear prompt us to take this path—or nonpath—for we don't have to think and act, we just sit back and let things happen to us. When you go against your own principles because it's easier to give in to friends than to argue or explain your position—or because you don't want to risk their disapproval, or worse, their ridicule—then you're following the path of no resistance. It's the dark way, the blind way, that's probably led by the spiritually blind.

Spirit Warriors

Creators need to be warriors—not of violence, but of the spirit. We need discipline, clarity, strength of will, and attention, the mindfulness of being aware of what we're doing and being present in the moment we're doing it. Creators I talk with in every field speak of the agony as well as the ecstasy of creation, the dark as well as the bright side of the process.

To go through the challenges of creation, to fit ourselves for the times when we seem to go dry, when the "boulders" in the path of our creation—as the historian of Christian doctrine Elaine Pagels calls them—seem too enormous to move or get around, we must not give up, but accept the challenge of their stolid resistance, go through or over or around them on our way to realizing the dream, the image, and inspiration that was given us to create. To do that, to realize our capacities as creators, we need to be at our fullest, most integrated state of being, and to keep growing and creating. When we are knocked down

---

CREATORS TALKING

"Before a massage, my own orientation is to get myself physically grounded, get my body in alignment and go through this series—first attaching my feet to the earth, and honoring the earth—I ask the earth for support. I get this from studying Native American meditation. After attaching to the earth I bring my energy up and ask for God's support; then I ask for a kind of thin membrane of protection that will allow me to stay receptive but filter out negativity and energy that's not mine. That's a challenge, because I absorb from people. I make a prayer, thanking God for his presence and that he may lead me through the process basically to continue the right path, that I can support the person on their path and bring them to the right alignment."

—ELIZABETH VALENTINE, MASSEUSE, PRESIDENT OF THE MASSACHUSETTS PROFESSIONAL BODY WORKERS ASSOCIATION and battered and distracted and defeated, as we will be along the way, day after day, we need to be able to call on all our resources in order to take up the challenge again, to pull ourselves up off the floor or out of the pit and—in that wonderfully simple, profound instruction of t'ai chi—return to the form.

I have said in workshops on creativity that writing is a form of meditation, in the sense that you are concentrating on only one thing, attempting to stop the usual jangle of distracting ideas, thoughts, fears, and hopes, and focusing on your breath or a mantra or a simple way of counting. In the actual act of writing you can focus only on the words you are putting down in sequence on the page, and those words, like an ongoing mantra, are filling up your mind. You can't be thinking of other things.

Taking that analogy a step further, I said in a seminar recently that "writing is prayer," in the sense that it is an act of devotion, of discipline of spirit in the act of creation. A professional writer who was present, who is also a very devout man of prayer, challenged me, saying quite adamantly, "Writing isn't prayer—it's hard work!"

"Well," I said, "sometimes prayer is hard work, too."

That same afternoon I happened to be at a used bookstore, and I saw on a bargain table a biography of Kafka by his writer friend Max Brod. I hadn't read any Kafka since shortly after graduating from college, yet I felt drawn to this book. Justifying it as a bargain, I bought it. The book was absorbing, presenting a side of Kafka I never knew about—one who enjoyed laughing, talking, taking outings in the country, going boating, meeting pretty barmaids. Brod also reported that Kafka wrote, in one of his journals: "Writing is prayer." I smiled, feeling affirmed; at least I wasn't the only writer who'd had the thought.

I do believe that writing, like any creative act done from the heart, whether it is a painting or a piece of music, a sculpture or dance or a homemade pie, a newly designed dress or a scientific discovery, is its own prayer, its own affirmation of the "animating or vital principal," the spirit in us all. Creation is prayer; to create is to pray.

Creation is prayer; to create is to pray.

In the Zone

If we are clear enough and open enough to let it come through, to be a vessel and channel of that creative force, it fills us up. That is the great paradox and irony; to be full, we must first be empty. We all know the great moments when we are "taken out of ourselves," when we are so absorbed in what we are doing—those trancelike times in skiing or writing, dancing or cooking, playing a piece of music or solving a problem in math or chemistry—it's as if we are not even present! It's as if we are the music, or the dance, or the mathematical equation; or that those things are "in place of us." We are so filled up by them we become them. Those are the transcendent moments, the "peak experiences" of life that we strive for and long for.

Athletes call it being "in the zone." Michael Jordan spoke about it after a game against the Portland Trail Blazers, game one of the NBA Finals in 1992, when he scored thirty-nine points, including six three-pointers.

Boston Globe columnist Michael Madden reported,

> Every athlete knows this feel. For a few precious moments, everything goes perfectly. No athlete knows how to summon this feel, except to mumble about "zone," as if this special feeling hibernates in some extraterrestrial zone, drops in once a year or so for a tease, then heads back to its "zone" for a rest. While the athlete tries his and her all to summon this feel back from its zone, it's never on call. It just shows up—well, when it wishes to show up.
>
> "Whenever this feel comes," said Michael, "you just cherish it. What it feels like is you're out there by yourself. When I got in that rhythm, it was like a . . . a . . . force.". . .
>
> Jordan had a smile wider and warmer than his usual one this day. He knew he had been touched by a force, and that was enough. He is now mature enough to know that the force calls its own recipients, rather than vice versa.
>
> "It's not something you go out and search for," said Jordan. "You don't come into the game and say 'I want to get myself into that zone.' You just relax and you just coax

yourself into it. You let the zone come to you. Then, when you're in that zone, you know it. And the next time that zone comes to me, I'm going to ride it as far as I can."

Jordan said he had tried to summon the feeling during a three-point shooting contest at an All-Star game once, but it didn't work, and he felt embarrassed by his performance.

Robert Parish, the former center of the Boston Celtics and student of t'ai chi, told me before he retired of his own experience with the zone: "It's like trying to find a good relationship. You can't go out looking for it, it just has to happen."

What is known as a "peak experience" or transcendence or inspiration—when some other force seems to take over—comes to all kinds of creators, from athletes to architects. The prize-winning architect Evans Woollen told me that when he's working on the design of a building,

> You know the solution exists somewhere—in some collective unconscious, and it's up to you to find it. Ridding the mind of other things—finding solutions—it's rather mysterious.
>
> It's coming through you, only—it's not knowing where it's coming from. It's a kind of spiritual thing—part of why I think solutions have their own life—they were born entering here, in me.

Many musicians speak of the experience of being empty and at the same time filled, of being an instrument used by a higher power in the act of creation. Judy Collins told me, "I feel I'm an instrument in writing—at the piano, I tape everything—the minute something starts I feel I'm 'taking dictation.'"

Many musicians speak of the experience of being empty and at the same time filled, of being an instrument used by a higher power in the act of creation.

Singer and songwriter Nancy Wilson says,

There are those magical times when it seems to pour right through you. That's the most incredible feeling I can imagine as far as songwriting. You're like the vessel or the instrument itself that somebody's playing—somebody or something. I don't have a specific name for it; there's a lot of names: Buddha, God, inspiration.

Singer Patti Smith said of such experiences, "I've had those moments when I do feel the voice coming through me, and I know it's coming from out there. . . . It's really special and it's not of me. . . . I get out of the way and it comes out fast and painlessly."

Biographer Sharon O'Brien described in an essay in the *New York Times Book Review* how, at a certain point in writing *Willa Cather: The Emerging Voice,*

> I experienced for the first time the process of writing as Cather described it—a submission to a creative force that seems to use the writer as an instrument. I had planned to write only a page or two, but the words kept streaming out, almost as if someone else were producing them. Writing became such a process of discovery that I couldn't wait to get to work in the morning: I wanted to find out what I was going to say.

A Story Is Given

I've experienced that same sensation in writing, most powerfully when I was living in a house by a pond in New Hampshire. After a decade in New York City I had wanted to live in the country, empty myself of the soot and noise and furor of city life, and experience fresh, clean air and quiet. I had saved up enough money to work exclusively on writing fiction and had spent the summer months toiling away at a long story that only a week before I had sent to my agent. I didn't yet have a new story in mind when I came into the living room one brilliant autumn afternoon and felt a surge of well-being and life and—well, creation—welling up in me.

I put my typewriter on a round table in the living room, pulled it over by the window where I could see the pond and the trees, and sat down to write. I had no idea what I was going to write, I just sat down and started writing. First the season came, and then a scene in the halls of my high school, and the feelings of that time and a girl—I wrote as if the story were already written and I was typing it out, and a little less than three hours later I stopped because I had come to the end, and I read the story over and cried. I cried because I had just "delivered" this story, I had emptied myself out in the most complete way—and I was full. I was full of joy and life and love and the sort of feeling Jesus described when he said he offered us life, more abundant, pressed down and overflowing.

That story was sent by my agent to *Redbook* magazine and they bought it and published it a few months later. The following year it was included in *The Best American Stories of 1966*. Looking back, I can see that in many ways I had prepared myself to be open to that story. I had made a hard and conscious move away from the city, which I felt was overwhelming me then, and into the countryside for the first time, taking many risks to try to follow a healthier path, to find a setting that might allow me to create the kind of stories I longed to write. That one was simply given to me, and I think I was able to receive the gift because I was in a place—in my life as well as geographically—that enabled me to receive it.

Oregon professor Robert Grudin observes that these experiences we call "inspiration" can't be made to happen by our own design; yet,

> even if we cannot specify or command inspiration, we can, I think, practice deserving it. The lives of people who are inspired or inventive possess a number of characteristics in common. Many of these characteristics are less inborn virtues (though seen together they look like "talent" or "genius") than plain habits, difficult to cultivate perhaps, but nonetheless far from superhuman. Collectively, these habits might be called an ethos of inspiration—not a birthright but a demanding and integral code.

The key, says Grudin, is "identifying fully with one's work and seeing it as an expression of one's own character. Such passion, which is generally more characteristic of artists and the self-employed than it is of salaried workers, can nonetheless be cultivated in any work that carries a high degree of responsibility."

The zone is possible for all of us, no matter what creative work we do.

You may not be able to go looking for it, but you have to be prepared for the zone of transcendence. You have to do the hard, nitty-gritty work of disciplined practice (emptying), as athletes like Jordan and Parish have done, so that when the zone comes to you, you can respond to it, you can move with it, be a good enough instrument of the force to let it move through you and with you. There is no use having the zone come to you if you are out of shape, hung over, or fuzzy from dope or lack of sleep. It would be wasted on you, if it came to you at all.

The zone is possible for all of us, no matter what creative work we do. But just as Michael Jordan and Robert Parish practiced the basics of their game and honed their skills to make themselves ready, so must all of us who wish to be creative, no matter what our field. Odette Bery, a chef who is also a teacher, points out,

> If you're a musician, or a painter, the technical skills required before you can use your own creativity are phenomenal. It's the same with a chef. A chef is more creative once the technical skills are there, and an understanding of basic food chemistry. It's easier for me to be creative than when I started out—the technical skills have to be there to back you up.

Commitment to and preparation for creativity are crucial. The sort of thing I'm talking about was stated perhaps best of all by Abraham Lincoln, when he wrote—with a vision of something larger than a basketball court or a short story: "I will study, and get ready, and maybe the chance will come."

Had he not done the preparation—including all that reading by the light of an oil lamp as a boy—the chance would not have come, and even if it had, he would not have been equal to the task. We can't just be bystanders, waiting for lightning to strike and give us great moments of transcendence. We need to carry out our part of the process; in other words, we need to be co-creators with the force, or spirit, or God.

The Freedom to Say No

The idea that less is more, of emptying being a way to fill up, is described by Rabbi Kushner in *To Life!*

> So many of the rules and rituals of the Jewish way of life are spiritual calisthenics, designed to teach us to control the most basic instincts of our lives—hunger, sex, anger, acquisitiveness, and so on. We are not directed to deny or stifle them, but to control them, to rule them rather than letting them rule us, and to sanctify them by dedicating our living of them to God's purposes. The freedom the Torah offers us is the freedom to say no to appetite.

This philosophy may underlie the phenomenon of the traditionally small number of Jewish alcoholics. A religious Jew, like Rabbi Kushner, "fills" himself with faith and personal power by depriving himself of the indulgences proscribed by the law of the Torah.

How powerful this faith can be is demonstrated by Rabbi Kushner's reaction to the tragedy of his son's painful and early death. He did not lose his faith but turned to it, and rather than the easy numbing of pain that many people would seek in drugs or alcohol, he wrote out of his own wrenching experience a book that would help millions of others around the world, of all faiths, deal with tragedy and loss in their own lives, by being able to survive those times: *When Bad Things Happen To Good People.* From his loss, he filled others with courage and spirit.

There is no filling up without emptying first; there is no emptying without being full.

Filling up, like emptying, has a different meaning on the spiritual path than on the other possible paths of life—like the path of least resistance, or the path to oblivion. On those paths, filling up would mean drinking till you're drunk, eating till you're sick, gorging yourself with whatever sensations pleased you at the first experience of them, without regard to consequences.

Most of the kinds of filling up I've described—from tasting food to meditation, silence, yoga, t'ai chi, and prayer—also involve emptying. Emptying and filling up are really parts of the same process—you can't separate them and have them make any sense; you can't, in fact, "have them" at all. There is no filling up without emptying first; there is no emptying without being full. I remember a Good Friday sermon of Reverend Scovel when he said that without the Crucifixion there is no Resurrection; the two events are finally one and the same event, different sides of the same story.

Sometimes "empty-full" depends on who is seeing it, and how. Gretel Ehrlich, author of *The Solace of Open Spaces*, points out that "the emptiness of the West was for others a geography of possibility." After a personal tragedy, Ehrlich left her city life and went to live in vast Wyoming, learning that "loss constitutes an odd kind of fullness; despair empties out into an unquenchable appetite for life."

Emptying and filling, we grow and create.

PART 3

Living the Creative Process

7

Creating: Five Exercises for Developing Your Creative Spirit

HOW DO WE GET ACCESS TO OUR OWN CREATIVITY?

When the myth about alcohol and drugs as stimulants to creativity was exploded for me, it was clear that other substances and addictive behavior were just as useless and even destructive in trying to evoke the muse. If having a shot of bourbon or a hit of coke didn't spark a story, it was obvious that gobbling a chocolate cake, having sex with a stranger, or starting a new relationship cycle was not going to call forth the spirit of creation.

The emptying of the myth left a question, a space in my mind, and I felt the impulse to fill it, to explore the mystery of how to summon our creative powers. Over the years, I had tried all the tricks I could think of in my own pursuit of the muse, from bourbon drinking to pencil sharpening, from gnawing a pipe stem to rubbing a worry stone someone gave me. Along the way I'd even stumbled on some useful techniques, easily passed along, but I had no idea what use they'd be to others (who probably knew them all and had even better ones). I sensed I wasn't going to learn much more by sitting in my room and staring at my word processor.

Community came to mind. Since I'd finished writing my book *Returning: A Spiritual Journey* in 1986, I'd been leading workshops in

Spiritual Autobiography at adult education centers, churches, and retreat houses throughout the country, from the Episcopal monastery of the Cowley Fathers in Cambridge to the Esalen Institute in Big Sur, California. I'd been surprised and delighted at the quality and substance of the stories people wrote about their own journeys. The writing in these workshops was far and away more interesting than what I had read in creative writing classes at colleges, graduate programs, and writers conferences. I'd learned that writing "from the spirit," asking people to look at their experiences from a spiritual perspective, was enlivening and productive, and had the effect of creating a kind of community among the participants.

I decided I'd try to create a new kind of workshop, with exercises designed to evoke people's creativity, and see what I could find out about accessing the creative spirit, not just for people who were writers, or wanted to be, but for everyone who was interested in exploring this mystery of creativity in their lives from a spiritual perspective (as opposed to the sort of workshop promising millions by writing best-sellers in your spare time, or "creating" fortunes in the stock market).

I designed a series of simple exercises for a workshop I called Creating from the Spirit. I've led it now in small and large groups around the country and found it fun as well as enlightening, and always fascinating in the creative work it evokes. I have not yet come across anyone who can't draw and write in response to the simple exercises; and in fact, the drawings and stories people have created are so rich and interesting, I think they'll inspire others to create too.

The work certainly testifies to what people can create in a circumscribed period of time. I limited all written exercises to twenty minutes, which I now think is itself an aid to creativity. When you have all the time in the world—when you take an assignment home and work on it for hours—you find it hard to get started. Then once you begin, all the internal editors emerge and start telling you to do it a different way, and you start second-guessing yourself, wondering what other people will think if you say such a thing—and by the time you finish (if indeed you ever finish) you may have watered down the work to the point where it has lost its original vitality.

I invite you as readers to now become participants, and follow the same basic rules as the people whose work you will read in the following pages. Set an alarm clock or an oven timer for twenty minutes at each exercise, and follow it strictly. When the buzzer goes off, if you aren't finished, take one more minute (no more than that!) and then, if you still aren't through, end by making three dots, to indicate you have more to say but for now you have to stop.

Ask a friend to join you. It's more enjoyable—and I think produces better creative results—if you do these exercises with at least one other person, or some friends, members of a church or a Twelve Step group, a writers' group, or any other group of people you know who might enjoy exploring their creativity. All you need is a supply of plain white paper (ordinary 8½-by-11-inch typing or copying paper will do just fine), a box of crayons for drawing, and a pen or pencil and notebook to write in.

This Is Not a Contest

Whether you do the exercises alone, with one or two friends, or in a group, stop for a moment before beginning and remember that this is not a contest or a guide to How to Succeed in the Arts without Really Trying. This is not a religious program, in the sense of being limited to any one belief or faith; it is based on the conviction that true creativity is born of the spirit, in the broad and varied ways I've defined and looked at that concept throughout this book so far. If you are in a faith community, by all means draw on its sustenance and experiences whenever they come to you. If you are not, don't feel left out. We all have a wealth of material, treasures of the spirit we simply don't bother to look for or cultivate.

Before beginning this exercise, take time to empty yourself of other concerns, of the mechanics of getting the paper and

> *I invite you as readers to now become participants, and follow the same basic rules as the people whose work you will read in the following pages.*

If you don't believe in God or the concept of prayer, simply meditate on a quotation of some kind that inspires you, perhaps one relating to creativity or creation.

crayons or pencils or other supplies you need, of getting yourself to a comfortable place to draw and write. Let go of your fears or expectations, your past experience with creativity, your hopes for what you may "get out of this." Inhale deeply, then breathe out all such concerns.

Now fill up by taking a few minutes to think about what "spirit" means to you, and how creativity relates to, and is part of, your own spiritual path. Take a few more deep breaths and close your eyes for a moment. Enjoy the wordless pause, the rest, the cessation of effort, and feel yourself filled with peace. If you have a short prayer you like, repeat it in your mind. I don't mean a prayer of petition. Don't pray "for" anything, like inspiration, or creative power, or a masterpiece flowing from your pen, simply put yourself in an attitude of prayer, of gratitude for being part of creation.

I like the way Rabbi Harold Kushner talks about the kind of attitude of prayer I'm suggesting in his book *To Life! A Celebration of Jewish Being and Thinking:* "We have learned to think of prayer as bribing God, pleading with God, or educating God." Prayer in the Jewish tradition, Rabbi Kushner explains, "is not 'talking to God' so much as it is using words and music to come into the presence of God in the hope that we will be changed by doing so."

If you don't believe in God or the concept of prayer, simply meditate on a quotation of some kind that inspires you, perhaps one relating to creativity or creation. If you know any lines of poetry you find inspiring, think of those. If nothing comes to your mind, simply think of the spirit, the breath of life, and concentrate on your own breath, being grateful for the gift of it, the gift of life.

Now take up your crayons and paper, with the freedom and pleasure they gave you when you first took them up in kindergarten. You will not be given a grade.

Enjoy.

EXERCISE 1

THE CREATION ROOM

Take twenty minutes to draw a picture—either as a drawing or floor plan, whichever allows you to put in the greatest amount of detail—of the room in which you first created something you liked. It may be your room at home or a room at school or an office or an attic; it may be a kitchen or garage or basketball court. You may have written a poem or song or story, or painted a picture, or perhaps you most enjoyed baking a cake or coming up with a new recipe for a tuna casserole; you may have built a model airplane, or fixed a car, or executed a new play in basketball or a new kind of shot. It doesn't matter what the object or act is as long as you created it and had a sense of satisfaction in the creation.

Take your time. Think back to the place where this creation occurred. Remember what the room was like, what furniture was in it, what pictures were on the walls. Was it cold in the room or hot? Was there a window, and could you see outside? What was the weather like? Was there any music playing, or could you hear anyone talking? What did it feel like to be in that room? What was it like creating something? Where did you get the idea? What materials did you use?

After you've taken twenty minutes to draw the room and remember all you can about it, share it with another person, and let them share their room with you. Each of you should take ten minutes to explain as much as possible about the room and what you created in it and what that was like.

After you have shared the room, take twenty minutes to write about the experience you had of creating something—or doing something creative in that room. Tell as much as you can about it.

Here are some of the things people wrote about the room in which they created something:

BEWITCHED
This room was the basement of our house; the orange thing to the right is a curtain dividing the basement in half—my father's workshop was on the right and the playroom (shown) was on the left.

My brother and sister and I spent countless hours playing and watching TV down here. I have many memories of creative occurrences in this room. The view is from the stairs—how I often saw it as I squatted down and peered under the ceiling into the room.

Right below the stairs, out of view from this picture, was a sewing machine. My mother made most of our clothes (as well as the ugly orange curtain—a color fashionable in the '60s; what it was doing in a room with green tiles on the floor, I will never know). I often took scrap bits of cloth and made clothes for my dolls. I designed and sewed them. Nothing fancy, but it made me feel proud when they came out well.

Another thing I did with my Barbie dolls was make them appear and disappear. My siblings and I were fascinated by magic. *Bewitched* was our favorite show, and we wanted to be magic too. So I rigged up a system with thread, tying one end to the railing on the stairs and the other end somewhere at the far end of the room. I attached Barbie to the thread and positioned my brother with her at the top of the stairs. Then, feigning ignorance of his presence, I said out loud, "Gosh! I wish I had a Barbie doll!" Then I wiggled my nose and whoosh! There she came—flying through space into my outstretched hand. Magic!

We were also big into skits and puppet shows. Whenever cousins, or kids whose parents were friends of my parents, came to visit, we would recruit them for our shows. Since I usually was the oldest, I was writer, director, and costume designer. Then at the end of the visit, after the adults had quit gabbing, we would perform the show. All of the creation and practicing was done in the basement.

This room was the setting for much of my childhood imagination.

—STEPHANIE CHASE

PAPA'S STUDIO

No place was more exciting. Papa's studio was in a corner of the basement of his house. There was always music in the room either from an old brown radio with its arch-shaped top or from Papa's violin. I loved this space. I particularly loved the different jars of colored water that were always on the counter next to where Papa worked.

Papa was a sweet and gentle person who loved it when I came to his studio. He would always put one of his old white shirts on me. He called it a work shirt. It would keep my clothes from getting paint on them.

I would sit at the counter next to Papa and watch him letter and paint. I never got tired of this.

Papa would offer me a box of brushes. He'd tell me to take any one I wanted. He'd give me paper and I would pick the colors of paint that I'd want to use. He'd always explain that when I used a color, I would need to clean my brush in the jar of water that matched the color I was using.

I loved this experience. I loved watching the color in the water become a little darker each time I washed my brush. The colors were beautiful. The colors in the water jars were as wonderful as the experience of my painting.

I don't remember any of my final products. Those weren't in any way as important as selecting the colors or cleaning my brush.

My favorite part of watching Papa paint was seeing him put one hand under the hand he painted with. He told me he did this so as to keep the paint from smearing and to steady his hand.

I can remember the thick smell of tempura paint and the smell of Papa's cigars.

One of my favorite parts of watching was when he'd take his violin from its old case and play "Turkey in the Straw." He'd play for me after he painted. He'd always put a handkerchief under his chin before he'd begin. His chin moved up and down and his mouth made shapes it never did when he talked to me. I always wanted him to play more and more.

It wasn't only the act of painting that I liked, it was the experience of being in this tiny room and watching Papa do his work. He would leave the room from time to time to clean the water that was on the counter beside him. Cleaning the brushes was very important to him.

Sometimes I'd watch him draw a picture first. It would be a sketch. He wouldn't press hard. Sometimes he'd erase with a soft tan eraser that he'd call an art gum. He would make little crumbs as he used it and he would brush these on the floor.

There was an old dark-green rug under the stool where he sat. His stool was wooden. It could turn all the way around and had a back for him to lean on. There were some round holes in the seat and the back. The stool where I sat didn't have a back. When I first sat on it he would put phone books on it to make it high enough for me. Mine couldn't turn.

We would listen mostly to opera as we painted. I loved to come here.

When I went away to camp there would be days that I'd receive letters from Papa. There were pictures that he'd painted for me in his studio.

—MARIKA GEOGHEGAN

FIRST STEPS

It was my birthday. There were two rooms in my grandfather's house involved in the earliest instance of remembered creativity. I was in one, which was in shadows because the light had been turned off. The door to the kitchen was open and the light was on, which bathed the middle of the living room with a yellowish glow and cast fuzzy shadows.

In the darkness of the living room, I could see a couch with a pillow on the right, where I had been sleeping. On the other side were two chairs and a floor lamp in between. Because it was dark I cannot remember the color. The room was dark because I had been left there to take a nap, and it was now after dark.

My parents and grandfather were in the next room; my mother was preparing dinner. I could watch them through the door, almost like watching through a window. They were talking and had their backs to me.

The kitchen had two windows at the far side of the room that I could see—it was dark outside the windows—four chairs next to the stove on the left. It was dark above the windows. The sink, stove, and refrigerator were all on the right. There were cupboards on the sink and counter top. There were dishes on the table, and pans were out for the food on the kitchen counter. The walls were white and the floor was a light-colored linoleum.

The kitchen was lit by a ceiling light that had a yellowish hue, probably from the bulb. There was a large pillar between the two rooms that almost filled the doorway.

Everything was very fuzzy because I am very nearsighted. This event occurred when I was about a year old. I woke up feeling a little groggy from the sleep and a little lost. We did not go to my grandfather's often, so the room was strange to me, especially in the dark.

I eventually realized that my parents were in the next room and I wanted to see my mother. I felt that she would come get me. When she didn't, I decided that she didn't know I was awake because the three adults were very engrossed in what they were doing and saying, I started to crawl across the rug, but was interrupted by the pillow.

I had been learning to walk, I felt that I could walk. but I did not know how. I decided to try. After a false start or two I realized that I had to counterbalance my weight in the place where I started to fall. I toddled off into the next room, past the pillow, and no one noticed me at first.

My dad say me first, then my grandfather. My mother turned when Dad said, "Don's walking." She screamed and scared me. I fell. My parents tell me I did not walk again for six months.

—DON MITCHELL

FURTHER EXERCISES: GOING TO NEW ROOMS

It turns out that everyone has an early memory of being in a room where they created something—though I know of no such memory earlier than Don Mitchell's recalling the rooms where he took those first steps when he was a year old!

Drawing the "creation room" and telling someone else about what happened there helps release that memory, and writing about it becomes a fascinating story, one that affirms our own creative powers. It also affirms that the source of creation is not alcohol or drugs. The story coming out of this process is itself an affirmation of the creativity we have access to right now, without any outside stimulants.

There is not only one "creation room." If you wish to draw more on your own creative history, draw other rooms in which you created something—in high school, or college, or your first apartment, or at camp, or a friend's house, or whatever place you remember as being a site of your own creativity.

Don't limit yourself to the type of creative activity you do most often. If you are a writer, think of other things you've created besides stories or poems; if you're a painter, recall creative acts that have nothing to do with paintings or art. Look at your creative experience in a larger way than the one that usually comes to mind. Think of meals you've created, trips you've planned, friendships you've formed, ideas or projects you've created in your community. Discover how much creating you do in the normal course of your life.

Draw the room where each of these creations had its origin or its completion. Each room will provide a picture and a story, as well as a new affirmation of your creative power.

How can you relate this exercise to your current creative activity? Think about the room where you now write or paint, keep a journal, meditate, or whatever creative activity you are practicing—or want to practice. Many creators find that going to the same place to create every day is helpful in evoking the aura of creativity. If you live in one room, as I have on different occasions, create a space in the corner of

It turns out that everyone has an early memory of being in a room where they created something

the room that is the focus of your creative activity. If you can, put up a screen to give it a sense of specialness, or spiritual privacy.

Once I was living in Greenwich Village and trying to write a novel at the same time that I was writing magazine articles to make a living. I felt stifled at trying to do both kinds of creating in the same room. The novel notes and pages got mixed up with notes and pages for articles. When I started to work on the novel, I'd begin to think about the article I was also working on. I couldn't shake my mind from one kind of writing to the other. I felt that the solution was to work in two different rooms, but I had no other room, nor did I have the money to rent one.

Then it occurred to me that a teacher friend was out of her apartment every weekday from eight in the morning until five in the afternoon. She might let me use it to work on my novel. She agreed, and we created a schedule. I worked on my magazine articles at home in the morning, and at noon walked six blocks to my friend's apartment, picking up a sandwich along the way, had lunch, and worked on my novel at her dining room table until she returned, then talked with her over a cup of coffee, and went back to my place.

It's as if a new physical space allows for another space in your own consciousness. I have heard that John Updike uses different rooms of his house north of Boston for the different varieties of writing he does—there's a room for novels, another for short stories, another for book reviews, and so forth. I admire Updike's creativity in setting up his house that way, but of course most people don't have the luxury of a room for each of their creative endeavors.

I am living in a one-room or "studio" apartment in the Village as I write this, and I have designated one wall for my word processor and "writing space." When I was working on a novel last spring, I had my most creative period when I spent a month in another city doing workshops on the weekend and writing every day during the week. When I return to the novel, I plan to use the Writers Room in the Village, where I can rent a cubicle for a nominal fee and have a separate place to work on that book—just as I used the Writers' Room in Boston to work on *New York in the Fifties* while I wrote articles, lectures, and workshop material back at my apartment.

Writers in cities like New York and Boston have joined together to seek grants or corporate sponsorship or donations of space to establish writers' rooms with office cubicles and desks for computers where they can go and work in silence, away from their apartments but in community, surrounded by other writers. The Writers' Room in Boston lost its foundation sponsorship in the general economic crunch, but Ivan Gold (former president of the Boston Writers' Room) organized some of the regular users of the room, and they found a new space to work in. It's a project that writers or artists of any kind in any community could create.

Places of Power

The space where we work is important. I've always had a sense of the places where I could write and where I couldn't write. There is no way to describe it. I have to go into a room and look around, and I know at once. I once went looking for a house to rent with a friend in the summer; one had everything we were looking for, except I knew I couldn't write in it. I didn't know why, I just knew it was true, and I knew it wasn't just some silly feeling to dismiss. I lost a whole summer once by staying in a place where I felt queasy about working from the first time I went inside. I should have listened to that instinct, and from then on I did.

"I think where you write helps," Rabbi Kushner told me when we talked about creativity. "There are two places in my house where I write, one in summer on the back porch, one in winter in my study. I suspect that being where the creative process worked well before increases the chances that it will again."

For the architect Evans Woollen, it's important to live for a while in the place where he's going to design a house or building. He has lived with clients, and he doesn't put pencil to paper until he knows them. At a school or college, he takes a room on campus and talks to as many people as possible.

We experience places almost the way we do people—some we immediately love, others make us uncomfortable, sometimes we change our minds (and emotions) about them as we get to know them.

Creative workers also have found inspiration from what Carlos Castaneda calls "places of power." There are some geographic sites in the world that have proved through the centuries to be such places—like Jerusalem, the sacred city of three great religions. There are also places of power for each of us, places that may not affect anyone else in the same way, but somehow touch us, stir our imaginations and our creative sensibilities.

Willa Cather experienced that feeling when she went on a two-week trip to New Mexico. She was so moved by the place, by the very look of the land, that she came back East inspired to write a book about it. She did research on the early settlement of that territory, and out of that knowledge, fired by the inspiration that being there had for her, wrote one of the great novels of our literature, *Death Comes for the Archbishop.*

We experience places almost the way we do people—some we immediately love, others make us uncomfortable, sometimes we change our minds (and emotions) about them as we get to know them. Some people inspire us, others put us in a dark mood. It's the same with places. I love Boston, and Beacon Hill, where I had an immediate sense of being home when I first saw it; yet I've always felt uncomfortable in Cambridge, just across the river. I know people who have the opposite reaction. It's a mysterious, individual matter; just because other people love a place doesn't mean that you will too.

I made a pilgrimage once to the island of Iona, off the coast of Scotland, because I'd heard it was a spiritual place of power. Saint Columba had used it as a base for his missionary work among the Celts in the sixth century, and it was thought to be holy. A member of my own church in Boston had experienced great peace and spiritual insight there. I found it to be the most bleak, barren, and depressing spot of land I'd ever seen. I had, in fact, an antireligious experience (I woke in the night to see a mental vision of a wall with the words "There is no God"), and I felt such inner turmoil I left there as soon as I could. I was later told that others too had had dark experiences there, and

> *If you think back on your experiences, you'll know at once your places of power.*

were relieved to get to the mainland city of Oban—so was I.

There is no way to predict in advance how a place will strike you (any more than a person's personality will strike you—think about blind dates!)

British novelist Christopher Isherwood, author of *The Berlin Stories,* on which the musical and movie *Cabaret* was partly based, surprisingly found his place of power in southern California. I met Isherwood in Hollywood in the late '70s, when he was in his seventies. This joyous, full-of-life man told me that he had come to the United States in the '40s and, to his amazement, was drawn to the desert landscapes of southern California. Though he had grown up in rural England, he said that when he saw the desert area south of Los Angeles, he felt he was home. He settled in Santa Monica with his longtime partner, artist Don Bachardy, and lived a rich, creatively productive, and successful life in a setting completely foreign to the England of his childhood.

We aren't always able to live where we feel drawn, and each of us has more than one place of power where we feel at peace, enlivened, full. If you think back on your experiences, you'll know at once your places of power. If you have a chance to spend time in one of them to work creatively, do it. If you don't have that opportunity, you still can conjure up the place with memory, journal notes, photographs, pictures, and books about it. These are sources of raw power that you can translate into creativity.

Where are your own places of power? Make a list of them. Write a paragraph about each place. See what place you'd like to write further about—or paint or photograph. What kind of music conjures up the place for you?

Spend a few minutes in contemplation about what you've learned and experienced about creativity from this exercise in drawing and writing about the "creation room." Contemplation is different from meditation, where you're trying to empty your mind and focus on a single word or mantra or image, or simply concentrate on your breath. In contemplation you just get quiet and relax, in the same sort of position of comfortable attention you would want for meditation, but then let your mind dwell on a particular object, in this case, the mystery of creativity.

Now that you've created some drawings and stories, what do you think is the source of your creativity? Was the story you wrote already in your mind, waiting to be told? Was it somewhere out in the atmosphere, waiting to be drawn into your own consciousness and written down? Did it "come through you" or "come out of you"? Are there stories in you—or "out there"—waiting to be told? How do you find them? Are they "given" to you? By whom or what? Why?

There are, of course, no "correct answers" to these questions, as on a test, but they are fruitful subjects for contemplation.

EXERCISE 2

STORY MUSIC

I have often used music in my own writing, not for evoking ideas, but for bringing back past scenes, places, people, and situations. When I was working on my novel *Going All the Way*, which was set in Indianapolis in the 1950s, before writing I would play records I loved from that era, like Chris Conner's album *Something Cool*, or Chet Baker playing and singing "My Funny Valentine," or Les Paul and Mary Ford's rendition of "How High the Moon." When I played that music and closed my eyes I could summon up the sounds, sights, smells, people, places, and faces I knew back then.

When I wrote *Home Free*, which was set in the late 1960s, I played the music I loved at that time—Judy Collins's *Wildflowers* and *Who Knows Where the Time Goes* albums, the Mamas and the Papas singing "Monday, Monday" and "California Dreamin'," Nilsson wailing "Without You." A rush of memories filled my mind with

When I played that music and closed my eyes I could summon up the sounds, sights, smells, people, places and faces I knew back then.

that music, scenes crowding in on one another—streets of Los Angeles, the beach at Venice, protest marches on Beacon Street in Boston.

When I started my book, *New York in the Fifties*, one album I played over and over evoked an apartment where I spent a lot of time in 1957 in Greenwich Village and brought back the feel, the outlook, the ambience of my life at that time. It was Miles Davis's *Sketches of Spain*, which I had played in that apartment and loved. The mood of that era comes back to me with that musical evocation.

When I decided to play that piece as a musical exercise in evoking creativity, I did not imagine it would bring back memories of Greenwich Village to anyone else but me, unless by chance someone else had lived there at the time I did and associated this music with the time and place.

The reason I decided to try it in this exercise was that it seems especially haunting to me, bittersweet and full of mystery and passion. My idea was to play it without naming its title or author or anything else about it, simply let people draw whatever scenes or colors it brought to mind, then ask questions after they had listened to it for a while, questions that might prompt their own ideas and stories, and see what came out of their own imaginations. It is fascinating to see what completely different and yet imaginative, colorful, and dramatic drawings and stories came out of people who listened to that same piece of music.

The same exercise and the same set of questions can be used playing any piece of music—as long as it doesn't have words. As soon as there are words, they will fill your mind, and your imagination won't have a chance to respond with its own ideas and images. Select a piece of music of your own—or if you are part of a group, it might be more fun to let one person select a piece of music and put it on without telling you beforehand what it is.

Before playing the music, sit quietly, to empty yourself of other sounds and noises and talk. Think about the power of music, how it can produce moods and feelings of joy, despair, excitement, peace, comradeship, loyalty, love, patriotism, and inspiration, and a sense of the sacred. Imagine what your life would be like without music! Think about the gift that music is in your life, how it adds beauty, harmony, color, and meaning. What is the source of this gift that we take for granted? How does music affect your spirit? How has music played a part in your own spiritual journey, your search for meaning?

When you put on your piece of music for this exercise, imagine the music moving throughout your whole body and mind. Imagine the music "filling you up." Think of the music as being inside you, and you being inside the music.

When you feel the music is part of you, absorbed by you, and you absorbed by it as well, respond to the following questions. Take your time in answering.

What kind of landscape do you picture with this music? Where should such music be played? What sort of scene and scenery does it evoke in your mind?

What sort of house or building would be in this setting? A log hut, a castle, a skyscraper, a tent, an apartment house? Or some other kind of dwelling altogether?

Who is in this building? What kind of people would be in a room in this place? What does the room look like? What do the people look like? Are they old or young, rich or poor, tired or exuberant?

What are these people saying to each other?

This is what some people wrote after listening to Miles Davis's album *Sketches of Spain*, without knowing the title or the musician, simply responding to the sound as they answered my questions:

REMEMBERING

When my father died the priest said prayers at the funeral home one of
the prayers asked for Robert to gather the pieces of himself together
that phrase stayed with me tagging along like a baby sister I listened to
the music and landscape appeared large grey rocks nothing green no
grass or trees I heard a funeral dirge but the notes were twisting the
ends of sadness like pieces of lemon and lime brighten a drink long flat
notes became all the pieces of Robert lying under those gray stones but
the notes climbing a staircase were lifting the stones halfway up suddenly
snake charmer music coaxing the pieces of Robert out from under the
climbing twisting notes singing it can be done until the music turned low
slow trying for the last time to draw Robert out crying at the end I could
almost hear bells the mood new I could see Robert all dandied up push-
ing open saloon doors and telling an off color joke then three long notes
death knells wailing I know I know I know

—E. J. MILLER LAINO

HONG KONG LOUNGE

When Ruth left him after twenty years of marriage, Dirk thought that he
would make a new start, far away from his familiar life in Miller's Falls,
Idaho, but Hong Kong was not what he'd hoped it would be. It had been
three years now and, though he had managed to land a clerk's job in the
Kowloon office of the Cathay International Bank, Dirk was more alone
than ever.

"Ah, Mr. Dirk, you're late tonight," said Sam Wah, the small, wiry bar-
tender at Hong Kong's Forty-Second Street Lounge.

"Yea, Sam, gotta pay the rent," Dirk replied, straddling the stool at the
center of the long, dark, teakwood bar.

Outside, the warm spring rain dissolved the smells of roasted meat,
spices, and brown eggs preserved in mud and horse urine into the soupy
mix that was Hong Kong. Here, inside the Forty-Second Street Lounge,
the only smells were whiskey and stale beer. The place was dark and
nearly empty except for a few couples leaning toward each other over
small tables against the wall, whispering words of love or plotting to separate some poor fool from his money.

A melancholy tune washed over the desolate floor littered with
matchbooks and napkins, carelessly dropped by earlier patrons. The dron-
ing, mellow horn emphasized Dirk's loneliness in another empty night.

—ALAN BODNAR

OUTLAWS
Place
Southwestern
deserty terrain
dry
flat
You can see a long way off
Room
Movie theater (belongs with a film)
People
Swarthy Mexicans w/bullets criss-crossed across self
hardened cowboys
loose frontier women
Bittersweet mood—success, but at what cost?
A movie.

The old West. New sheriff and his sidekick come to town to rid the area of lawless bandits. They are met with resistance from the incumbent authorities who are working in cahoots with the outlaws.

Not your usual shoot-'em-up movie, but a conflict of wills and values. More subtle, covert action. In addition, good and bad guys are not clear. There is a bittersweet tone to the setting. Is what the sheriff's doing truly good? Are the "outlaws" truly bad?

The sheriff and his deputy prevail. They win. Perhaps they even shoot and kill the bandits. But at what cost? The music plays as they ride off into the sunset, leaving the audience with the unsettled feeling that there was no winner.

Be still my friend.

These great trees are prayers.

—Stephanie Chase

FURTHER EXERCISES: LISTENING FOR IDEAS

It always amazes and moves me after listening to the music and then hearing what people write—the scenes, stories, plots, characters that weren't there fifteen or twenty minutes before. Where did they come from? Did they come from the music? But how did the music create such different places and faces and words? How did these people hear the same piece of music and create from listening to it stories of Hong

Kong, the Wild West, the desert, lovers and sheriffs and farmers and fires, sunsets and marshes and wakes and spirits and trees?

Where did it come from?

What an unexpected, incredible, colorful, dramatic well of stories and sights and places we all possess! What is the source of it? Is the music we hear instilled in us? Does it become part of us—our mind, our consciousness, our unconscious? Does it become part of our soul, our spirit? There is a category of sacred, or spiritual, music, but beyond that, is all music spiritual, or "of the spirit"?

Listen to more music. Try the exercise with different types of music. Here are some ideas of some of the kinds of music you could listen to while "writing out of" the music: symphonies, cantatas, sonatas, etudes, jazz, rock, heavy metal, country and western, sacred music (hymns without words). Listen to music of different ethnic backgrounds, nationalities, and cultures, and write "out of them." The only music that I think doesn't work for this process are songs with lyrics, rap, and opera, because they have words, which create their own scenes and messages.

Invite a friend to do the exercise with you and bring his or her own piece of music; in a group, take turns in letting each person supply the piece of music that everyone uses to "write from."

Summon new landscapes, people, stories. They are there for the playing of each new piece of music.

You will never run out.

If, like me, you're not trained in music, speak to a friend who plays a musical instrument about how they create as musicians. While writing prose seems to almost come naturally to me, the whole concept of writing music is one of the deepest mysteries I can imagine. I was fascinated to read about the creative process of Maria Schneider, a jazz composer, arranger, and band leader. She has written for the Woody Herman Orchestra and was an assistant orchestrator and arranger for Gil Evans (the title piece of her debut album, *Evanescence,* is dedicated to him).

Listen to music of different ethnic backgrounds, nationalities, and cultures, and write "out of them."

Schneider told *New York Times* reporter Sheila Rule,

> If I have one idea, I try to put down all sorts of possibilities that the idea could be manipulated into. Then I draw arrows to things, what fits on top of what. Then it becomes like a puzzle. I may come up with contrasting ideas that intuitively fit, but I have to intellectually try to see why. When it all comes together, when I listen to my pieces at the end, it's like they did exist before but I had to find them.

Ask yourself how this process relates to your own creative work. How could you apply it to your own creative work?

Here's another exercise to use with music.

Pick out a piece of music that to you is "of the spirit." It need not be what anyone else defines as spiritual, it only matters that it evokes that kind of response in you.

Play the music, and as in the first exercise, let the music come inside you, and try to feel yourself inside the music.

Think about the idea of music as prayer.

While listening to your piece of spiritual music, and letting it fill you up, write your own prayer, a prayer that comes out of the music, as the story you wrote came out of the music. It doesn't need to be a prayer of petition, it may simply be a prayer of thanks, or appreciation, or joy, rejoicing, praise. It could be a prayer of participation in the universe, as a co-creator of life, at least of your own life and of those whose lives you touch and are touched by, twine and are intertwined with. Let the music "pray in you" and for

Let the music "pray in you" and for you, and let your prayer come out of it.

you, and let your prayer come out of it. Just listen, and when you begin to fill up, let the words of your prayer flow out on the paper. Whatever comes is your prayer.

EXERCISE 3

LOOKING CLOSE

> *"Miracles . . . seem to me to rest not so much upon*
> *faces or voices or healing power coming suddenly near to us*
> *from afar off, but upon our own perception being made*
> *finer, so that for a moment our eyes can see and our ears*
> *can hear what is there about us always."*
> —WILLA CATHER

For most of us, nature is background. In fact, most of life is background. We buzz by it, in cars or planes or just walking swiftly to work or a party or dinner or whatever destination, not noticing who or what we see, paying little or no attention to the world we live in.

Nature is part of the world's creation, just as we are. Though we may pay it homage culturally or politically—we're dedicated to preserving the rain forest, warding off the greenhouse effect, stopping the pollution of lakes, rivers, and streams—we don't bother to look at any of it except for a glance, if that.

Nothing is more creative than nature, more evocative of creation and the creative process, more a living metaphor of creativity. If we want to learn, it is there to teach. But first we have to learn to look. One of the most powerful exercises I know is to go out and actually "look close" at an object in nature—a leaf, a twig, a flower, a rock.

Writers think they know how to look; in fact, they pride themselves on their ability to see, especially reporters, whose job it is to notice details. Many aspiring novelists first work as reporters for the very reason that they hope to hone their ability to observe, to see and record what is in a particular scene, place, event. Sometimes, though, I think we writers get lazy and sloppy in our looking. We assume we are looking when, in fact, we are letting our eyes slide by and over and through the details that may hold the key to the importance or understanding of the story.

I have come to think that scientists are better at looking for the telling detail, the key to the mystery. Their own work is dependent on it. Without looking, scientists would not be able to do their job. The expertise and power that a scientist brings to bear in "looking close" was brought home to me, thanks to a man who took one of my workshops at the Rancho La Puerta health spa. He had done this exercise in "looking close" and said it reminded him of the way good scientists are trained to look close. When he got home he thoughtfully sent me a marvelous essay by a scientist about how he was trained in this discipline.

This essay is from a book of memoirs about the great Harvard professor and scientist Louis Agassiz (*Louis Agassiz as a Teacher*, edited by Lane Cooper), written by his former students, who themselves became scientists and professors of science. This recollection of Professor Agassiz teaching a student how to look at a fish describes so powerfully the discipline of looking close, and its rewards, that I now read it in my workshop before sending students out to look closely at some object in nature.

The Lesson of the Fish

"Take this fish," said [Professor Agassiz], "and look at it; we call it a haemulon; by and by I will ask you what you have seen."

In ten minutes I had seen all that could be seen in that fish, and started in search of the Professor—who had, however, left the Museum . . . nothing was to be done but to return to a steadfast gaze at my mute companion. Half an hour passed—an hour—another hour; the fish began to look loathsome. I turned it over and around; looked it in the face—ghastly; from behind, beneath, above, sideways, at a three-quarters' view—just as ghastly. I was in despair; at an early hour I concluded that lunch was necessary; so, with infinite relief, the fish was carefully replaced in the jar, and for an hour I was free.

On my return, I learned that Professor Agassiz had been at the Museum, but had gone, and would not return for several hours. . . . Slowly I drew forth that hideous fish, and with a feeling of desperation again looked at it. I might not use a magnifying-glass; instruments of all kinds were interdicted. My two hands, my two eyes, and the fish—it seemed a most limited field. I pushed my finger down its throat to see how sharp its teeth were. I began to count the scales in the different rows, until I was convinced that it was nonsense. At last a happy thought struck me—I would draw the fish; and now with surprise I began to discover new features in the creature. Just then the Professor returned.

"That is right," said he; "a pencil is one of the best of eyes." . . .

He listened attentively to my brief rehearsal of the structure of parts. . . . When I had finished, he waited as if expecting more, and then, with an air of disappointment:

"You have not looked very carefully; why," he continued more earnestly, "you haven't even seen one of the most conspicuous features of the animal, which is as plainly before your eyes as the fish itself; look again, look again," and he left me to my misery.

I was piqued; I was mortified. Still more of that wretched fish! But now I set myself to my task with a will, and discovered one new thing after another, until I saw how just the Professor's criticism had been. The afternoon passed quickly; and when, toward its close, the Professor inquired:

"Do you see it yet?"

"No," I replied, "I am certain I do not, but I see how little I saw before."

"That is next best," said he, earnestly, "but I won't hear you now; put away your fish and go home; perhaps you will be ready with a better answer in the morning. I will examine you before you look at the fish."

This was disconcerting. Not only must I think of my fish all night, studying, without the object before me, what this unknown but mostly visible feature might be; but also, without reviewing my discoveries, I must give an exact account of them the next day. . . .

"Do you perhaps mean," I asked [the next day], "that the fish has symmetrical sides with paired organs?"

His thoroughly pleased "Of course! Of course!" repaid the wakeful hours of the previous night. . . . I ventured to ask what I should do next.

"Oh, look at our fish!" he said, and left me again to my own devices. In a little more than an hour he returned, and heard my new catalogue.

"That is good, that is good!" he repeated, "but that is not all, go on"; and so for three long days he placed that fish before my eyes, forbidding me to look at anything else, or to use any artificial aid. "Look, look, look" was his repeated injunction.

This was the best entomological lesson I ever had—a lesson whose influence has extended to the details of every subsequent study; a legacy the Professor has left to me, as he has left it to many others, of inestimable value, which we could not buy, with which we cannot part.

See for Yourself

You can now make your own "scientific" discovery by picking out an object in nature and looking at it to see what you can learn about it, what a period of concentrated observation will reveal to you that you didn't see at all on first glance. Now that you have read of Professor Agassiz's lesson, it will surely not seem unreasonable when I ask you to take at least twenty minutes to observe your natural object. Time after time, though, people will get bored after the first five or ten minutes, assure me there is nothing more to see about this piece of bark, or stone, or pine cone. Like Professor Agassiz, I can only instruct them to look again, to keep looking.

This simple exercise is one way to waken us to the immense possibilities of nature as a stimulant to our own creativity—and to the enrichment of our experience. Before setting out, sit quietly, and empty yourself of your preconceptions about familiar natural objects and what they look like. Tell yourself you are going to look with fresh eyes, as if you have never before seen a tree, a leaf, a fallen branch, the bloom of a rose or a violet. Think about Professor Agassiz's lesson, and how the student's continuous looking kept revealing more and more, even though he thought he had seen everything there was to see. Read again the quotation from Willa Cather on "Miracles."

Set out with a pencil and notebook to search for an object in nature to bring under your gaze. You can find it in your own backyard, or any field or vacant lot or city park. If you can't do this, use for your study a piece of fruit or a vegetable—a stalk of broccoli, the sections of an orange, a bunch of grapes.

Look at it up close, steadily, for at least twenty minutes. As you do this, try to forget about yourself and concentrate your full consciousness on the object you're examining.

Elissa Mintz, a technical writer in Boston, explained her use of this process in a paper she wrote in my creativity workshop: "When I need to accomplish something, complete something, I can only do it by looking outward—by losing as much of my sense of self as I can and looking at the thing itself, the thing as it is."

Take notes on everything you can observe about it—color, texture, smell, taste, how many leaves or seeds or sections it has, how it is divided, markings on it, everything you can discover about it.

Pretend you are taking these notes so you can describe this object to a person from another planet who has never seen such a thing before and doesn't know what it is, or what it does, or is—or is not—used for. Discover it for yourself for the first time. After you think you have noted everything there is to know about it, look some more, see if there is anything further you can learn about it.

After you have studied the object for at least twenty minutes (take more time if you wish), jot down answers to the following questions about it:

What else does it remind you of? Does it remind you of anything in your own life—any experience you've had, any

> *Tell yourself you are going to look with fresh eyes, as if you have never before seen a tree, a leaf, a fallen branch, the bloom of a rose or a violet.*

emotion or idea? Does it remind you of anything else you have heard or read about? What kind of character would your object be if it were in a story?

Now draw the object, and see what more you can learn from the new "eye" provided by the pencil. If you are doing this with someone else, or in a group, show the picture of the object you have drawn to the other person or another person, and tell them what you learned about it.

Take twenty minutes and write about the object you have drawn. Write either a description of what you saw and learned, or a story, inspired by what the object reminded you of, or what you discovered from it.

Another way of writing about it is to imagine you are speaking for the object. Write its own story—if that grape, or leaf, or stone could speak, what story would it tell?

These are some of the things people wrote about their experience of looking close:

FEEDER OF NATIONS
I chose to approach this exercise from the perspective of trying to describe a common fruit or vegetable to someone from another planet.

I feed nations
Yet I began life underground
A small swelling on a hairlike strand of root
One of a thousand hairlike strands of root
The roots of my mother
She stands aboveground
Small and greenleaved
Under a bowl of cool, spring sky
The warming fingers of the spring sun pluck at the winter coldness
   of the earth
I swell into a tiny sphere
Then grow marbleized
Nourished by the dark earth
I swell again
Above my head

My mother opens herself to the sun
And bursts out with blossoms
Small, white and yellow flowers
Among which bees hum I, however, burrow deeper into the warm, brown earth
And swell
I am a large sphere and solid
An earthworm burrows by
I interrupt her journey, a hard, brown sphere in her path
She inspects me, then
Burrows blindly on in search of another worm
A fat, white grub pushes up and nibbles on me
But I am hard and bitter, and she pushes away
A caterpillar samples a strand of my mother's roots
But it, too, is bitter
The caterpillar propels himself to the surface
Bursting out into the hot hum of summer
There, he attaches himself to the underside of one of my mother's leaves
Rolls himself up and encloses himself in a hard shell
And hangs there, secretive and hidden
Beneath him, in the dark, I continue to swell
I have grown a skin
A thin, brown skin enclosing the white meat of my core
Above, the world hums with the sounds of summer
The hard shell of the caterpillar splits
The creature inside heaves and struggles
A leg is thrust out, an antenna unfurls
A thin, fragile wing flops loose
Soon, amidst the hum and heat of summer
The creature spreads his thin and trembling wings
Brilliant orange and black.
And, in a while, lifts off
To float and flutter on the hot summer breezes
To browse on the sweetness of the summer flowers
I am alone in the dark
And now, I feel a pull and a stretch
I am losing my roundness and becoming oval
My brown skin thickens
I stretch my oval self and become full of the fat sweet hum of summer
Full of the nourishment of the rich brown earth
I lie in the dark, brown earth and rest

Above, my mother is slowly dying
Her leaves brittle and edged with gray
She droops
And then, with the first cool wind of autumn
I am pulled violently from my resting place
The hands of a small child grasp me
Wrench me from the umbilical cord that has attached me to my mother
   all summer
Above me curves the bowl of a deep, blue sky
The air no longer hums
Its summer work done, it has become quiet
Waiting and resting before the challenge of winter
The child carries me away
I am washed
The rich, brown earth scrubbed from my skin
I lie glistening on a table
Rich with the nourishment of the deep, brown earth in which I formed
   and grew
One end of me is sliced off
It contains a small knot
And in this small knot is the Essence of my Being
The rest of me is placed in boiling water
Within that moist, hot world, the white meat inside my skin softens
I become soft and white
I am broken open and given to the child to eat
I have a gentle taste
Soft and white, with a faint memory of the brown earth in which I grew
I release my taste into the mouth of the child
The child is nourished by my soft, white meat
Filled with the nutrients I have drawn from the rich, dark earth

Next spring
The small piece of me set aside will be planted
From the small knot of the Essence of my Being contained there
I will push a green tendril up through the dark earth towards the
   warming fingers of the sun
I will sprout leaves
And thrust down into the earth a thousand hairlike roots
I will become the mother

Thus, I do feed nations

—PAM MONANTY

TULIP

Vivid red leaves. Inside: flaming yellow; star-shaped at bottom of the red cup. Six little stamens of what I think of when I hear the word, and a paler yellow kind of extension of the stem but a little thicker, exactly in the center. Six vivid red petals, not leaves. Two are torn, dog-eared; did they grow that way? Some stamen dust rests on the yellow cup contrasting magnificently. A little tulip colony. Now there are four flowers. Yesterday I counted 6 bulbs ready to bloom. Looks like one plant was torn from this clump of life and another green stem was clearly ripped from the plant. There are 3 more scraggly-looking pieces of this pie. I don't know if they'll make it to adolescence. Tough neighborhood. Rhododendron tree behind it is looming and messy. And the dreaded tiger lilies are now just a lot of green pointy leaves growing taller by the minute, threatening to bloom. But these tulips, I call them roses. They're glorious and majestic. The 3 shorter flowers are distinctly different from the bigger, bolder, older, more defined flower leading the pack. The soil is moist but doesn't look nourishing. And now I see a stream of ants down there busily circling nothing.

I left the house deciding to choose something to stare at (for the assignment), maybe while driving in, and these tulips called to me— stopped me in my tracks on my way to the car, thankfully inspiring me and forcing words from the pen and paper, stopping all other thoughts.

There they are, now I'm across the way, in the car. They exist before and after me, without me at all.

No. They were not here before now. Not last year or the other 3 years I've lived here. When the green clump first staked its claim on the patch of dirt by the porch steps I puzzled over how they came to be and suddenly remembered: Nancy. Last year we spent all hours together but went our separate ways and now rarely speak. Seed catalogues last year planted her hope in the world and she planted their seeds. She's moved away but this little package of life was her doing. Maybe she mentioned it to me, and like so many words, rolled off of me, and were trampled underfoot.

They remind me of a poem by Danny Siegel, something like, "my defiant shabbos rose"—maybe black, and something about a buttonhole and rebellion; and of Li-Young Lee's poetry book called Rose. And Benjamin Tammuz: "... the rosebush next to the bench has opened three red eyes during the night and looked out onto the street, shy and happy." Tulips don't get the press roses get, and maybe it's better for their character. They are the first hearty spring flowers after the crocuses who clear their way through the days where frost is still likely to pounce and stifle tender, young beauty.

If it were a character in a play, it'd be a long-legged woman full of surprises—unnoticed at first but slowly, from the first opening, blooming into a gorgeous, vibrant, and steadfast individual.

LOOK AGAIN: TULIP 2

The messy clump of green has been one surprise after the next.

Each sign of more life made me curious. I have to say I was expecting very little but pleased at the thought of Nancy's work/gift. At first the bulbs were dark red, not promising. And the proximity to each other odd—literally a clump, one on top of the next, as if randomly tossed in my direction by Nancy walking old Scout, tugging at him to stop walking nose in the ground and get on with it.

No these aren't prim and proper Boston tulips, in manicured lawns in a row: yellow-red-yellow-red, arrogant and untouchable. These are flawed and forgiving flowers she planted.

I'm hurt by the senseless destruction of part of their little colony. Trying not to take it too hard, but tension with the downstairs neighbors mounts as the temperatures rise, doors and windows open, and all signs of life are amplified obnoxiously ending the privacy of winter. I'm thankful for the end of that privacy which usually feels like isolation, but when the grass is greener my perspective shifts. I blame it on the neighbors because they bug me and hate me—and they monopolize any outdoors there is in this little urban suburb yard. They make it a dump—tossing cig butts and scattering broken toys and pieces of fence.

The poor clump really looks trampled and torn at. A slightly gaping hole where part of the plant once lived and a broken off stem are evidence of the crime. These are otherworldly gifts of love from a friend and they've been violated, terminated. The pigeon poop piles up and suffocates any attempts at plant life farther down. But this spot was the right one for planting. Nancy's oddly unassuming and humble. You'd never know she's a musician who is asked to perform all over the world. She is not impressed with herself and often seems clumsy and in need of direction—but she's like this tulip—surviving and shining, eager to please.

—LISA HURWITT

FURTHER EXERCISES: SEEING MORE

Just as there is no end to the music you can hear, there is no end to the objects in nature you can look at—trees, flowers, twigs, buds, rocks, fruit, vegetables, bulbs, bushes, vines, plants—and we haven't even gotten to bugs and animals! Each time you look close, as you have in this exercise, you will see new connections to your own experience, find new stories, ideas, analogies, metaphors.

There is another fruitful and creative way to look at such objects in nature. I learned this from a nun whom I had sought out for spiritual direction. I went in hopes of learning exotic mysteries about arcane paths to God, keys to spiritual understanding I had never dreamed about as a mere Protestant. I felt that a Roman Catholic nun would have all the answers in this realm, would be an expert in such matters. I was prepared to do whatever she asked me to do, even if it involved such artifacts as beads and incense.

She told me to go look at a tree.

"Look at a tree," she said, "and try to think why God made it, what he had in mind when he created it."

She told me to sit down and meditate this way while looking at the tree for twenty minutes, and to write down all the things that I observed about it. I have to admit, I was a little disappointed, since the assignment seemed so mundane. Look at a tree. Is that all? I thought maybe she gave me such an easy assignment because I was a Unitarian; she figured I wasn't up to much more than a tree.

I dutifully went off to the Boston Public Garden, one of my favorite places of power, and sat down in front of the biggest tree I could find. I closed my eyes, took a deep breath, put in my mind the question of why God would make this tree. With that in my head, I raised my eyes to look at it.

I was overwhelmed. I felt as if I had been pushed backward by the force of the tree. It was so complex, so intricate in design, so hugely various—from the patterns of bark that in themselves seemed like pictures and hidden murals, to the top of the limbs and the panoply of leaves, the pattern of limbs—the whole thing seemed far too huge and complicated for me to begin to perceive in the way the sister had instructed me.

I decided to look for something simpler, something on a par with my own primitive level of spiritual understanding. After looking around, I settled on grass. A blade of grass. This plain, small object seemed the thing most suited to my own level of perception. Of course, I wasn't sure I could single out the exact same one each time I looked,

"Look at a tree," she said, "and try to think why God made it, what he had in mind when he created it."

but I could try; I could stare at the same patch of grass and observe the blades as best I could.

I went back to the same spot every day for two weeks and meditated on the blades of grass for twenty minutes each day. I kept discovering new things all the time—different shades of green, different thicknesses and textures, the way the grass moved in the wind, how blades bent toward and away from one another, the sense of the aliveness of each separate blade. I wrote in my notebook, as Sister had instructed, the words that described the qualities of God as I imagined God was manifested in the grass that she/he created: "tenacious," "resilient," "communicating," "alive," "dancing," "dependent," "surprising," "reaching," "responding."

Originally I had planned at the end of the two weeks to pick a blade of the grass to tape in my notebook. But by that time I felt such a relationship with the grass that I felt its aliveness, and the idea of tearing off a piece of it seemed a cruel and unfeeling thing to do. If, before I had meditated on the grass for two weeks, anyone had told me I'd have such misgivings about tearing off a blade, I'd have thought they were balmy. That's how deeply looking at it changed me.

I also began to see other things in a deeper way. After my meditation sessions, I would look around at the rest of the garden. One day I looked into the eyes of a squirrel and he looked back directly into mine. I felt a connection, as if we were both creatures together, and that I was made of the same "stuff," or material, as he was; and as the grass I was looking at, and the trees, stones, birds, insects, animals. I felt a part of the scene, not just an outsider observing it but an integral part of it, part of the world, the whole creation.

You may want, having done the exercise in looking close, to try now looking in a meditative way at an object of nature to see—as the nun instructed me—what God had in mind in creating it. If you don't believe in God, simply contemplate it from a spiritual point of view. Ask yourself, why it was created? How? By whom, what, where, when?

What does it have to tell you? Even if you don't believe in God, you can look at a tree or blades of grass or flowers or bushes and think about their place in creation.

Do this for two weeks and write what you learn in your journal every day. What do you see that you didn't see before? At the end of the two weeks, write a letter to a friend, telling about the whole experience. Invite a friend to go with you to a park, garden, field, or wooded area, and pick out an object in nature to study closely for twenty minutes, writing down everything you can see about it. Then tell each other your discoveries. Write about them.

Peace in Nature

One of the benefits of looking close at something in nature is simply the pleasure of being outside in the natural world. Most people find peace and relief there that refreshes them, like business executive Arnold Hiatt, who likes to walk in the woods and on the mountains, and sail on the ocean.

We can find peace and refreshment in other places as well. When I gave a workshop in Spiritual Autobiography at Sing Sing prison for a group of men studying for a degree from the New York Theological Seminary, I found a depth of spirit and creativity in a place that would seem to stifle such elements. I went to inspire the men; but with their patience, faith, and striving to create something useful out of their time in confinement, they inspired me.

One of the men of this group, Billy L. Griffin, wrote,

> The most spiritual incidents that I recall are those surrounding my staring out the window and watching the stars after my nightly prayers. Everything was so peaceful, so tranquil. These times were of great value to me, especially after a troubled or hectic day.
>
> I'd just sit at the window, watching the goings-on of my neighbors as they wound down their days. They seemed to move slower. Lights went out, the noise of television and radios stopped. . . .

The night sky was always dark and clear. I'd locate stars and wonder if they were planets or not. I'd look for constellations, especially the big and little dippers. I'd often reflect on how tiny I and the world was. This was usually my point of departure as I would muse over different topics without trying to force the issue. Wherever my mind went, I followed until I was too tired and ready for sleep. And sleep would be so good.

A man in the group who signed his paper "Fred" wrote,

Growing up in South Carolina's rural farm land, daily I would go to one or the other of my two favorite hide-a-ways and meditate. One of those areas was near a brook behind a pasture which ran beneath a line of shade trees. The other was in a patch of woods about a quarter of a mile from my grandfather's house. These two places were special to me, there I could commune with God—who in those moments was nature at her finest.

Another man in the group wrote of going out in a rowboat to the middle of the lake in Prospect Park in Brooklyn and lying back and floating, finding a sense of peace.

Looking Close in Your Work

We don't need to restrict looking close to the wonders of the earth and sky. It's a practice that also helps us be creative in our work, regardless of what it may be.

Architect Evans Woollen tells how his mother pointed out buildings to him as a child, reacted to them with laughter or scorn, and got him interested so that he looked closer at them. Looking close is part of Elizabeth Valentine's technique as a body worker, which she developed by learning anatomy through studying sculpture. Chef Odette Bery says the best experience for learning to be a creative cook is watching other people prepare food.

Watch. Be awake and aware, and discoveries will unfold before you.

EXERCISE 4

FINDING INSPIRATION FROM OTHERS' CREATIVE WORKS

When I was eight years old, I read a book at the Broad Ripple Branch of the Indianapolis Public Library (my favorite place in the neighborhood, aside from Wally's Grill for hamburgers) called *The Bears of Blue River*. I was so moved by it I wanted to be a pioneer like the hero, Bowser Brent, and if I could not go back in time to do that, I wanted at least to go on a real canoe trip into the woods and camp out and live on fish I caught myself. I did that twelve years later with my friend Joe "The Fox" Hartley. We went to Great Sand Lake, Ontario, above the Lake of the Woods, and camped for a week without seeing any other human beings, and lived on the Northern pike and muskies we caught. In a sense that whole trip, that marvelous adventure, came out of my reading *The Bears of Blue River*.

All of us have read books that moved us that way, have heard music and seen movies and plays, looked at paintings and sculpture that have influenced our lives. Remembering how we were affected by the creative works of others gets our own creative juices flowing, bringing back memories of what happened and who it happened with, and how we and they changed, or were surprised, or inspired, or illuminated by what we heard or read or saw.

Creation begets creation. Many writers I know have told me that when they're stuck in their own work or feel they've hit a dry period, they turn to books or stories or poems that have inspired them in the past, to tune in to that wavelength of creativity. Even when the creative spirit seems dammed up in us, or gone dry, we can sense it, even sometimes revive it, by reading books whose own creative power has moved us on a deep level.

Think back to some of those special creative works that had a special influence on you.

Think back to some of those special creative works that had a special influence on you. Take twenty minutes to write about what it was like when you read that book or heard that song or saw that painting, and were deeply touched. Write about how it felt, and how it affected you.

This is how some people responded to that question:

OPEN SESAME

In San Francisco in 1969, I journeyed through a retrospective show of the work of van Gogh. At that time I was living in a Yoga Ashram under a discipline of poverty, chastity and obedience; a daily routine not unlike that of the monastery here.

It was a traveling show with a tremendous amount of his work in it. I have met many people who saw this memorable show during the years it went from place to place. Each one of these people shared my wonder at it.

I had some very good art teaching and doing but was not at all thinking of being an artist when I went to this show.

It seems like it was 50 rooms. Each work is quite small, a jewel. The show was arranged chronologically. I began quite early in my parade around the walls to be profoundly affected. Each brush stroke was exquisite; each canvas amazing. If you go close up to a van Gogh anywhere you will see what I'm talking about. The paint is laid exactly so the bumps of paint are sensuous beyond description and a field of wheat will have been painted with thousands of these precise touches. The color is intense, simple, direct, clear. The drawing of shapes is a harmony of the spheres. To move from painting to painting and from room to room was to take a journey from which there was no returning.

I have studied van Gogh's work and life and have come to know that he regarded colors as symbols; the background colors of all his portraits are chosen to harmonize with the subject. Did you know he painted at night with a candle on his hat? A barroom scene was painted in garish yellow-green, red to give a hellish aura to it; I find this painting beautiful anyway. His colors are uncomplicated. They support rather than distract. Many great colorists use very obvious, mostly complementary color schemes. This was the first time I fully comprehended the spiritual power of painting.

—SUSAN ANDERSON

THE SECRET GARDEN

I read this book when I was perhaps 10–12. I don't even remember the story but I do remember the feeling. I loved that the book took place somewhere else and at a different time. I remember identifying with the little girl even though I can't recall her character totally. But most of all I loved that she has discovered this secret place. A place of beauty and mystery. It had a forbidden quality to it and I loved her courage and curiosity to explore and to continue to go there. This garden was attractive to her in the same way this book had an attraction for me. I just wanted to know more about this place. Perhaps I longed for such a place. But I needed my own space. I know that I was not told to read this book. I was not reading it because I was supposed to. I wanted to and it didn't matter if it won me any approval. That was the same kind of feeling the little girl had for her secret garden. This was important to me because I remember feeling for the first time interested in a book on my own that was a new side of me. I don't think I ever finished the book. But it had captured something in me that had been untouched and today I still feel grateful for this book.

—M. WHITEFORD

Recalling Inspiration

Thinking back to books, songs, stories, sculptures, dances, plays, movies that have moved us never fails to touch a creative spark. It reminds us of the power of creativity, how it not only produces aesthetic pleasure, but also acts on our lives and influences our actions, understanding, emotions, intellect, and spirit.

Whenever you are stuck for ideas or inspiration, think back to one of those works of art or literature that altered your own life, and write about what it was, how you experienced it, and what happened as a result. Soon you will be in the realm of creativity—first, the one created by the work that moved you, and then your own, as you create the story of how this work changed (recreated) you.

Creative people use others' creative works for their own inspiration, as well as for learning their craft. Author-attorney Alan Nolan felt "released" by reading Salinger's *The Catcher in the Rye* and J. P. Donleavy's *The Ginger Man,* novels that broke rules and gave him the courage to try something original. When therapist and author Claire Douglas feels bogged down in her writing, she reads the work of writers she loves, like the nineteenth-century novelists Edith Wharton and Henry James. Chef Odette Bery sometimes gets inspiration from reading recipe books.

Make a list of some of the books, movies, poems, plays, and other works of art that have inspired you. Think about your actual feelings when you experienced whatever work it was. Remember the emotion, the "spirit" of it.

Pick one of the books you put on your list and read it again; get back in touch with the feelings it evoked in you.

Keep your list and add to it. Note in your journal what events or experiences inspire you as they occur.

Here is a list of some of mine that may help you create your own list. You'll undoubtedly think of examples in each of these categories you like better than mine!

BOOKS:
The Bears of Blue River by Charles Major
The Red Badge of Courage by Stephen Crane
Let Us Now Praise Famous Men by James Agee
The Magician of Lublin by Isaac Bashevis Singer
Reaching Out by Henri Nouwen
A Palpable God by Reynolds Price
Body and Soul by Frank Conroy

MOVIES:
Yankee Doodle Dandy
The Graduate
The Razor's Edge (updated version starring Bill Murray)
My Left Foot
The Commitments
Carrington

OPERA:
La Bohème by Giacomo Puccini

SYMPHONY:
The New World by Antonin Dvorak

JAZZ WORKS:
No Sun in Venice by The Modern Jazz Quartet
Straight, No Chaser by Thelonious Monk
Sketches of Spain by Miles Davis
A Love Supreme by John Coltrane

PLAYS:
Darkness at Noon by Sidney Kingsley, based on the novel
    by Arthur Koestler
The Iceman Cometh by Eugene O'Neill
The Real Thing by Tom Stoppard
Blown Sideways Through Life by Claudia Shear
Angels in America by Tony Kushner

SONGS:
"Suzanne" by Leonard Cohen, sung by Judy Collins
"Just Like Tom Thumb's Blues," by Bob Dylan, sung by
    Judy Collins
"Anticipation," sung by Carly Simon

POEMS:
"Things of This World" by Richard Wilbur
"Live or Die" by Anne Sexton
"The Key to Everything" by May Swenson

Keeping a Journal

Are you keeping a journal? It's a good seedbed for creativity. A journal is a place where you can put down anything you want, without any rules. A journal provides the chance to kick off your shoes and not worry about what the neighbors think. It's only for you. If you want to share it or any part of it with any particular person, that's fine. But here's the basic rule for enjoying and getting pleasure and inspiration from your journal: Don't write for posterity! Or even your best friend, or loved one.

As soon as you become self-conscious, and worry how your journal is going to sound to others, you might as well forget it. What do you write in it? Thoughts, ideas, scenes, snatches of overheard dialogue, wishes, memories, jokes, poems, recipes, dreams—anything you want, in any style or form you want. Some people write in their journal every morning, or at night before going to bed. Others use it when the spirit moves them. You can make up your own rules about how to use it, as well as what and how to write in it. If you skip a day or a week, don't let this discourage you. Nobody knows! Return to it when you feel like it.

I always use a loose-leaf notebook with lined paper, probably because I'm accustomed to writing on lines like I did when I started school. Many people prefer to have a bound book with blank pages, which is easier to draw on. Bill Donaldson, who served as chair of the religious education committee at my church, suggests "a blank unlined book, a pen for writing, a different pen for drawing, such as a wide blue calligraphy felt tip." Many of the people who come to my workshops use many different colored pens or crayons to draw with in their journals.

A journal also is good place to write down quotations you want to remember from books, newspapers, poems—whatever strikes you. These can be a good source of ideas and inspiration, as well as a record of what you were thinking about, what was meaningful to you at a particular day, month, and year.

You might record movies or plays you saw, books you read, outcomes of sporting events you attended, or events you read about or watched on TV that were meaningful to you. What's in the news that you want to remember? Clip out a picture that meant something to you from a magazine and paste it into your journal. Be creative.

A journal is a key creative tool for many people. Author Ivan Gold feels journals are important for getting memories down; he sometimes segues from his journal right into the book or story he is working on. Judy Collins says, "The opening line from a journal can be the beginning of a song."

Dream Doors

Dreams have always been a part of the human story; they are part of the Bible and sacred books of other religions; Freud and Jung saw in dreams keys to understanding our own nature. There's a renewed interest in dreaming and what it can tell us—books, workshops, courses, lectures, and theories of dreaming abound. Stephen LaBerge of Stanford University is the exponent of "lucid dreaming"—a technique of becoming conscious in our dreams that we are dreaming. The advantages, he says, are that we can alter the "script" of the dream, have it come out the way we want it. These methods and results are described in his books *Lucid Dreaming* and *Exploring the World of Lucid Dreaming.*

I've resisted attempting that practice, feeling that interfering with my own dreams isn't a good idea. This is not based on anything more than my own instinct and has no scientific or spiritual basis. What I do practice is telling myself to remember my dreams when I go to sleep, and this usually works. On waking it's necessary to jot down key phrases or scenes from the dreams, or they quickly evaporate like wisps of smoke.

Judy Collins believes the main access points to her creativity are her journal and her dreams. Therapist Claire Douglas writes down dreams and meditates as a way to get ideas. Chef Odette Bery has dreams with recipes. Architect Evans Woollen had a dream about the form of a monastery he was commissioned to design.

One of my own most powerful dreams had a great influence on my creativity. After my nonfiction publisher had turned down my first attempt at a novel, I was devastated.

I kept on writing fiction secretly, not telling anyone but a few confidants. One morning I woke at dawn and felt

As soon as you become self-conscious, and worry how your journal is going to sound to others, you might as well forget it.

exhilarated, because I had just had a dream in the form of a novel. It began with a title page; then came a simple story with a beginning, middle, and end, and then a page that said "The End." It was like a signal from my inner self telling me, You have a novel in you. I knew then I would write it—not the story of the dream, but the novel "in me" I wanted to write. It was seven more years until I did, but I always remembered the dream, and the dream helped me believe.

Even if we remember our dreams, how can we use them? Some therapists make creative use of dreams to deepen the dreamer's understanding. I think that even without such aid we often get insights about ourselves, and sometimes about our work, from dreams. If you want to explore that further, look for one of the many workshops on dream analysis or interpretation offered at most adult education centers.

Tibetan lamas have taught "dream yoga" for centuries to help their students develop mindfulness in daytime living and get a sense of the illusory nature of life. What if our waking life is a dream too? Or our dream life is actually the "reality"? What if everything is a dream? Fred Alan Wolf, author of *The Dreaming Universe,* is a quantum physicist who asks the ultimate question these other questions raised by dreaming lead to: If life is a dream, who is the dreamer?

Here are some simple exercises for experimenting with your own dreams as creative possibilities:

Keep a dream journal for a week. Write down everything you can remember about your dreams. Draw with pens or crayons scenes from your dreams, or feelings of dreams. See if there are any stories in the dreams. What do they tell you about yourself? About your relation to the universe? Share your dreams with a friend. Ask about his or her own dreams. Use one of the groups you are in—or form a new one—to read about dreams, and get together to draw, write, and share about dreams.

Even if we remember our dreams, how can we use them?

EXERCISE 5

DRAW A ROAD MAP OF YOUR CREATIVE JOURNEY

Our whole lives are studded with creative activity—creations of others that have moved us, as well as creations of our own. To get in touch with your continuing creative experience, the way it has moved through your life and still moves you, take a large piece of paper from a drawing pad and use your crayons to illustrate as colorfully as possible the course of your creative journey.

Before starting to draw, spend a few minutes of quiet. Think of the people and circumstances that led you to this point—of drawing a map that will enable you to look at your life as a creative journey. Think of all the gifts you've been given that have enabled you to make such a journey, to create in so many different ways. Jot down some of the highlights you want to include—times when you were opened up creatively by someone else's work, or when your own creativity blossomed; when you acted creatively in your job, or relationship, or family life; creative activities outside of the arts, like creating ways of service to the community or to other individuals. Think in the broadest terms possible of your own creativity, and decorate the map of your journey with the signs and symbols of your creative development and growth, the high points (as a mountain peak) or low points (as a mine shaft) of your creative pilgrim's progress.

Let your imagination flow, and don't stint with the crayons; the more color the better.

After drawing the map, share it with someone else. If you are doing these exercises by yourself, show your map to a family member or a friend and explain what the symbols are. Take them with you along the route of your creative journey.

After drawing the map and sharing it, take just ten minutes to write about one of the points you drew on your creative journey. Of course, it can't be a whole story, only the beginning. It demonstrates that every point on the map is a story, that each creative act can produce another (the story of the creation).

FURTHER EXERCISES: MAPPING NEW TERRITORY

Keep the road map of your creative journey. You can look at any point on it at any time and find a story. Each turning point gives you the ideas, emotions, drama, and insight of a creative experience that moved you, turned you, opened you up in some way.

You can write "off of" the map for a long time, remembering and recharging your own creativity.

Start a new map. Draw the new creative experiences that occur during the coming week, and if you aren't aware of any occurring— create some! Look at what and how you created things in the past. Revise and retool those creative ideas and experiences you liked, or that seem relevant now.

Don't think of creativity in a narrow, confining way when you draw your maps. Remember how other people play a part in your creativity—and you in theirs. When asked about the factors that helped him break his long creative block, novelist Ivan Gold said, "It's got to do with love, confidence . . ." His wife, Vera, his son, Ian, his writer friends, a publisher who believed in him (Seymour Lawrence) and offered that belief in the form of a contract with an advance against royalties for an unfinished manuscript—all were part of the chemistry of his creative rebirth.

Religious historian Elaine Pagels, who tackles the biggest subjects in her books (like *Adam, Eve, and the Serpent*), said of her creative work, "It's lonely—it's important to have people in your life who know what it's all about—I know they're there."

None of us creates in a vacuum. People are part of our creative journey, giving us not only encouragement and support, but ideas we couldn't see ourselves, even though they are right in front of our noses. My publisher, Seymour Lawrence, wrote me when he read an essay I did on James Baldwin and said, "That should be part of a book on New York in the fifties!" It seemed a natural. Why didn't I think of it? Sometimes it takes others to tell us what's right in front of us.

Editor Andre Schiffrin called radio host and interviewer Studs Terkel when he read some interviews Terkel had done with people in

South Africa in which they told the story of their village. Schiffrin suggested he do the same thing with "an American village." That's how Terkel's first book, *Division Street*, was born.

We could all make a map of where we met the people who helped, inspired, and supported us in our journey!

Each turning point gives you the ideas, emotions, drama, and insight of a creative experience that moved you, turned you, opened you up in some way.

Think of different kinds of creative maps you could make of your life. A couple who did this workshop with me in Palm Beach, Florida, told me they are making a creative map of their relationship, and are going to continue to draw it, reminding themselves to keep creating it as they live it, and not simply "let it happen" or get boring or fall into a rut.

Here's another exercise for partners: Each person draws a map of the way she or he would like the relationship to look if it were the greatest relationship imaginable! They show their maps to each other and see how and where the maps could merge into a great relationship for both partners at the same time.

Taking off from that idea, you could make a creative map of your job, your family life, your service to the community, your education, your pursuit of art, music, sculpture, writing, acting, or filmmaking. Map what has occurred up to now; how this part of your life went in the past year, the past week. Then draw a future map, how you would like it to look if you could map it any way possible. What stops you from following that map? Create ideas and methods for making that map unfold in your life the way you design it.

Failure as Opportunity

Sometimes your attempts at creativity have failed—and others will fail in the future—whether with your work, or art, or relationships. No road map of a creative journey is a series of triumphs. All of us suffer disappointments, frustrations, and downright defeats in our creative life as well as in any other aspect of life.

Think of different kinds of creative maps you could make of your life.

So has every other creator in the history of the world.

When you are brought down by one of those inevitable defeats, remember the great tradition you are in! James Joyce, like many writers, was a "failure" in his own lifetime. Some creators are fortunate enough to have their rejected work vindicated in their lifetime. When Julia Child submitted *The Art of French Cooking* to a publisher, she was told that Americans would never be interested in French cooking, and besides, the book was too long. It was bought by another publisher and became a phenomenal best-seller.

Joan Didion's first novel, *Run River*, was turned down by thirteen publishers; Norman Mailer's third novel, *The Deer Park*, was turned down by five publishers, even though his first, *The Naked and the Dead*, had been a best-seller. Kurt Vonnegut's first best-seller, *Slaughterhouse Five*, was turned down by two of his previous publishers before being accepted by a new one.

As I read through the interviews I've done with creators, it struck me how many of them mentioned some failure or other, which usually opened a new door, though it wasn't visible at the time.

Elaine Pagels wrote poetry as a teenager and now describes herself as a "failed poet," but the world knows her as an outstanding writer of religious history. Odette Bery was turned down for a teaching job by Garland Junior College, but later, as a well-known chef, taught cooking there. Yoga teacher Danielle Levi-Alvares worked on a novel for a while but felt better when she gave it up, deciding she was more creative in her life than in her writing. She later got to translate one of Thich Nhat Hanh's books into French.

Sometimes failure persists, we bottom out, and the world gives up on us. But always there are those who rise again—who hear that voice that says, "Get up!" John Frankenheimer, the director of some of the most commercially and artistically successful films of the 1960s—*The Manchurian Candidate, The Bird Man of*

Alcatraz, and *Days of Wine and Roses*— found himself at sixty-four in 1994 "trying to pick up the pieces of a career that went awry," according to a *New York Times* article by Bernard Weinraub.

Every turning point, whether of success or defeat, creates new openings—new opportunities to create.

The occasion of the interview was Frankenheimer's return to television (considered "Hollywood's bottom rung"), where he had started out in the '50s. Weinraub reported that "personal difficulties, including alcoholism, left [Frankenheimer] tormented for years and plagued his career." Talking about it with what Weinraub called "unusual candor and without a trace of bitterness," the director said, "I have to rediscover myself, reinvent myself." Frankenheimer said he'd had a drinking problem but "straightened out in 1981," and "from that day on I haven't had a drink."

"The 1980s were spent putting my life back together," the veteran director said.

> But look, I don't want to cast myself as a victim in any way because I'm not. I've had a terrific career and a long run. And if you keep stepping up to the plate, sooner or later you get a hit. And sooner or later you get a home run. The important thing is to be resilient enough to keep stepping up to the plate. And I'm stepping up to the plate.

It reminded me of Henry James's injunction to himself in his journal after his own big failure: "Produce; produce again; produce again better than ever and all will be well."

Every turning point, whether of success or defeat, creates new openings—new opportunities to create.

8

Doing It Day by Day

IF WE CAN CREATE STORIES, PICTURES, AND SONGS, TRANSFORM RAW FOOD into gourmet meals, steel and cement into soaring buildings, why can't we use our creative powers to enhance our own daily lives? If we can learn through exercises and conscious use of our senses to gain access to our creativity for making books, paintings, and buildings, why can't we call upon this spirit within us to enhance our moment-by-moment experiences in order to live them more fully— more creatively?

Here is a rough blueprint for doing that, created from one person's own idiosyncratic experience and outlook. Try it, and see if any of the ideas or suggestions could be applied to your own life. Then, with this as a model outline, create a blueprint of your own.

I. Waking

For many of us, this is not as easy as it sounds, and in fact may be the most challenging part of the day.

I am not a morning person. I have never in my life jumped out of bed immediately upon waking, pointed eagerly toward the window, and exclaimed, "Look, the sun!" My natural tendency is to pull the covers up over my head and hide.

Ever since I can remember, clear back into childhood, my process on waking has felt more like some interior ancient reenactment of the whole human drama, going back to protozoic times, rising through the slime, struggling up from the sea to reach land, crawling inch by inch over the dry terrain, and then, millions of eons later, by performing a miracle of will and coordination, rising to stand and then move forward on only two legs! That's the part where I actually manage to get my feet off the bed and onto the floor, stand up, and propel myself, step by step, to the bathroom, where, in the mirror, I confront some strange, sleep-ridden hallucination that reminds me of the theory that God formed his creatures from clay.

My mood was shifted—uplifted—for the morning challenge a decade ago when I came back to Boston from Hollywood and discovered a radio program that began at seven o'clock in the morning with bird calls (repeating them again for later risers at eight o'clock, and every hour on the hour till noon). I bought a clock with a radio alarm and set it for the station with the bird calls—a program called *Morning Pro Musica* hosted by the sonorous, deep-voiced Robert J. Lurtsema, a cultural hero of New England. Following the bird calls, one was not jolted by some harsh, staccato, speeded-up standard announcer's rap, but soothed by the amazingly slow, low, dulcet tones of Robert J. He played mostly classical music, music that rolls into your consciousness with the richness of spirit of the masters, Beethoven, Brahms, Bach, Vivaldi, Telemann, Albinoni, Pachelbel . . .

BIRDS, NOT BUZZERS

Such music brings a noble mood, a sense of the variety and possibilities of life, the power of beauty, and the capacity of humans to create it, with horns, drums, harpsichords, pianos, strings, woodwinds, each of these instruments conceived, invented, created by some mere creature or combination of creatures as mere as myself, then mastered and imagined in intricate combinations by some composer (think of the intricacy of such composition), then performed and led and produced in concert, pouring over us and into us (if we allow it) with the whole force of creation.

Wake to bird calls.

Wake to bird calls. The sound is gentle, sweet, melodious, relaxing yet interesting, a nonshock way to lure you into the day, as opposed to the rude shove of an alarm or the hard bump of a buzzer, both of which begin your day with a nasty jolt. If you live in the country, or some quiet place where birds outside your window provide your wake-up call naturally, all the better. If you don't have that advantage, buy a bird-call record. If you can do it, or know someone who can, rig your record player or CD so it goes off at the time you want to wake by playing the birds' music, followed by other music you find uplifting, whether it's the classical style or not, whatever stirs you, gives you a sense of the spirit—the animating or vital principle.

INSCRIBING THE DAY

One day Robert J. announced after the bird calls that he was going to play a piece by Bach called "Christians, Inscribe the Day!" The idea struck me, and I could feel a tingle of anticipation at what it suggested. To be stirred by it, you don't have to be a Christian. (If you're not, substitute Buddhists, Jews, Muslims, or just People—or simply say your own name with it, as in "Dan—inscribe the day!" or "Alice—inscribe the day!") What moves me is the concept that we stand at the beginning of a new day, and instead of just letting that day happen to us, roll over us (sometimes it seems like an oncoming freight train), it's actually possible for us to inscribe the day—to make our mark on it, cause something we want to happen in it, take some action that will affect it. That's not a bad thought to have on waking.

Inscribe the day.

How?

Write down something you'd like to make happen in the day that you hadn't thought of before.

Get up a half hour early and write in your journal—thoughts, observations, ideas, descriptions, names, places. Read a writer's journal or notebook to see how he or she organizes and categorizes subjects and lists and ideas. Some of my own favorites are the notebooks of F. Scott Fitzgerald, published at the end of his unfinished novel *The Last Tycoon*, in the edition with an introduction by Edmund Wilson. Fitzgerald loved to keep lists, ideas, overheard snatches of dialogue he might use later in a story.

As well as being a record of our daily journey, a journal can be like a creative warehouse of parts that can later be assembled to make a story, play, script, or novel, or a place where the creator of a fiction can rummage to find just the right missing part for a work he or she is constructing at the moment (a line overheard in a coffeehouse, a description of dawn at the beach, an experienced emotion of anger or love that may fit one of your characters). Or one of those stored parts may serve as the spark for a new creation.

If you have a meditation practice, and are accustomed to doing it in the morning, that is obviously part of a powerful beginning of the day. If you don't have such a practice, or you like to meditate later in the day, at least take five minutes to be still. Breathe in and out, become aware of your breathing. Settle. Be still, before becoming active. Center yourself before moving out into the whirlwind of work and the world that will push and pull you in different directions.

2. Eating Breakfast

Sit down before you eat.

It's not only more relaxing, it's more civilized. Rabbi Harold Kushner explains in his book *To Life!* that, though it is little known, "there is a Jewish law forbidding us to eat standing up. Animals eat standing up. Human beings turn the act of ingestion into a much more dignified one. They sit, they offer a prayer of thanks, they eat their food in a leisurely manner rather than gulp it as animals do."

This is part of the larger purpose of the Jewish laws, Rabbi Kushner explains, "to teach us how to take the ordinary and make it holy."

> *Center yourself before moving out into the whirlwind of work and the world that will push and pull you in different directions.*

If you eat at home, listen to music you enjoy.

Light a candle. Eating dinner by candlelight makes it special, an occasion. It never occurred to me to eat breakfast by candlelight until my friend and favorite photographer, Theresa Mackin, invited me for breakfast once and lit two candles at the table before serving bowls of oatmeal with raisins. (Theresa has taken most of my book jacket photos since 1985 and always creates a way to make me smile and not look goofy. She is one of the most creative people I know.) It was lovely. Why shouldn't breakfast be special sometimes? What's the occasion? It's a new day, a day that never existed before in the entire course of history, and you are alive in it.

Why not celebrate? Why not honor the day, and the meal, and your partner or family or roommates—or yourself alone—with this glow?

A PAUSE THAT REFRESHES

Before you begin to eat, take a moment to stop, breathe, and think about what you're about to eat. Some years ago I began to silently offer a prayer of thanks for my food, my health, and my life before eating breakfast in the morning. If not a prayer, then a meditation of thanks is appropriate and empowering, a quiet acknowledgment of the life force, the abundance of the world that provides this sustenance, the fuel or power that keeps you going.

When you eat, notice how it tastes. Food isn't just fuel that we ingest because we need it to operate, it also provides enjoyment. If you don't enjoy what you're eating, think about what you might have for breakfast the next day that you would like better. Don't just use food as background you take for granted, but take the pleasure as well as the sustenance from it.

Read cookbooks, or books about food and cooking, for other people's ideas, new ways of doing things. A whole new world of appreciation opened up to me back in 1971 when a friend pressed on me some books by M. F. K. Fisher. The books had intriguing, witty titles like *How to Cook a Wolf*,

When you eat, notice how it tastes.

With Bold Knife and Fork, and *Consider the Oyster.* "You must read these books," my artist and writer friend Eve Babitz told me. "They're like Proust—but with recipes!"

Ms. Fisher was a great storyteller, and she wove her tales around food and cooking and eating, making me freshly aware of the wonders of taste and the joy of eating—not just gourmet meals but homemade dishes like meatloaf with catsup. Fisher continued writing marvelous books until her death at age eighty-four in 1992, and she heightened my awareness of the fun of eating, the downright pleasure of it.

Before rushing out the door, stop for a moment, go back and sit down on your bed or in a comfortable chair. It only takes a minute to do this, but just taking a deep breath, centering, bringing yourself into focus, is relaxing and reassuring before moving out into the world.

3. Going to Work

If there is any way to walk or ride a bicycle to work, by all means, do it. If you have to drive, or take taxis or buses or subways, notice the people you see. Imagine their stories. See how they dress, what they read, what their body language tells you. Listen to what they say.

People evoke ideas. Look at them. Listen to them.

"You've written fourteen books and hundreds of articles and stories—where do you get your ideas?" someone once asked me.

"Walking down Charles Street," I said. (That's Main Street in the neighborhood where I lived in Boston.)

It's even all right to smile at people you see on the street.

I know you'll say that's dangerous today, especially in the city, but you can make a pretty good guess at a person who isn't going to get hysterical if you smile at them. Trust your own instinct. It's especially all right to smile at a waiter or clerk in a store or the place where you buy a newspaper.

WHEN I CHANGE, YOU CHANGE

Here's a way to test a philosophic principle. Vivekananda says, "When I change, you change." This simple-sounding phrase has the deepest

You don't have to wait for the troublesome people in your life to mend their ways, or get out of their rut, or alter their attitude toward you. Change yourself, and they cannot remain unaffected by it.

and most far-reaching implications. It means you don't have to wait for the troublesome people in your life to mend their ways, or get out of their rut, or alter their attitude toward you. Change yourself, and they cannot remain unaffected by it.

Test this principle in the smallest way—smile at someone and see what happens. Does their expression remain the same? See if in this minuscule way you can demonstrate one of the powerful truths of human behavior: When I change, you change. It may enable you to see how the principle works in much larger ways, with people much closer to you, people important in all aspects of your life—boss, employee, wife, husband, friend.

Take with you on the bus or subway a book you have already read whose ideas inspire you, whose thoughts make you look at things in a deeper (or "higher") way, give you an angle of vision you usually don't get when you're going to or from work. I've carried around a book with many underlinings, called *Abandonment to Divine Providence*, written by Jean-Pierre de Caussade, a seventeenth-century French Jesuit whose letters to nuns of that era seem to speak to my current condition in America! I'll never forget standing on the subway platform of the Red Line stop at Charles Street in Boston at a time of particular distress in my life, waiting for a subway I thought would never come. I pulled Caussade's book from my briefcase and opened it, by chance, to this underlined passage: "All things conduct you and support you. Your way is lined with banners as you advance along it in your carriage. All is in the hand of God."

A smile broke across my face as I imagined a big, flapping banner unfurling out from the subway platform, and a carriage rushing up from out of the tunnel underground. I went to Cambridge feeling royal. When I got off at the Harvard Square stop, the full, deep tones of a cello playing a lovely, plaintive melody greeted me, and I stopped to listen to a young man with long hair making music there in the subway cavern. Before moving on I emptied the coins from my pocket into his open cello case, and went on my way, feeling lighter.

Carry a seashell with you. Take a small shell from a beach and keep it in your pocket. Throughout the day, when you take something out of your pocket, touch the shell and remember the beach, and the sun, and the water. Let the warmth and refreshment come back to you. Think of the ocean, and how immense it is compared to whatever problem you are dealing with at the moment.

4. Working

Whether your work is physical, mental, social, or solitary, before starting it, take a moment to think about what you want to accomplish. If the work you have to do that day seems overwhelming, play a "witness" game with yourself. In meditation, the "witness" part of our mind is the part that observes our thoughts and feelings, which separates us from them, gives us some distance from them and control over them. Imagine for a moment that you are an outside observer, watching you do your work. Visualizing yourself doing it brings a distance and a kind of relief, lifting the weight or burden of the task. From time to time during the day play the witness, observing yourself doing the work and standing aside from it, as if you were watching it in a play or a movie.

In a sense you are the director of your own movie—the movie of your life.

You do the casting by choosing your friends and associates, you scout the locations when you decide what apartment or house to rent or buy in what city or landscape or neighborhood; you're also the musical director (what radio station do you listen to, what CDs or records do you play?) and the art director (you choose the clothes you buy and what you wear on a given day). As such you not only guide it, you can give it whatever interpretation you want.

In a sense you are the director of your own movie—the movie of your life.

PLAY A NEW ROLE

You can see your role in any particular situation—work, marriage, relationship—as hero or heroine or victim, and when you view it this way you have an opportunity to alter it, whether in interpretation or in action. How? Remember, you write your own lines; nobody hands you a script to memorize at the beginning of the day. You are free to "change your character," speak in a different way, express different thoughts and opinions, challenge others or accept them. The freedom of this becomes evident when you are aware of it, conscious of your opportunity.

A few years ago I heard Arlo Guthrie interviewed by Robert J. Lurtsema (now retired from Boston radio, unhappily for his fans). Arlo is the folksinger son of Woody Guthrie and the author and singer of the '60s hit song "Alice's Restaurant," which became a popular movie about the life and times of him and his friends. Arlo was living again in the old church that was featured in the movie, writing new songs, gathering new friends in good projects of peace and music. Robert J. asked Arlo if there was going to be a movie about his new life and times.

"Oh, there's another movie, all right," Arlo said quite matter-of-factly. "I'm just waiting to see how it turns out."

All of us have movies of our lives ongoing; I had a new one begin a few years ago when I moved to New York without any definite return date, deciding to take it one year at a time. Look at the turning points in your own life, and the new ones you know are coming—see how you are living your own movie. See how you can direct it in a creative way—include a scene or a person who wasn't otherwise going to be in the movie of your day, and see how the whole thing changes.

MAKING DIALOGUE SING

You can change the whole meaning of your movie and affect your relationship to all the other characters in the "cast" not only by what lines you say, but how you say them. I am not speaking theoretically; I am thinking of Karen Monti Lindo at *New Age Journal*. People called expecting the usual rote—often rude—boring and bored announcement. Instead they got music, as well as information.

Something like that alters your mood, it makes you think of other possibilities, it surprises you out of apathy. It reminds you that someone out there is alive, and likes it, and wants to make it more likable for you too. I can think of no better example of creating with the spirit than the way Karen Monti Lindo answers the telephone at her office.

EVERYTHING COUNTS

When I lead workshops in Spiritual Autobiography, I am struck by the small but significant incidents people remember and write about that involve some phrase or deed of kindness someone did for them, or they did for someone else, and how it changed a mood, a day, a life, created a turning point. One woman wrote of going to a restaurant for a Christmas-season lunch when she was ten years old, with a girlfriend, and the harried waitress was nice to them even though they were kids and the place was crowded, so they pooled all their change to leave her a tip, and knowing it wasn't enough, they wrote a note of thanks on a napkin as well.

Looking back through the window, the kids saw the waitress smile as she picked up the change and read the note. A small thing. Yet it brought a moment of pleasure to people's lives—not just the waitress, but the two girls, one of whom remembered it years later, when it

Lives may later turn on a smile, a frown, a hand stretched out in friendship or support.

brought new pleasure to a roomful of other people who heard the story. The thought comes to me over and over when I hear such stories that the smallest gesture we make to someone has a meaning, a resonance: Everything counts.

Lives may later turn on a smile, a frown, a hand stretched out in friendship or support.

F. Scott Fitzgerald once observed, "It isn't given to us to know those rare moments when people are wide open and the lightest touch can wither or heal. A moment too late and we can never reach them any more in this world. They will not be cured by our most efficacious drugs or slain with our sharpest swords."

Bear that in mind when you go out the door. Remember it when you open the next door. Look around you and see the people. They aren't just background and decoration for your movie set. Pay attention to them. Honor them. Remember, each one is the star of his or her own movie, just as you are of yours.

"By being kind to others—if it's done properly, with proper understanding—we benefit as well," writes the American Buddhist nun Pema Chödrön in *Start Where You Are.* "We are completely interrelated. What you do to others, you do to yourself. What you do to yourself, you do to others."

Former Chicago Bulls coach Phil Jackson believes that leadership "means treating everyone with the same care and respect you give yourself—and trying to understand their reality without judgment." When we begin to be aware of our relatedness, Jackson says, "we begin to understand, directly, remarkably, that we're part of something larger than ourselves."

5. Taking a Break

The Writers' Room, where I went to work most every day when I lived in Boston (I like to go to the office too, like everyone else!), was a series of cubicles with desks and computers or typewriters, in office spaces located in the Transportation Building, a state agency. It has now moved to State Street. It was an atrium-style building, and outside the offices was a wide walkway with tables and chairs. During the course of the day many of the office workers came out for a break and drank coffee and smoked cigarettes. The smoke was tangible and smelly and I walked through as if it were a gauntlet.

It saddened me to see the faces wreathed in smoke. I knew—as a formerly continuous smoker—that smoking not only makes the throat and gums sore, it numbs and lulls and dulls rather than wakens or alerts the mind (not to mention causing disease and death).

A ONE-LUNG SHOCK

I know this is an addiction and is not easy to stop—some say it's harder to end than alcohol. My own was ended by an unexpected shock. A friend came to visit me who had just had an operation to have a lung removed. I thought, with such a drastic result of his chain smoking, he would have stopped. Though I still smoked a pipe at the time, and it was making my gums sore and my teeth yellow, I was putting off the time I would give it up. When my friend Paul came to visit, I was shocked to see that he was still smoking. He would take a puff of his cigarette, then he would break out into terrible deep, hacking coughs, and then he would squirt some kind of medicinal spray down his throat.

This went on all during the evening, and when I woke the next morning my living room was filled with that fog and stench of continuous smoke. I wanted to get out of the house, and I went for a walk in the Boston Public Garden, taking in deep breaths of fresh air. I was clenching my own pipe in my teeth in anger at Paul, who seemed bent on destroying the one lung he had left. Suddenly I took my pipe from my mouth and threw it into a trash bin. That was it. I have never smoked since. Now when I write, instead of fiddling with pipe and tobacco, I chew on those wooden toothpicks called Stimudents, which serve me just as well. I think the shock of my friend's self-destruction, before my very eyes, shocked me out of my own addiction to tobacco.

BEING A TREE

My favorite work break is doing a yoga balance posture called the Tree. You simply stand, balanced, then shift the weight of your body to your right leg—fix your eye on an object on the wall in front of you—and lift your left leg with your right hand, bracing the left foot against the right leg, letting the left knee bend to the side. If you can stand that way, slowly lift your arms in the air, straight up, and hold the posture. Now you're the tree. Hold the posture for a minute or so, or as long as you can, and then switch to the other side. It gives both centering and balance and leaves you refreshed.

If you don't feel you can stand up and "be a tree" in your office without getting kicked out or jeered, you can always breathe at your desk. I mean consciously taking deep breaths, counting slowly on the inhalation and exhalation, getting long steady breaths that calm and center you. This, too, helps you think more clearly, and create.

6. Lunchtime

Instead of going to lunch one day, go to a museum, art gallery, or exhibit of sculpture, drawings, or photography. Look at the artwork on an empty stomach.

Often necessity is the mother of invention in creative thinking. Hardship sometimes forces us to new ways of perceiving things. Hemingway had some great ideas when he was writing about his art, rather than alcohol or violence or his idea of man-woman relationships. (We can lose valuable insights if we throw away all of Hemingway because of the booze in his books.) When "Papa" was a young writer in Paris, he sometimes skipped lunch to save what little money he had, and to take his mind off his hunger he went sometimes to the Luxembourg Museum.

Hardship sometimes forces us to new ways of perceiving things.

He says in his memoir of that time, *A Moveable Feast*, that hunger increased his appreciation of the artwork he saw: "All the paintings were sharpened and clearer and more beautiful if you were bellyempty, hollow hungry. I learned to understand Cézanne much better and to see truly how he made landscapes when I was hungry."

Hemingway found that all his perceptions were heightened in those days when he was hungry, and when he went in that condition to visit Sylvia Beach's bookstore on the Rue l'Odeon, "The photographs looked different and you saw books that you had never seen before."

EATING LESS AND SEEING MORE

To see what we have never seen before exercises and flexes the creative muscle, making it more powerful to use in our own artistic creation. I don't recommend going hungry all the time, which saps the strength and makes us ill, but try at least occasionally to heighten your perception on purpose. Instead of going to lunch one day, go to a museum and notice what more you see and experience. Afterward, write what happened in your journal, describe what you saw, what you felt, and what you understood as a result of the heightened perception brought on by the temporary hunger.

"Hunger is healthy and the pictures do look better when you are hungry," Hemingway said, and immediately added, "Eating is wonderful too and do you know where you are going to eat right now?"

Hemingway can hardly wait to tell us where he is going to eat—the hunger increases his appetite as he goes to a restaurant called Lipps, and reports, "Every place I passed that my stomach noticed as quickly as my eyes made the walk an added pleasure." He takes pleasure in the food as well as the art, ordering potato salad and reporting with obvious delight, "The pommes a l'huile were firm and marinated and the olive oil delicious. I ground black pepper over the potatoes and moistened the bread in the olive oil. . . . When the pommes a l'huile were gone I ordered another serving and a cervelas. This was a sausage like a heavy, wide frankfurter split in two and covered with a special mustard sauce."

Michael Jordan, an artist on the basketball court was kidded by his teammates for "eating like a bird." Jordan's reply: "Birds can fly."

You don't have to starve to be an artist!

On the other hand, you don't have to gorge yourself, either. Michael Jordan, an artist on the basketball court, whose ability to jump and "hang" in midair has earned him the nickname "Air Jordan," was kidded by his teammates for "eating like a bird." Jordan's reply: "Birds can fly."

LOOK THROUGH ARTISTS' EYES

Another way to go to a museum and see more than you ordinarily would see—without even being hungry!—is to invite an artist you know, or a teacher of art, to take you on a personal tour, show you some of their own favorite paintings, and tell you what it is they admire in them and what their own understanding is of the painting and the artist who painted it. Artists and art teachers often enjoy doing this, and can show you things—ways of seeing the artwork—that to the untrained, unschooled eye are a mystery.

If you don't know any such artist or art teacher, get a small group of friends together who would also like to learn to see more, and ask everyone to contribute a sum of money so you can offer payment to a painter or art teacher in your community to take you on such a tour. I know how much fun and how literally "eye-opening" this experience can be, because I've done it.

Every year the Beacon Hill Civic Association in Boston holds an auction to raise money for its work, and neighbors donate their services to be bid on—someone might offer to come to your house and cook a French dinner for twelve guests, another might play the piano at your party, someone else could take you sailing in Boston harbor. One year a local psychiatrist offered six hours of family therapy! Paul Taylor, who is an art professor at the University of Massachusetts at Boston and a distinguished art critic and author, offered to take a group of people on a tour of the Boston Museum of Fine Arts, showing them his favorite paintings and talking about why he appreciated them. My novelist neighbors, husband and wife James Carroll and Alexandra Marshall, won the bidding for that service and invited me and nine other friends to go on the tour.

I never took art appreciation in college, and I feel embarrassingly uneducated about art, mumbling with every other philistine in the world only that I know what I like—but I don't even know why.

What do the other arts have to teach you about your own?

The tour with Paul Taylor made me see every painting he talked about in a new way and made me realize how much I was missing.

I also saw that as a writer I was losing out on what I could learn creatively from painting that would apply to my own craft and art with words. Reading of Hemingway's days in Paris, I realized he was not just creating his innovative style by learning from other writers—literary mentors like Gertrude Stein and Ezra Pound. He was also learning about literary style from looking at the artwork of the great French painters. He wrote that he "was learning something from the painting of Cézanne that made writing simple true sentences far from enough to make the stories have the dimensions that I was trying to put in them. I was learning very much from him but I was not articulate enough to explain it to anyone. Besides it was a secret."

In the same manner of opening up to unfamiliar arts through a professional practitioner, ask a musician friend to prep you before going to a concert with you, explaining the kinds of things to notice and listen for—no matter what instrument or music they play. Afterwards tell what you heard, and listen to what your friend heard that you weren't even aware was going on (the next time you will be). A friend who did this said, "A jazz guitarist once taught me wonderful things about Mozart's string quartets."

What do the other arts have to teach you about your own? The poet Baudelaire immersed himself in art and found in paintings, sculpture, music, and poetry "the concordant parts of all the arts and the similarities in their methods." What are the similarities in the methods of the other arts to your own? How could you apply them to your own art, your own work, your own relationships—your own life?

Another discipline to exercise on a lunch break is simply "noticing." Being aware—noticing—is a crucial part of our creative power.

Noticing is also a kind of meditation, for when we are paying attention to who and what's around us, we are taken out of the ego-trap of our tiring self-absorption. Anthropologist John Murra, who taught at Vassar and Cornell, used to tell his students to "notice the different way people from other countries and cultures open doors, light cigarettes, greet you, say good-bye. It gives you clues about their culture and its suppositions."

Architect Evans Woollen learned from his mother as a child to notice buildings; the architect who designed the SkyDome in Toronto got his idea for the concept from looking at a lobster shell; biologist Louise Emmons discovered the meaning of the calls of African squirrels by watching them closely for a year and a half; chef Odette Bery notices how people approach their food. Hemingway noticed people and places for his use as a writer, saying of his days in Paris, "I would be listening to other people and noticing everything, I hoped; learning, I hoped."

Listening, noticing, and learning also make everything more interesting. It is boring to walk around the block at lunch break if you

---

CREATORS TALKING

"There are different ways to get quiet before writing. Sometimes, on my Sierra Club calendar, I record the events of the day before. This helps to clear my mind, to empty it. I say I had dinner with so-and-so, wrote in the afternoon, got an upsetting call from someone. There's only about an inch across the page to write these things in. But it helps me get rid of them, stop thinking about them.

"Sometimes I sit on the floor in the middle of the room and meditate. It doesn't feel like emptying out so much as opening up. My need is, Let me open. I run before breakfast so I can sit still and not notice my body. I can sit all day, but my real writing doesn't come till around four in the afternoon. I can't get there till this long time. I sit there—starting at ten—I have lunch at my desk; the real writing is from four to six."

—MARCIE HERSHMAN, NOVELIST, TEACHER, AUTHOR OF
TALES OF THE MASTER RACE AND *SAFE IN AMERICA*

just remain inside your own head and let the interminable chatter of automatic non-thought carry you along with it—the past regrets and future worries, the should-haves and would-haves and might-have-

See if you can find, as Baudelaire did, "the religious intoxication of great cities."

beens and never-will-bes that clog and clutter our mind and numb us. We can interrupt that boring tape by looking, listening, noticing, learning from people, places, faces, all around us.

Baudelaire loved to walk the streets of Paris, and he urged artists to paint urban landscapes, reminding them, "The life of our city is rich in poetic and marvelous subjects. We are enveloped and steeped as though in an atmosphere of the marvelous, but we do not notice it." (There's the tip to notice again.) We complain so much about cities now that we hurry through them without paying attention, averting our eyes, keeping our heads down, longing for some pastoral vista and losing the richness of what's around us.

Woods and fields and lakes are not the only places of inspiration. Reverend Cecil Williams, the magnetic minister of San Francisco's Glide Memorial Church, which welcomes people of all faiths, backgrounds, races, and nationalities, preaches that God is in the sidewalks, the crowds, the nitty-gritty of the city. On Easter he leads the children on an urban Easter egg hunt to show that it is even more miraculous to find such prizes on the pavement instead of in the grass.

Take another look at the streets and sidewalks you see every day on the way to and from work. Hunt for your own miracles. See if you can find, as Baudelaire did, "the religious intoxication of great cities."

RETURNING TO THE FORM

Some people do a class in aerobics on their lunch hour. Some are lucky enough to have a yoga or t'ai chi class near where they work. If you don't have such a class available to you at lunch hour, be sure to do one after work at least one evening a week. It can transform many aspects of your life. The benefits go far beyond the hour or so you are actually in the class.

Just as there are destructive habits like smoking and drinking on a regular basis, there are also healthy habits, routines that refresh us.

The segments of our lives should flow together, rather than remain compartmentalized. Yoga and t'ai chi have the power to flow into your behavior in all areas of your life and work, giving you ways to move, and be, and even create, in the form and rhythm of these powerful disciplines.

After work, if you don't have a class in aerobics, t'ai chi, or yoga, try a half hour of exercise on a stationary bike or rowing machine, or just go jogging, walking, or bicycling for that length of time, and then take a long shower. Doing this is not tiring but enlivening, and it gets to be a habit that you miss if you do without it. This purpose can be served in many ways—dance classes, or any of the varieties of body awareness methods, like Feldenkrais or the Alexander Technique.

ADDICTED TO HEALTH

Just as there are destructive habits like smoking and drinking on a regular basis, there are also healthy habits, routines that refresh us. I have seen a new kind of criticism lately, people putting down Twelve Step programs because they are "addictive," only replacing one habit with another, and that physical exercise does the same thing, creating addictions to running, jogging, or bicycling. This criticism is made as if there is no difference between getting drunk or riding a bicycle. What madness! I am grateful for my healthy habits. I am happy and proud to be so addicted to riding my stationary bike every day for a half hour that if I don't do it I feel stale, grubby, and cranky. I am trying now to get addicted to doing a yoga routine every day too, instead of just during the once-a-week class I attend. Bring on such addictions! They are the way of discipline, the way of the creative warrior seeking the fullness of life.

Pay attention to the senses. When we're not numbing them with tobacco and alcohol, we are free to use them for our enjoyment and to expand our own creativity.

7. The Evening Meal

Use your nose, your sense of smell. Different scents evoke entire eras, scenes, events, people in our lives.

Don't forget the sense of taste. At least one night a week take the time to create your own meal from natural food instead of the frozen or canned stuff. At a hardware store, for a dollar or so you can get a metal steamer to put at the bottom of a pan. Put in an inch or so of water, put the collapsible metal steamer over it, put raw vegetables on it, and steam them. If you're like me, you may have never known the real taste of vegetables until you've steamed them. You can steam carrots, beets, corn on the cob, broccoli, and bring out the true flavor. Don't drown them in sauce, just experience the natural taste. It may be a revelation!

Another way to increase your sense of taste and appreciation of food is to participate in a Silent Meal. Invite a friend or friends. Play music in the background, but agree not to talk during the meal. You will have an opportunity to concentrate on the food, to really taste it, perhaps for the first time. I have taken part in Silent Meals that are held once a week at the Rancho La Puerta health spa. Each time is a relaxing, restoring experience, a time of fellowship with the other people gathered in silence at such a meal, a whole other dimension of community and communion.

TASTE, TOUCH, SMELL

Taste for inspiration and ideas. We think of playing music for inspiration, but we often forget that Proust got the inspiration for his great work, *Remembrance of Things Past*, by eating a madeleine—a cookie—that brought back to him the memories of childhood, the very taste of what it was like. (Bring back your own childhood sometime by tasting tapioca!)

Use your nose, your sense of smell. Different scents evoke entire eras, scenes, events, people in our lives. See what memories the following smells evoke for you: wood smoke, bacon frying, Vicks salve, coffee boiling, patchouli perfume, lemons, wet grass, motor oil, the sea. There are stories in the memory of each aroma.

Try using scents for inspiration. Here's how a woman who took my workshop in Austin, Texas, used scent to evoke a childhood taste that inspired creativity. Patricia Speier wrote:

> Being in my grandmother Speier's kitchen was a spiritual experience. I say spiritual because I felt safe and connected in that place, and I also felt the glow of anticipation and the hope of magic there. Magic sometimes came in the form of cupcakes, iced with vanilla buttercream frosting. About a year ago I casually picked up a vanilla-scented votive candle while shopping. Immediately I was transported back to my grandmother's kitchen; I could absolutely taste those cupcakes. Now I buy those candles by the dozen. I have one in my bathroom that I light first thing in the morning. Lighting that candle each morning is a prayer. I bask in its delicious aroma while I shower and dress. I keep another candle in my study next to the computer. I don't light it every time I turn the computer on, but only when the work I am doing calls for communion with the muse. Lighting a vanilla votive ensures the presence of the creative spirit, even if it does not ensure a quality product.

Burning incense when you meditate provides refreshment. A writer I heard about brings in a pot of fresh soil from her garden every day and puts it by her desk to inhale the scent while she works, making her mind feel awakened and inspired. Balzac used to keep a rotting orange by his desk to smell for freeing his imagination.

See what the thought of touching these things brings to mind: a wool blanket, a cashmere sweater, tree bark, silk, autumn leaves, a baseball glove, corduroy, leather, a shell, a stone. Keep a stone by your desk for a while, and when you're stuck, pick it up and rub it. Maybe an idea will come out.

"Texture can be very evocative," Judy Collins said in an interview with Bonnie Allen for *Ms.* magazine.

It's like the madeleines that Proust speaks of—you taste something and it sets off a whole series of images. Color, fabric, scent, texture, the sight of something . . . they each can set up a whole series of creative thoughts for me. So they're part of the way I'm stimulated to write my music. They're all very much connected.

As well as using your senses, use your heart. Connect with other people. At least one night a week do something that makes you part of a community. It's part of being human. It's part of being creative. What communities can you become a part of and be expanded and enlivened by? How can you make a contribution to other people, to your own community?

Remember the wisdom Albert Schweitzer passed on to a graduating class of medical students: "I don't know what your destiny will be, but one thing I know, the only ones among you who will be really happy are those who have sought and found how to serve."

8. A Time to Create

In the busy schedule that most of us must keep, one of the most difficult disciplines is to find time for our creative work. Some brave souls get up early in the morning to write, paint, draw, compose, or play music for an hour. When I was writing articles for *Esquire* back in the early '60s, I wondered how Gay Talese was able to turn out so many superb pieces for the magazine while he held a full-time job at the *New York Times*. I was a full-time freelancer, able to use my time as I chose, but he had to report for work every day at nine o'clock in the morning. When I asked him what his secret was, he said, "I get up at four-thirty in the morning."

I want to make clear that I never got up at four-thirty in the morning to go to work, but I know it's humanly possible because Talese did it—until he had his first best-seller and was able to leave his reporting job at the *Times*. If we want to do something badly enough, we can always find a way.

The way to become a knight is to act like a knight.

Richard Blanco, a poet in the graduate writing program at Florida University, goes off by himself on his lunch hour from his full-time city engineering job and works on his poetry. His fellow workers know and respect what he's doing and support his efforts and his need to be by himself at that time.

During the time of my first job after college as a reporter for a weekly newspaper, I would go back to my room at a local rooming house and work at night and on weekends, hammering away at the fiction it would take nearly another decade to publish, but which gave me experience, practice, and the knowledge that I was writing, and, thus, a writer.

The way to become a knight is to act like a knight, the legendary professor Mark van Doren told his students at Columbia when he lectured on Cervantes's *Don Quixote*. By the same token, the way to be a writer is to write; to be a painter you must paint. And the biggest problem for many people is to find the time.

The standard wisdom is that you have to do your artistic work every day. Certainly that is ideal. Getting into a rhythm, a routine, by doing the same creative process every day is tremendously powerful and works for many kinds of disciplines. Explaining his process for creating the nightly monologue on *The Tonight Show*, Jay Leno told an interviewer for *Entertainment Weekly*, "It's a 24-hour thing. If I think of something, I'll make a note. And then when I go home I put them on cards. It's like lifting weights. You've got to do it every day."

CREATORS TALKING

"If you smoked reefer when you were writing, it seemed like all your ideas were brilliant. But when I read what I'd written with that, it's so bad—even the typing is bad. It's like when you're on a trip with acid—you get the façade of brilliance—but if you're doing it a lot, you don't even remember the brilliance was only a façade."

—JILL NELSON, JOURNALIST, AUTHOR OF *VOLUNTEER SLAVERY*

Not everyone has the freedom to work in his or her chosen creative field every day, however; but that doesn't have to stop anyone. If you can't do it every day, do it when you can. Do it on weekends, do it on vacations, do it on "sick days," on slow days at work, and on holidays. Stay up all night to do it, or get up before dawn to do it. Fight for the time, and take what you can make.

Many people find a way to produce their art and hold down a full-time job, and/or raise children. The late Kay Boyle was a distinguished and highly productive novelist, short-story writer, and journalist who raised five children and, during the time I knew her in the 1950s, taught school full-time. One of Kay's daughters, the painter Clover Vail, works by day in a legal office and paints at night and on weekends. (It's not a matter of genes, but of commitment.) The flamboyant novelist Harry Crews taught himself to write by churning out "practice" novels while he served in the Marine Corps. Malcolm X and Eldridge Cleaver wrote in prison. Today at Sing Sing prison I know men who are creating fine art, in painting and writing, in circumstances and atmosphere hardly conducive to creativity. Yet they create. They not only survive, they create.

You can too.

Commitment is the key. If you're not clear about what that is, or what it means to be committed, here is the best explanation I know, written by W. H. Murray, author of *The Scottish Himalayan Expedition*:

> Until one is committed there is hesitancy, the chance to draw back, always ineffectiveness. Concerning all acts of initiative (and creation), there is one elementary truth, the ignorance of which kills countless ideas and splendid plans; that the moment one definitely commits oneself, then Providence moves too. All sorts of things occur to help one that would never otherwise have occurred. A whole stream of events issues from the decision, raising in one's favor all manner of unforeseen incidents and meetings and material assistance, which no man could have dreamt would have come his way.

I have learned a deep respect for one of Goethe's couplets: "Whatever you can do, or dream you can, begin it; / Boldness has genius, power, and magic in it."

FIND YOUR PRACTICE

Try to find a meditation practice that suits you, and make it a part of your routine. Find a place to sit and meditate. Think about the natural world. Think about what Einstein meant when he wrote:

> My religion consists of a humble admiration of the illimitable superior spirit who reveals himself in the slightest details we are able to perceive with our frail and feeble minds. That deeply emotional conviction of the presence of a superior reasoning power which is revealed in the incomprehensible universe forms my idea of God.

Meditate after reading this passage from the Book of Job (12:7–10):

But ask the beasts, and they will teach you;
the birds of the air, and they will tell you;
or the plants of the earth, and they will teach you;
and the fish of the sea will declare to you.
Who among all these does not know
that the hand of the Lord has done this?
In his hand is the life of every living thing
and the breath of all humankind.

9. Going to Bed

Before you go to bed, put a notebook and pencil beside you in case you wake with dreams or thoughts you want to write down. Read Edmund Wilson's book *Night Thoughts* to see how creative he was with these middle-of-the-night ideas. Read some books on dreams and dream work to enable you to remember your dreams and use them creatively in your life and art. (Notice in the interviews with creators how many

people use dreams, and how they incorpo-
rate them into their creative work.)
Remember a line from Baudelaire: "Sleep
is full of miracles." He noted in his journal
that "one must desire to dream and know
how to dream. The evocation of inspiration. A magic art."

Before you go to bed, put a notebook and pencil beside you in case you wake with dreams or thoughts you want to write down.

Give thanks for being part of creation,
for being blessed with the animating or
vital spirit that enables you to create. Read something you find
empowering, affirming, and wise. Remind yourself you belong here,
on this planet, and that your own role here is as important to the people you touch in your own daily life as is the president's, or any Nobel
Prize winner's. It's especially important to remind ourselves of our
worth when things are not going smoothly, when our plans seem to
run up against brick walls, when our messages don't seem to penetrate.

When Cardinal John Henry Newman left the Anglican Church at
the height of his influence to become a Roman Catholic, he was subjected to scorn and rejection. He lost old friends and was thrown in
with strangers who suspected his motives. In this dark time he wrote
to himself a message that I find strength in myself. Most of us, at some
time or other, need and can find comfort in this powerful affirmation:

> God has created me, to do Him some definite service; he
> has committed some work to me which He has not com-
> mitted to another. I have my mission—I may never know it
> in this life, but I shall be told it in the next. I am a link in a
> chain, a bond of connection between persons. He has not
> created me for nothing. I shall do good. I shall do His work.
> Therefore I will trust Him. Whatever, wherever I am. I can-
> not be thrown away.

9

New Models: Creators of the Spirit

I WAS INTO MY THIRD BLOODY MARY WHEN THE WRITER HOSTING THAT SUNDAY afternoon soiree said I was mistaken, Dostoyevsky was not an alcoholic—in fact, he hadn't even been a big drinker. The shock and disillusionment must have showed on my face, for everyone burst out laughing. One of my other writer friends pointed at me and said through his cackling laugh, "You're mad that Dostoyevsky wasn't a rummy!"

It was probably twenty-five years ago, but I can see that room now, as I can taste the thickish film of tomato juice on my tongue and feel the vodka at the roof of my head. It seemed like a silvery substance up there, like mercury, coating the very inside top of my cranium and causing a slight ringing sound that would grow more piercing as the day wore on. It would combine with the white bright light of the winter afternoon to create a headache of killer intensity, but still I drank on, even though I didn't even like Bloody Marys. I took whatever alcohol was offered in whatever form or concoction, and once I started, I would no more imagine stopping than ripping off my clothes and jumping into a snowbank. Are you kidding? Don't even offer me coffee, it cuts the high, stops the iron-locomotive progress of the booze fueling me along like a runaway train until I crash into bed and oblivion.

I was lucky to survive. Too many writers, some of them friends of mine, crashed right into their graves while riding the booze train. Instead of burying any more artists and writers, let's bury the myth that booze is a muse, that alcohol and drugs are a spur to creativity. The path to creativity begins with clarity, which means clearing the mind and body of substances that numb the senses and cloud perception.

The old model of creativity was booze, drugs, and deterioration of the work as well as the physical and mental condition of the creator, leading to early death, as with Dylan Thomas (thirty-nine) and F. Scott Fitzgerald (forty-four), or somewhat extended life with self-inflicted injuries and abuse of the body leading to hospitalizations, as with Faulkner, or mental aberration and suicide, as with Hemingway. The myth was propagated that illness and early death were not only glamorous, exciting, and noble, but necessary for the act of creation itself, like a sacrifice to the gods, trading health and sanity for art and literature.

The new model of creating from the spirit replaces numbing with enlivening, by replacing drugs and alcohol with clarity, by using all the techniques that bring us into that state. A process of emptying, filling, and creating enables us to tap into our spiritual resources, our deepest selves, for inspiration and sustenance. The clarity prized by recent creators who recovered from drugs and alcohol and wrote about it, like Raymond Carver, and those who never bought into the old model, like Toni Morrison, supports and validates the new model of creativity.

As I explored the subject for this book and became aware of the myth that creativity was restricted to the arts, I saw that I could learn from teachers and practitioners in many different fields. The old idea that people in the arts are the only creators is a good example of a restrictive myth, one that limits possibilities. Getting rid of such myths gives a liberating feeling, opening doors and entire vistas that weren't visible before. That's been part of the fun of "living into" the new model of creativity based on clarity. (By "living into" I mean aspiring toward, having your actions be consistent with your goal—a concept and term I learned from Landmark Education courses.)

Being T'ai Chi

Some of the new mentors I found inspiring in the way they create their lives and work were in the new fields I was starting to explore, like t'ai chi.

I was lucky to have as a teacher David Zucker, who really embodies t'ai chi. In the way he moves and holds himself, in the clear, low-key manner in which he speaks, David seems to exemplify the concept of centeredness. There's a feeling that if you pushed him down, he would simply bounce back up to his original position without any effort, by means of some internal balance. As well as teaching t'ai chi, David is a creator in theater, an actor, mime, and director, and his centeredness is integrated in his work.

I asked him once to tell me how a man who grew up a Catholic in Chester, Massachusetts, became a teacher of t'ai chi as well as a sixth-degree black belt master of the Zen martial art of swordsmanship called Shim Gum Do.

"In the late '60s and early '70s," he said, "I got interested in spirituality through Zen and Taoism. I used to haunt the bookstores for books on those subjects. I saw this book on something called t'ai chi, which I'd never heard of before. It said it was 'meditation in motion,' and since I was a very active person—I began doing mime and acting in college at UMass/Amherst, then got an MFA in theater at Brandeis—it seemed right up my alley."

He bought the book on t'ai chi, found a Chinese master of the art in Cambridge, studied for several years, and began to teach it to his friends, then to classes at the Boston Center for Adult Education.

"Before I got into t'ai chi," David told me, "I did a lot of drugs, a lot of marijuana. I'm totally antidrug now. There's a very big difference in my lifestyle since I started t'ai chi, but it was a gradual change. I don't know how much to attribute directly to t'ai chi, to Zen, or to Christianity. It was all a kind of a turn to God."

T'ai chi has been called a form of self-defense, yet in studying it I never had the sense I was learning anything that might fend off a mugger. There are no kicks or yells or punches involved in the graceful movements of the form. I asked David how it could be used in self-defense.

"In t'ai chi, you learn to confront in a positive way," he explained.

> You dance with the other person, you turn it into a dance. Since I started doing t'ai chi, I've never been in a fight in which I've had to physically defend myself, but I've been in plenty of situations where I could have been killed if I hadn't reacted spontaneously and immediately—like car accidents that were avoided when I saw headlights coming at me down the other side of the street and reacted instinctively. T'ai chi becomes an art you use daily, rather than waiting for the one moment of your life when you use it in self-defense. I tell people it's a waste of their money if they're learning it for self-defense because they'll maybe use it once in their life or maybe never use it—but in fact that's the highest form of self-defense, if you never have to use it.

David tries to do his t'ai chi at least a half hour every day, but he says,

> In a sense I'm always practicing, because even when I'm not doing the actual choreographed form itself, any movement I do can be t'ai chi. If I'm in the kitchen and I reach for the cupboard, I try to open the cupboard with my whole body. In t'ai chi, you unify your body from the soles of your feet to the top of your head, you try to move as one unit. I can do that walking down the street—I still slip on the ice but I don't fall down anymore, because I've learned to keep my weight low. Anything I do all day is a dance of a sort because my body is moving around.

I recommended t'ai chi to my minister, Carl Scovel, and he took a class at a time when David didn't teach, and was not altogether satisfied with the experience. I urged him to take it with David so he would see the real thing, and the next year he did, and thanked me. Some time after that Carl gave a sermon in which he talked about the distinction between teaching and being. To illustrate his point, he used the difference in taking a t'ai chi class with his first teacher, and then with David Zucker. The first teacher, Carl said, was a good man, completely competent, who taught t'ai chi in a clear, able manner. The difference between the class with him and the class with David, Carl explained, was that "The first man teaches t'ai chi; David is t'ai chi."

A Writer's "Palpable God"

In a similar way I came to admire the novelist Reynolds Price, who not only writes precisely and eloquently, in essays as well as fiction, about his faith as a Christian, he is that faith. I first knew Price's work as a talented writer of fiction from his first novel, *A Long and Happy Life,* a kind of tour de force that was printed in its entirety in *Harper's* magazine when it came out in 1962. I admired it, but I hadn't followed Price's later work, so I was surprised and intrigued when Carl Scovel (my minister, pointing yet again to the right clue) loaned me a book by Price he thought I'd enjoy, called *A Palpable God.*

The book begins with a long essay, "The Bible as Narrative," which tells how Price came to a crisis in his faith and his work. To address it, he wrote literal translations from the Greek of Old and New Testament stories of the Hebrew-Christian Bible. These compose the rest of the book. I had not known Price was a practicing Christian, and I was impressed with the passion and strength of his faith, its central place in his life and work. I began to read the rest of his novels. I found

CREATORS TALKING

"In my own work, I'm always torn. Do I want to be a real artist, or do I just want to entertain? Do I want to go for developing a story psychologically, or just get a really good laugh out of the reader? I hope I end up doing both."

—DAN LICARDO, SHORT-STORY WRITER

in them an underlying theme of humans engaged in the quest for meaning and understanding, grappling with God and the Christian faith they were born into in the American South. These are not overtly religious novels; yet religion is a part of them, as it is a natural part of the daily lives of the characters, even though they may not even be churchgoing people, even though they may feel, as character Kate Vaiden does, that faith is not easy, that sometimes in trying to pray and be in touch with God she feels "like Helen Keller in a barrel."

I was shocked and dismayed to learn from a newspaper story that Price was stricken in 1984 with "an astrocytoma in his spinal cord" that resulted in paraplegia, and that he was confined to a wheelchair for the rest of his life. The disease struck him while he was in the middle of writing the novel *Kate Vaiden,* one of his most ambitious and accomplished works (it would win the National Book Critics Circle Award for fiction). He not only finished the book, he made the occasion of what others (like me) would have taken as a tragedy to be a blessing. The publisher's description of his career for his 1987 book of essays, *A Common Room,* reports that as a result of his physical incapacity, "The new access of time and energy has enabled him to complete two novels [*Kate Vaiden,* followed by *Good Hearts*], a collection of essays, and a trilogy of plays called *New Music.* He continues teaching at Duke."

I wanted to meet such a man. I had given my workshop in Spiritual Autobiography to the Cowley Fathers in Cambridge, and I offered to give it at their retreat house in Durham, North Carolina, where Reynolds Price was living, in hopes of getting to meet and talk with him. I had that privilege in October of 1989.

I wrote to Price and asked to meet him for dinner. He suggested a local Mexican restaurant, where he was driven by an assistant, a graduate student, in his specially equipped van with a ramp for his wheelchair. Price had written that he was born in Macon, North Carolina, "a village edged by cotton and tobacco fields but split down the middle by the Seaboard Railway," in 1933. That was the year after I was born; yet he seemed not only much wiser in understanding and intellect, but at the same time as youthful in spirit (evidenced by a genuine enthusiasm for life and work) as any person I know, of any age. His main preoccupation and enthusiasm that evening was that his trilogy of plays was going to be put on the following week at a theater in Cleveland, and he was looking forward to going there to see the production. It was clear that his physical limitations would not prevent him from carrying out any aspect of his work.

He continues to use what others would call his handicap as an opportunity to create. To try to relieve some of the pain produced by his condition so he could sit and write for longer periods, Price went to a hypnotist. During the sessions he not only eased the pain in his back but found that the hypnotic trances brought memories of early childhood that had never been accessible to him before. When the hypnotic therapy was successfully completed, Price asked the hypnotist if he could work with him using the same technique to bring back other early memories. The hypnotist agreed, and out of those trance-induced memories, he recovered from his past the material for a brilliant autobiographical memoir, *Clear Pictures*. Since then, Price has completed two more highly praised novels, *The Tongues of Angels* and *Blue Calhoun*, as well as a uniquely powerful personal account of his experience with cancer, *A Whole New Life: An Illness and a Healing*. He continues to work and produce at the highest level, at the peak of his artistic powers. Reynolds Price is a heroic example of one whose body-spirit, even in crisis and physical restriction, has led to creative fulfillment and triumph. Price embodies his religious faith, acts it in his life and work, and when he writes about it, as he does in his essay "At the Heart," his words carry the weight and ring of earned authority:

> The most difficult and constant of our struggles is with ourselves, with our predictable but always surprising tendency to choose the wasteful course, our busy devastation of other creatures and of the planet itself, a succession of errors that blinds us to the rare glimpses God permits of his moving hand. When those choices have led us into

harrowing dark nights of the soul, and he and our fellows seem absent or unwilling to help, then the next likely cry—parched and blameful—is "Abandonment! No just God could treat me thus."

But as the mystics of many creeds assert, God does not entirely abandon us. He does however take us seriously; even more terrifying, he loves us and craves our love. A great part of what we call evil is not the result of divine sadism or fickle disappearance but of the reverse.

We steadily flee a creator who can tend both the slow wheel of the galaxies and our own feverish escape while he awaits our return. For his own purpose as he waits, he may hide behind all but impenetrable screens—holocausts, individual agonized lifetimes—but the merciful intent of his hand is eventually discernible by any patient witness.

And the tale he is choosing to tell himself and all creation will not finish but will amend and augment itself, blossoming ever more grandly like the radiant choruses of Mozart's *Magic Flute*, swelling to transform a world of farce, trial, pain—unfolding with unimaginable and individually appropriate rewards for each worthy creature (perhaps for all human creatures if each—as seems increasingly possible—was bought by the sacrifice of his only son), a goal of unbroken justice and joy for all creatures known to God by name.

Toni Morrison's Monument

Whether his theology is yours, all people of spirit can find in Reynolds Price's life and work a nobility of faith as well as achievement, a large and courageous vision of a quality and scope I have witnessed in other writers working now as well. I heard it in the voice and message of Toni Morrison when she came to receive the Melcher Book Award, given annually by the Unitarian Universalist Association for the book that "most advances the cause of liberal religion." I served on that committee when, for the first time in the history of the award, it was given for a work of fiction, Morrison's novel *Beloved*. I had until the judging avoided reading the book, thinking I already knew about slavery, or knew enough, and didn't see the point in being further depressed by hearing another dramatization of its evils. But when I read the novel—with increasing fascination and compulsion to finish—I realized I had essentially known nothing at all of slavery, certainly never had plumbed the depths of its dehumanizing horrors and blasphemy of soul until I was compelled to do so by the genius and compassion of the novelist.

After our committee announced its award in the spring of 1988, we learned that *Beloved* had won the Pulitzer Prize. We worried that the growing and well-deserved success of the book and increasing fame of its author would make it unlikely that she would come to Cambridge that fall to receive our own less-prestigious award.

Toni Morrison did come, though, explaining at a reception in her honor that she wanted to acknowledge the Melcher Book Award in person because it was especially important to her that the novel was recognized for its religious value. She spoke to an overflow crowd at the Unitarian Church in Harvard Square (two hundred others were turned away), telling with brief, sure, eloquent delivery that it wasn't until she had finished a book that she really knew the reason she had written it. When she finished *Beloved* she realized she had written it as a "monument" to the slaves. There are many monuments in this country, she

---

CREATORS TALKING

"A lot of scientists wouldn't agree with me about the creative aspect of science. They think it's a lot of facts—but Einstein felt it was mostly intuition. It is—you're faced with so many bits of information, and you have to decide which is important. You have to extract out of the data, and it takes intuition to see what's in it. After you get the answer, *then* you work on proving it. You create in your mind—I believe these things exist and I have to make an order out of it. Create an order."

—DR. LOUISE EVANS, BIOLOGIST, AUTHOR OF
NEOTROPICAL RAIN FOREST MAMMALS: A FIELD GUIDE

said; monuments to generals, to soldiers and sailors, to presidents and captains of industry. There are monuments to people who freed the slaves, but there are no monuments to the slaves. "Not even a bench," she said, "on the Mississippi River."

And so she dedicated her book to the sixty million people who died as a direct result of slavery.

Now there is a monument to their memory, a monument that may finally be more lasting and memorable than the monument to the presidents carved out of Mount Rushmore.

Ms. Morrison took questions from the eager, admiring audience, answered them succinctly and gracefully and with the dignity and command of moral as well as literary vision. Yes, it was hard to write the book, she said; it was sometimes very painful, and sometimes she wanted to stop. At those times she heard the voices of her ancestors saying, "You think what you are doing is hard? Putting words on paper? Think what we did!"

And she would take up her work again, and continue. She explained that she had to set for herself the highest standards because she was writing this for her ancestors. Knowing that, she said, she could not write "junk." "They are not interested in junk," she said, with withering contempt for the shabby, the sloppy, the less than first rate.

Hearing Toni Morrison that night was one of those experiences that made me proud of being a writer. I called my friend Marcie Hershman, who was struggling to write her own "monument" to ancestors who had died in the Holocaust, to tell her about the evening. Marcie had returned from a trip to Germany with her brother Rob, which had wakened something in her, stories of people who lived their daily lives during the Holocaust. Marcie had completed one of the stories, which was published in the magazine *Tikkun,* and she had continued to write other stories set in the same fictional town of that era; and yet it was a struggle. It was difficult and painful to recreate in her imagination that time of destruction to people of her own family. She had even been tempted to stop, to put the whole project away, give it up. I told her what Toni Morrison said about how hard it was to write

Beloved, and how she heard the voices of her own ancestors saying to go on, to remember how much harder it had been for them, and that her book was a monument to them. Marcie said she knew exactly what was meant, and it was helpful to hear Morrison's experience. Marcie did continue and finished her powerful novel, *Tales of the Master Race.*

Passing on Morrison's words to Marcie was not the one crucial factor that enabled her to complete her own monument, forge her own moral vision in fiction, but it helped; it was one of the many messages of meaning and encouragement and courage, and I felt honored to serve as the conduit. I was reminded of the idea of spirit moving from one place to another, through the work of writers like Morrison, who are its purveyors, who reach beyond what seems possible and bring it, a kind of moral lightning, down to us.

From Death to Healing

Another book born out of personal pain transformed into a moral vision of meaning to people of all faiths, or no religious belief at all, is *When Bad Things Happen to Good People.* I first read the book when I was part of a small prayer group that met once a week at King's Chapel. We took turns sharing with one another poems or psalms or passages from the Bible or books we were reading that we found insightful and helpful in our lives. A young man whose father and brother had both died in the same year read to us from this book and spoke about how its understanding of personal tragedy had helped him in dealing with his loss. It was shortly after that I met the author, Rabbi Kushner.

In his book *To Life!* Harold Kushner again writes out of his personal struggle to understand and live by a religious vision. He explains,

> When my wife and I learned that our three-year-old son had an incurable illness that would cause him to die young, I could not accept the notion that God wanted this bright, innocent child to suffer and die. But I could believe that, in the face of genetic misfortune, God could give us the

strength to cope, to survive and ultimately transcend the tragedy. Unable to keep my son from dying, God showed me how to redeem his death from being a statistic and forge it into a book that would bring healing to millions.

As often happens, creation was forged out of pain, the pain was transformed, and it transforms others. It was not the creation that caused the pain, but rather that turned it into something else, as in a process of alchemy—for creation is a kind of alchemy, not by heating and mixing of ores and metals, but using the even more precious lodes of spirit and imagination.

I started writing this book about new models of creation without an outline, without knowing who or what I would use to make a point I had not yet articulated even to myself. I decided to just plunge in. I didn't know I'd be writing about my old t'ai chi teacher, followed by two Christians and a Jew, or two novelists and a rabbi, or three writers with religious themes. I only went for whom and what I admired and had moved me personally. Now I see something else these people have in common as well as their creativity and spiritual attunement— their moral vision of the universe. The writers, like the t'ai chi teacher, are all people who strike you at once as deeply centered, people whose bodyspirit conveys a confidence, not of egotism but of vision, and whose voices also convey a power, a strength, not of volume but of clarity. In their person as well as their work they portray conviction, balance, wholeness, awareness, and a sense that their life and art and spirit are fully integrated, are one.

All have known their own dark night of the soul and easily could have remained in darkness or emerged broken or resentful or both, but all have come back from it bearing meaning and story, not only for themselves but for others. That is the work of the spirit and how it moves, guiding us—in the Navajo phrase—"on the gleaming way." That is the way of creation.

> *As often happens, creation was forged out of pain, the pain was transformed, and it transforms others.*

Let a Joy Keep You

We needn't search for suffering to inspire us or seek pain to prod us into poetry. As M. Scott Peck said in the opening sentence of *The Road Less Traveled,* which struck a chord of recognition in millions, "Life is difficult." Our measure of suffering and pain will find us; we needn't glorify it, wallow in it, or sink beneath it; rather, we have the choice of creating ways to deal with it, to transform it.

Creation not only can transform pain and bring joy, it also is born of joy, like the story I wrote in New Hampshire that autumn afternoon from a feeling of fullness and gratitude, of delight in being alive in that time and place and all the times and places before, the splendor of all that life pouring through me. Joy is the essence of John Cheever's last novel, written while he was finally living and writing sober, just as Raymond Carver celebrated the joy in his decade of living and writing sober in his poem "Gravy."

We can't all transform our pain into works of art, but we can find joy in our own expressions—writing, painting, sculpture, dance, music, and more. Beyond the traditional creative arts are millions of different creative possibilities every day: in the work people talk about in these pages, from cooking a meal to designing a building, from answering an office telephone to giving a massage; in sports, sales, teaching, and science, any field offers a chance for creation. So do the materials around us, the stuff of daily life.

I remember a King's Chapel church retreat called Zen and the Art of Bread Baking, led by Sue Spenser, who left lawyering to become a minister and served for several years as our seminarian. She had the idea for this retreat, and got us all to participate in pounding the dough that we would bake into rolls and bread for breakfast. There was joy in sinking my fingers into that dough, kneading it and shaping it, "being with" the feel of the stuff, the raw material I knew would rise and transform to bread. I reveled in the wonderful gooey play of it, the fun of whapping it around as others were laughing and doing the same

Creation not only can transform pain and bring joy, it also is born of joy.

with their own dough, a general joyousness in the big camp dining hall, bringing back memories to all of us. Scenes returned to me of long-forgotten taffy pulling, followed by other delights of home creation: my mother canning tomatoes for winter in the steam of our kitchen, my father and mother and I making our own

Whether it is lighting a candle over oatmeal at breakfast or staying up all night to write a story or a song, creating transforms our lives and the lives of others.

root beer, which we proudly poured into bottles we capped ourselves, which later exploded in the basement, making us think for a moment we were under attack, and then exploding with our own laughter.

The sudden joy of that laughter dispelling the sometimes sadness of our small white green-roofed house with all the passions contained within evokes a line of Carl Sandburg I loved as a boy, words accompanied in memory with the goose-bump wonder and mystery of the *New World Symphony* that called up a love of the land I was born in and love of friends and family past and present, an exhortation and blessing, all summoned by the memory of making bread, that simple act of creation: "Let a joy keep you."

Being Part of the Flow

The whole earth lies around us and a universe spins in our heads, all available to use for our own creation, moment by moment, day by day. Whether it is lighting a candle over oatmeal at breakfast or staying up all night to write a story or a song, creating transforms our lives and the lives of others. We ignore its power and accessibility at the price of joy, of life itself.

Living free of the myths of creativity does not answer all questions or solve all problems, nor does the clarity that is part of creating from the spirit ease all pain. In fact, clarity sometimes makes us feel pain that we once numbed with quick fixes of booze and drugs, but that pain is usually a warning, a message whose disregard may lead to more serious, deeper trouble. With clarity we feel more of everything, including the natural joy to which we are also heirs.

In shedding the myths of creativity, in "living into" creating from the spirit, I, of course, still blunder and stumble, experience the doubts and self-delusions of the human condition. But I have never felt more free. I feel part of a larger flow that is not just of my own creating, but a flow I've helped create my opportunity to be in. This feeling comes through my workshops, which feed and inspire me, and passes on into my writing, as in this book. The chance to be of use, to share my experience in community with people through speaking and writing words, is not only privilege but deep pleasure. I feel and enjoy it more fully now than I ever have in my life.

Not long ago I had a dream in which I was standing by the ocean, talking with people wiser than I—they were some kind of sages—who asked me what I wanted, how I wanted the rest of my life to be.

"I want to be a wave," I said.

When I woke, I knew what I had meant—that I wanted to be part of something larger than my petty self, something of service to others, to all. It meant not to simply create for my own ends, my own ego, but to do so in a way that was part of creation itself, as a genuine "co-creator" with the spirit—the life force, God, whatever name one uses. George Bernard Shaw expressed this sentiment in a way that I'd endorse as the highest goal of creating from the spirit:

> This is the true joy of life, the being used for a purpose recognized by yourself as a mighty one; the being a force of nature instead of a feverish selfish little clod of ailment and grievance complaining that the world will not devote itself to making you happy. I am of the opinion that my life belongs to the whole community and as long as I live it is my privilege to do for it what I can. I want to be used up when I die, for the harder I work the more I live, and I rejoice in life for its own sake. Life is no "brief candle" to me. It is a sort of splendid torch which I have got hold of for the moment, and I want to make it burn as brightly as possible before passing it on to future generations.

I add my own "Amen."

Credits

GRATEFUL ACKNOWLEDGMENT IS MADE TO THE FOLLOWING FOR PERMISSION to reprint previously published material:

Addison-Wesley Publishing Company, Inc.: Excerpts from *Minding the Body, Mending the Mind* by Joan Borysenko. Copyright © 1987 by Joan Borysenko, Ph.D.

The Boston Globe: Excerpt from "Jordan Stepped into Another Dimension—The Highlight Zone" by Michael Madden.

Cornell University Press: Excerpts from *Louis Agassiz as Teacher* by Lane Cooper.

Cowley Publications: Excerpts from *A New Christian Yoga* by Nancy Roth. Reprinted by permission of Cowley Publications, 28 Temple Place, Boston, MA 02111.

Constance H. Gernson: Excerpt from "On a Swim to Find Serenity" by Constance H. Gemson, *New York Newsday.*

Donadio & Ashworth, Inc.: Excerpt from "Tomatoes" by Laurie Colwin, *Gourmet Magazine,* August 1992. Copyright © 1992 by Laurie Colwin.

Grove/Atlantic, Inc.: "Gravy" from *A New Path to the Waterfall* by Raymond Carver. Copyright © 1989 by the Estate of Raymond Carver.

Index

Ford, Mary, 158
Forum, The, 76–77
Fox, Matthew, 130
Frankenheimer, John,
    190–191
free will, 11
freedom: from confusion,
    76; emptying and, 140;
    from myths, 130–131,
    219, 231–232;
    restriction and, 92–93
Freud, Sigmund, 23, 77, 185
friendship, 83–84
Frost, Robert, 84

G
Gablik, Suzi, 52
Gandhi, Mahatma, 43, 45
Gattuso, Joan, 78
Gemson, Constance H., 112
gender: inequality, 54, 61;
    myths about, 49–54;
    yoga and, 122
geography, 156–157
Glastonbury Abbey, 99, 100,
    101
Goethe, Johann Wolfgang
    von, 216
Going All the Way
    (Wakefield), 125, 158
Gold, Ivan, 47, 50, 155, 184
Gold, Vera, 57
graffiti, 127–128
Graham, Barbara, 33
Graham, Martha, 63
Greene, Graham, 63
group energy, 58–60
Grudin, Robert, 37, 112, 138
Gubaidulina, Sofia, 18
Guerrilla Girls, 52–53
guides. *see also* teachers:
    benefit of, 74;
    blind, 133; seeing
    through artists' eyes,
    179–186; self as,
    199–200
Guthrie, Arlo, 200

H
Hamill, Pete, 37, 82, 85–86
Hart, Mickey, 20
Hartley, Howard, 73
Hartley, Joe "The Fox," 179
Hawking, Stephen, 126–127
Hawthorne, Nathaniel, 35
healing, 28–29, 110–112, 130
health and medicine. *see
    also* addiction; alcohol

and drugs; healing;
    suicide: depression, 36;
    lifestyle changes, 10,
    210; meditation and,
    115; smoking, 203
Heard, Gerald, 5
Hebert, Michelle, 108
Hemingway, Ernest, 23, 41;
    in Paris, 204–205, 207;
    suicide of, 219; views
    on sexuality, 62
Henri, Robert, 10, 13–14, 35
Hepburn, Katharine, 63
Hershman, Marcie, 12, 208,
    227
Hiatt, Arnold, 11, 43–44, 98,
    177; quoted, 108
Hicks, Bill, 21
Hildegard of Bingen, 130
Hindu tradition, 116
Hines, Gerald D., 10
Holiday, Billie, 95
Hollywood, 40, 45, 72, 117,
    191; Wakefield's flight
    from, 125
Home Free (Wakefield), 62,
    159
homosexuality, 51–52
Horne, Lena, 63
human beings: clarity and,
    87; creativity and, 11,
    32, 140; spirit-
    endowed, 6
Hyde, Lewis, 30

I
incense, 212
inspiration: exercise for, 179–
    186; Grudin's view, 138
Iona (Scottish island),
    156–157
Irving, John, 43
Isherwood, Christopher, 157
isolation, 55–60, 77

J
Jackson, Phil, 97, 113, 202
James, Henry: discipline of,
    34; failure of, 17–19,
    191; influence of, 55,
    182; plays of, 16;
    "spirit" and, 30
James, William, 17, 23
James at 15 (TV series), 45,
    72
Jamison, Kay Redfield, 36
jazz musicians, 18–20
Jen, Gish, 11, 60, 83

Jerusalem, 156
Jesus, parables of, 89, 131,
    132
Joan of Arc, 43
Johns, Jasper, 52
Jones, Thom, 55
Jong, Erica, 37
Joplin, Janis, 13
Jordan, Michael, 135–136,
    206
journalism, 7–8
journals, 176–177, 183–185,
    186, 194–195, 205, 216;
    Collins's view, 7; Gold's
    view, 51
joy, 230–231
Joyce, James, 14, 190
Jung, Carl, 185

K
Kahlo, Frida, 52
Kafka, Franz, 134
Kerrigan, Nancy, 131
Kidder, Tracy, 55
King, Martin Luther, Jr., 43,
    45
King's Chapel (Boston), 73,
    94, 96, 228, 230
Kingsley, April, 9
Kripalu Center, 103–104
Kumin, Maxine, 38, 55, 60
Kushner, Harold, 11, 126;
    on Jewish dietary laws,
    92–93, 195; on prayer,
    148; quoted, 25, 155,
    228–229; on Torah, 140
Kushner, Tony, 51

L
LaBerge, Stephen, 185
Lahr, John, 21
Larkin, Philip, 18
Layton, Elizabeth, 63
Leavitt, David, 50
Lee, Li-Young, 173
Lehmann-Haupt,
    Christopher, 35–36
Leno, Jay, 214
Levi-Alvares, Danielle, 10,
    20, 190; Wakefield's
    experience with, 11
Lewis, Norma, 18
Licardo, Dan, 222
Lincoln, Abraham, 139
Lindo, Karen Monti,
    200–201
listening exercise, 162–165
Live Aid, 57

About SKYLIGHT PATHS Publishing

SkyLight Paths Publishing is creating a place where people of different spiritual traditions come together for challenge and inspiration, a place where we can help each other understand the mystery that lies at the heart of our existence.

Through spirituality, our religious beliefs are increasingly becoming a part of our lives—rather than *apart* from our lives. While many of us may be more interested than ever in spiritual growth, we may be less firmly planted in traditional religion. Yet, we do want to deepen our relationship to the sacred, to learn from our own as well as from other faith traditions, and to practice in new ways.

SkyLight Paths sees both believers and seekers as a community that increasingly transcends traditional boundaries of religion and denomination—people wanting to learn from each other, *walking together, finding the way.*

We at SkyLight Paths take great care to produce beautiful books that present meaningful spiritual content in a form that reflects the art of making high quality books. Therefore, we want to acknowledge those who contributed to the production of this book.

PRODUCTION
Tim Holtz & Bridgett Taylor

EDITORIAL
Amanda Dupuis, Martha McKinney,
Polly Short Mahoney & Emily Wichland

COVER DESIGN
Drena Fagen, New York, New York

TEXT DESIGN
Susan Ramundo, SR Desktop Services, Ridge, New York

PRINTING AND BINDING
Versa Press, East Peoria, Illinois

Spirituality

Who Is My God?
An Innovative Guide to Finding Your Spiritual Identity

Created by *the Editors at SkyLight Paths*

Spiritual Type™ + Tradition Indicator = Spiritual Identity

Your Spiritual Identity is an undeniable part of who you are—whether you've thought much about it or not. This dynamic resource provides a helpful framework to begin or deepen your spiritual growth. Start by taking the unique Spiritual Identity Self-Test™; tabulate your results; then explore one, two or more of twenty-eight faiths/spiritual paths followed in America today. "An innovative and entertaining way to think—and rethink—about your own spiritual path, or perhaps even to find one." —Dan Wakefield, author of *How Do We Know When It's God?*
6 x 9, 160 pp, Quality PB Original, ISBN 1-893361-08-X **$15.95**

Spiritual Manifestos: *Visions for Renewed Religious Life in America from Young Spiritual Leaders of Many Faiths*

Edited by *Niles Elliot Goldstein;* Preface by *Martin E. Marty*

Discover the reasons why so many people have kept organized religion at arm's length.

Here, ten young spiritual leaders, most in their mid-thirties, representing the spectrum of religious traditions—Protestant, Catholic, Jewish, Buddhist, Unitarian Universalist—present the innovative ways they are transforming our spiritual communities and our lives. "These ten articulate young spiritual leaders engender hope for the vitality of 21st-century religion." —Forrest Church, Minister of All Souls Church in New York City
6 x 9, 256 pp, HC, ISBN 1-893361-09-8 **$21.95**

Jewish Spirituality: *A Brief Introduction for Christians*

by *Lawrence Kushner*

Lawrence Kushner, whose award-winning books have brought Jewish spirituality to life for countless readers of all faiths and backgrounds, tailors his unique style to address Christian's questions, revealing the essence of Judaism in a way that people whose own tradition traces its roots to Judaism can understand and enjoy. Offers Christian readers tools to strengthen their own faith.
5½ x 8½, 112 pp, Quality PB Original, ISBN 1-58023-150-0 **$12.95** A JEWISH LIGHTS Book

The Geography of Faith
Underground Conversations on Religious, Political, and Social Change

by *Daniel Berrigan* and *Robert Coles;* Updated introduction and afterword by the authors

A classic of faith-based activism—updated for a new generation.

Listen in on the conversations between these two great teachers—one a renegade priest wanted by the FBI for his protests against the Vietnam war, the other a future Pulitzer Prize–winning journalist—as they struggle with what it means to put your faith to the test. Discover how their story of challenging the status quo during a time of great political, religious, and social change is just as applicable to our lives today. 6 x 9, 224 pp, Quality PB, ISBN 1-893361-40-3 **$16.95**

Spirituality

Inspired Lives: *Exploring the Role of Faith and Spirituality in the Lives of Extraordinary People*

by *Joanna Laufer* & *Kenneth S. Lewis*

Contributors include *Ang Lee, Wynton Marsalis, Kathleen Norris*, and many more

How faith transforms the lives and work of the creative and innovative people in our world.

In this moving book, soul-searching conversations unearth the importance of spirituality and personal faith for more than forty artists and innovators who have made a real difference in our world through their work. 6 x 9, 256 pp, Quality PB, ISBN 1-893361-33-0 **$16.95**

Women Pray
Voices through the Ages, from Many Faiths, Cultures, and Traditions

Edited and with introductions by *Monica Furlong*

Many ways—new and old—to communicate with the Divine.

This beautiful gift book celebrates the rich variety of ways women around the world have called out to the Divine—with words of joy, praise, gratitude, wonder, petition, longing, and even anger—from the ancient world up to our own time. Prayers from women of nearly every religious or spiritual background give us an eloquent expression of what it means to communicate with God. 5 x 7¼, 256 pp, Deluxe HC with ribbon marker, ISBN 1-893361-25-X **$19.95**

Zen Effects: *The Life of Alan Watts*

by *Monica Furlong*

The first and only full-length biography of one of the most charismatic spiritual leaders of the twentieth century—now back in print!

Through his widely popular books and lectures, Alan Watts (1915–1973) did more to introduce Eastern philosophy and religion to Western minds than any figure before or since. Here is the only biography of this charismatic figure, who served as Zen teacher, Anglican priest, lecturer, academic, entertainer, a leader of the San Francisco renaissance, and author of more than 30 books, including *The Way of Zen, Psychotherapy East and West* and *The Spirit of Zen*. 6 x 9, 264 pp, Quality PB, ISBN 1-893361-32-2 **$16.95**

Simone Weil: *A Modern Pilgrimage*

by *Robert Coles*

The extraordinary life of the spiritual philosopher who's been called both saint and madwoman.

The French writer and philosopher Simone Weil (1906–1943) devoted her life to a search for God—while avoiding membership in organized religion. Robert Coles' intriguing study of Weil details her short, eventful life, and is an insightful portrait of the beloved and controversial thinker whose life and writings influenced many (from T.S. Eliot to Adrienne Rich to Albert Camus), and continue to inspire seekers everywhere. 6 x 9, 208 pp, Quality PB, ISBN 1-893361-34-9 **$16.95**

Spirituality

Three Gates to Meditation Practice
A Personal Journey into Sufism, Buddhism, and Judaism
by *David A. Cooper*

Shows us how practicing within more than one spiritual tradition can lead us to our true home.

Here are over fifteen years from the journey of "post-denominational rabbi" David A. Cooper, author of *God Is a Verb*, and his wife, Shoshana—years in which the Coopers explored a rich variety of practices, from chanting Sufi *dhikr* to Buddhist Vipassanā meditation, to the study of kabbalah and esoteric Judaism. Their experience demonstrates that the spiritual path is really completely within our reach, whoever we are, whatever we do—as long as we are willing to practice it. 5½ x 8½, 240 pp, Quality PB, ISBN 1-893361-22-5 **$16.95**

Praying with Our Hands: *Twenty-One Practices of Embodied Prayer from the World's Spiritual Traditions*
by *Jon M. Sweeney*; Photographs by *Jennifer J. Wilson*;

Foreword by *Mother Tessa Bielecki*; Afterword by *Taitetsu Unno, Ph.D.*

A spiritual guidebook for bringing prayer into our bodies.

What gives our prayers meaning? How can we carry a prayerful spirit throughout our everyday lives? This inspiring book of reflections and accompanying photographs shows us twenty-one simple ways of using our hands to speak to God, to enrich our devotion and ritual. All express the various approaches of the world's religious traditions to bringing the body into worship. Spiritual traditions represented include Anglican, Sufi, Zen, Roman Catholic, Yoga, Shaker, Hindu, Jewish, Pentecostal, Eastern Orthodox, and many others.
8 x 8, 96 pp, 22 duotone photographs, Quality PB Original, ISBN 1-893361-16-0 **$16.95**

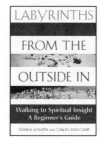

Labyrinths from the Outside In
Walking to Spiritual Insight—a Beginner's Guide
by *Donna Schaper* & *Carole Ann Camp*

The user-friendly, interfaith guide to making and using labyrinths— for meditation, prayer, and celebration.

Labyrinth walking is a spiritual exercise *anyone* can do. And it's rare among such practices in that it can be done by people together, regardless of their religious backgrounds or lack thereof. This accessible guide unlocks the mysteries of the labyrinth for all of us, providing ideas for using the labyrinth walk for prayer, meditation, and celebrations to mark the most important moments in life. Includes instructions for making a labyrinth of your own and finding one in your area.
6 x 9, 208 pp, b/w illus. and photographs, Quality PB Original, ISBN 1-893361-18-7 **$16.95**

Other Interesting Books—Spirituality

God Within: *Our Spiritual Future—As Told by Today's New Adults*

Edited by *Jon M. Sweeney and the Editors at SkyLight Paths*

Our faith, in our words.

The future of spirituality in America lies in the vision of the women and men who are the children of the "baby boomer" generation—born into the post-New-Age world of the 1970s and 80s. This book gives voice to their spiritual energy, and allows readers of all ages to share in their passionate quests for faith and belief. Sometimes irreverent—but always *relevant*—this thought-provoking collection of writings, poetry, and art showcases the voices that are defining the future of religion, faith, and belief as we know it. 6 x 9, 176 pp, Quality PB Original, ISBN 1-893361-15-2 **$14.95**

Releasing the Creative Spirit: *Unleash the Creativity in Your Life*

by *Dan Wakefield*

From the author of *How Do We Know When It's God?*— a practical guide to accessing creative power in every area of your life.

In this passionate, personal guide, award-winning author Dan Wakefield explodes the myths associated with the creative process and shows how everyone can uncover and develop their natural ability to create. Drawing on religion, psychology, and the arts, he teaches us that the key to creation of any kind is clarity—of body, mind, and spirit—and he provides practical exercises that each of us can do to access that centered quality that allows creativity to shine. 7 x 10, 208 pp, Quality PB, ISBN 1-893361-36-5 **$16.95**

God Lives in Glass: *Reflections of God through the Eyes of Children*

by *Robert J. Landy, Ph.D.*;

Foreword by *Sandy Eisenberg Sasso*, author of *God's Paintbrush*

Children from around the world show us God in ways we may have forgotten.

How do kids imagine God? In many and diverse ways full of wonder and rebuke, in ways that grownups may have forgotten. In ways that you will be delighted to remember. This full-color book of insights celebrates the unique spirituality of children, allowing adults to take an eye-opening look at our own faith, religion, and spirituality—and to rediscover a fresh, enlightening perspective. 7 x 6, 64 pp, HC, Full-color illus. ISBN 1-893361-30-6 **$12.95**

Or phone, fax, mail or e-mail to: SKYLIGHT PATHS Publishing
Sunset Farm Offices, Route 4 • P.O. Box 237 • Woodstock, Vermont 05091
Tel: (802) 457-4000 • Fax: (802) 457-4004 • www.skylightpaths.com
Credit card orders: (800) 962-4544 (9AM–5PM ET Monday–Friday)
Generous discounts on quantity orders. Satisfaction guaranteed. Prices subject to change.